The War of 1812

A Compact History

The War of 1812

A Compact History

by

Major James Ripley Jacobs, U.S.A. (Ret.)

and

Glenn Tucker

Editorial Coordination by

Historical Evaluation and Research Organization

Hawthorn Books, Inc.   Publishers   New York

The authors wish to express their appreciation for permission to reprint maps in this volume:

The maps on pages 49, 133, and 146 are from *Military Heritage of America* by R. Ernest Dupuy and Trevor N. Dupuy. Copyright © 1956 by McGraw-Hill Book Company, Inc. Reprinted by permission of McGraw-Hill Book Company, Inc.

The map on page 181 is from *Poltroons and Patriots,* Vol. II, by Glenn Tucker. Copyright © 1954 by The Bobbs-Merrill Company, Inc. Reprinted by permission of The Bobbs-Merrill Company, Inc.

Contents

Foreword

Take a large chunk of commercial rivalry; add equal portions of stiff-necked arrogance and land-grabbing greed; season with the valor of ignorance. Such was the recipe that produced the War of 1812—the war that should never have been.

One might, with reason, call this a stupid war. In the first place, large segments of the peoples of England, Canada and the United States were bitterly opposed to it. In the second place, the United States declared war against England for a variety of causes, the most important of which, and the most popular in the United States, was freedom of the seas. Yet when the two tired nations struck hands in the Treaty of Ghent some two and a half years after the ferocious bloodletting had ended, the freedom of the seas was not even mentioned.

Yet there is another side to the coin. The war settled several moot questions. The solidarity of Anglo-Canadian resistance to invasion expunged forever from the minds of American expansionists any hope of annexing England's North American colony by force of arms. In turn, the amazing combat superiority displayed by the vastly outnumbered U.S. Navy in single-ship duels and the

7

recrudescence of the U.S. Army when properly led gave forceful proof to British extremists that any thought of reconquering the lost thirteen colonies was equally the stuff dreams are made of.

And, in finality, despite the silence of the Treaty of Ghent on the subject, America's darling tenet, freedom of the seas, was in fact established. Never again would a ship of the Royal Navy molest American ships or sailors.

For Canada, the war was a catalyst. In the process of their self-defense, the Canadian people took the first step on the long path that would finally lead to national independence within the British Commonwealth.

Americans should particularly remember that the War of 1812 marked the glorious coming of age of the United States Navy. They should take heed, too, of an object lesson presented. The shocking inefficiency of our Army and militia gave stark warning of the futilities of wishful thinking and the valor of ignorance then governing our wobbly scheme of national defense.

High drama marked the progress of the struggle. Instances of splendid leadership and amazing personal bravery were matched by hideous examples of blatant cowardice, stupidity and senility. Andrew Jackson, Winfield Scott, Oliver Hazard Perry, Thomas Macdonough and a host of others on the American side stood with England's Isaac Brock and Canada's Charles de Salaberry in sharp contrast to William Hull, Henry Dearborn, James Wilkinson, William H. Winder, Henry Proctor and their ilk. Nor can one miss, through the powder smoke, the presence of the great and gallant Tecumseh, chief of the Shawnee Indians.

The story in all its vivid color is told in this book, a fusion of the independent efforts of two competent American historians. Major James Ripley Jacobs, U.S.A. (Ret.), chronicler of the beginnings of the United States Army, writes of the land battles, and Glenn Tucker, ardent admirer of the early sailing United States Navy, relates the encounters on the high seas and the Great Lakes. Their products have been happily wedded by a group of associated scholars of the Historical Evaluation and Research Organization of McLean, Virginia.

R. Ernest Dupuy
Colonel, U.S.A. (Ret.)

The War of 1812

A Compact History

1

Background and Causes

of the War

Few on either side of the Atlantic truly wanted the War of 1812, but none sought aggressively to avoid it by intelligent negotiation, and none seemed in advance to weigh the consequences if it came. As icebergs might float and bump, so aimless drift brought the two nations crashing together. As the Connecticut *Courant* aptly put it, "We view the declaration of war as we view the cataract at Niagara—as one of the wonders of the world."

Though border incidents and hostilities between settlers and Indians in the Northwest abounded, the gradual breakdown of peaceful relations between the United States and Great Britain over a period of more than ten years resulted mainly from commercial controversy, land-grabbing and numerous episodes at sea.

The resumption of the Napoleonic Wars in 1803 brought about mutual blockades both of Great Britain and France and of their respective colonial possessions. In consequence, American commercial and maritime interests attempted to make financial hay through neutral trading with both adversaries. As a result, warships of both sides preyed on American merchant ships. Yet President Thomas Jefferson's Embargo Act of 1807 and Non-

11

Intercourse Act of 1809 produced only anger in his own United States, for these measures stultified efforts of American industrialists to gain foreign trade supremacy. Meanwhile, depredations on American shipping continued, with the French just as guilty as the British—with one vital exception: Britain's practice of search and impressment, through which American ships were searched by British war vessels and American seamen shanghaied into the Royal Navy.

The high-handed overhauling of the unprepared American frigate USS *Chesapeake*, 38,[1] off the Norfolk Roads in June 1807 by HMS *Leopard*, 54, and the forceable removal of four alleged deserters raised a fever of rage in the United States. The outrage was revenged in May 1811 off Cape Charles when the USS *President*, 44, searching for a British frigate that had impressed sailors from a merchantman off Sandy Hook, overhauled and as roughly gunned down HM sloop of war *Little Belt*, 20, with nine British sailors killed and twenty-three wounded.

Meanwhile, on the Northwest frontier, Shawnee chieftain Tecumseh, with the not very covert assistance of British authorities in Canada, made war against the encroaching American frontier settlers. William Henry Harrison's victory at the Battle of Tippecanoe in November 1811 quenched that fire, but the irritation abetted the efforts of greedy American expansionists to acquire Canada (and Spain's Florida, too). The election of 1810–1811 had brought a "war hawk" administration into power, and President James Madison and his Cabinet began making preparations for war.

French inroads on American trade were overlooked in the rise of anti-British sentiment in Congress. So, too, were belated British diplomatic efforts to ease the unemployment and distress at home caused by the trade break with the United States. On June 1, 1812, the President asked Congress for a declaration of war on Britain, on four major grounds: impressment of American seamen, violation of American neutral rights and territorial waters, blockade of United States ports and British refusal to revoke the Orders in Council of 1807, which barred all neutral trade with France and her colonies. Despite objections by the New England

[1] The number following a ship's name indicates the number of guns she was assigned.

states (except Vermont), New York, New Jersey and Delaware, Madison's recommendation was approved by Congress. War was declared June 18.[2]

Neither nation was in position to wage a major war. Great Britain was already involved in a life-or-death conflict with Napoleonic France. The impoverished United States was relatively unprepared, and in January 1812 Secretary of the Treasury Albert Gallatin had estimated that the normal fixed expenses of government for the coming year alone would run to more than $3.5 million in excess of current revenues. (As it turned out, before the war ended the United States borrowed some $98 million; the nation was saved from bankruptcy only through Gallatin's financial deals with John Jacob Astor, Stephen Girard and other American financiers.)

Besides a chronic lack of funds, the American government started the war with a tiny Regular Army, inadequate in numbers, poorly trained and poorly led. In July 1812 there were only 6,686 regular officers and men; in September 1814 the Regular Army reached a maximum strength of 38,186. Between 1812 and 1815 a total of 527,654 regulars, volunteers, rangers and militia served at one time or another. Unfortunately, the majority of these—some 458,463 militia—were men whose military training was limited to an annual 24-hour jamboree on village greens. In addition militia operations were commonly restricted to the confines of the respective states and their use subject to the whims of state governors.

The caliber of these governors and their interest in the general welfare differed widely. Governor Daniel B. Tompkins of New York, for example, tried intelligently to prepare his militia to meet both state and national needs. Faced with the possibility of invasion from the north, Tompkins delegated to his brigade commanders the authority to call out their militia in emergency. On the other hand, Governors Caleb Strong of Massachusetts and Roger Griswold of Connecticut were obstructionists, several times refusing to turn out militia on federal call. Vermont's Governor Martin Chittenden tried to keep all his militia at home. In one instance he specifically ordered a battalion of

---

[2] On June 23, 1812, Parliament did suspend the Orders in Council, but that was too late.

Vermont militia on active duty to leave the front forthwith—
an order the battalion deliberately refused to obey.

In sum, the militia were poorly trained, irregularly paid and
seldom on active duty for more than a month or two at a time.
When they operated together with regulars, unified action was
often thwarted by contentions over rank and privileges. Before
the war, the few regulars had been kept so busy policing the
frontier that no plan had ever been devised to use them as a
training corps for the militia or to combine both harmoniously
into well-integrated units.

The Army did possess one small asset: the handful of young
men who had emerged from the United States Military Academy
since its inception in 1802. These young professional junior
officers—there were 106 of them—would prove their worth before
the war ended.

But leadership in the Army high command was moribund in
1812. The senior officer, Brigadier General James Wilkinson, a
sinister, double-dealing character, was in temporary limbo following a court-martial for treason, in which he had received the
Scotch verdict of "Not Proven." Wade Hampton, next in line,
was a nonentity. When the Army was increased for the war, both
were by-passed; Henry Dearborn and Thomas Pinckney, prominent civilians who had had some Revolutionary War experience,
were put into uniform as major generals. Nine additional brigadier generals, mainly old crocks, some of whom had seen Revolutionary service, were appointed. Only one of these would shine
militarily: William Henry Harrison.

Such was the assortment of generals who would attempt the
invasion of Canada so devoutly desired by the war hawks, which
American political leaders fondly expected to be a pushover. No
general staff existed, of course. Plans were approved and campaigns plotted by the President and his Secretary of War.

The U.S. Navy, although small and for years strangulated by
economy-minded politicians who had no concept of sea power,
was something else again. Its nucleus, as the war broke out, was
seven frigates (not all in commission), ten sloops of war and a
few smaller craft.[3] Their quarterdecks were manned by a small

---

[3] Not counted here are sixty-two shallow-draft gunboats built for coast defense but
absolutely useless in any naval conflict.

group of professionals, most of them still young, but veterans of the wars with the Barbary pirates in the Mediterranean and of the quasi-war with France in the West Indies.

Two ingenious naval architects—Joshua Humphreys and Josiah Fox—together with another talented naval draftsman, William Doughty, had been responsible for the original six frigates: *Constitution, United States* and *President,* all 1,576-ton 44s; *Constellation,* 38, of 1,265 tons; and near-sisters *Chesapeake* and *Congress,* both 38s, of 1,244 and 1,268 tonnage respectively.

The numerous American shipyards at once set about a crash construction program, but the superiority in numbers of the Royal Navy, whose far-flung fleets dominated the world's waters, could not be overcome. Perforce the U.S. Navy's role became that of the *guerre de course*—commerce destruction—against terrific odds.

The United States had a high potential for producing matériel for both the Army and the Navy. Timber was plentiful, and the necessities of a maritime nation were provided by numerous ship chandleries along the eastern coast. There were many gun makers; powder mills flourished; iron foundries were numerous. Government arsenals at Harpers Ferry, Virginia, and Springfield, Massachusetts, were adequate. So, too, with food-stuffs: the nation's agriculture was strong.

However, poor land communication presented problems in distribution. When coastwise traffic was barred by the British naval blockade, there were additional bottlenecks to the flow of supply. As for clothing, American cloth manufacturers had increased their output since the Embargo Act of 1807 had interrupted European traffic, but not sufficiently to supply war needs. In consequence the poorly clad troops would suffer. Poor performance by venal contractors of food and clothing, under haphazard control, added to the discomforts of troops in the field.

These problems became almost insuperable when it came to undertaking any invasion of the wide wildernesses of Canada. Yet invasion of Canada was the only offensive land operation open to American arms in a war with Great Britain. Furthermore, annexation of Canada was one of the aims of the war hawks.

British North America at the time was divided into two principal parts: Lower Canada, reaching from the Atlantic Ocean to the Ottawa River—today's Quebec province—and Upper Canada, west of the Ottawa. Lower Canada contained the majority of the population, approximately 335,000, and was in easy contact with Great Britain. Upper Canada, with few towns of importance and a white population of only some 95,000, was dependent upon Lower Canada for manufactured goods and other supplies, all transported over the St. Lawrence River—Great Lakes waterway. Land communications were abominable for long-distance hauls; wheeled transportation bogged down in summer, while drifted snow and extreme cold impeded movement by wheel or sled in winter.

It was thus imperative that the British keep open the St. Lawrence–Great Lakes waterway. Any American interruption of that communication line would prevent a westward British military encirclement and invasion of the vulnerable Ohio valley. American control of the St. Lawrence River itself would also interdict not only communications with Britain but also the cattle supply route from the New England states—the major source of fresh beef for British troops in Canada. Actually, as the British governor general, Lieutenant General Sir George Prevost, himself declared, during the war two-thirds of his men were dependent upon this supply of contraband, smuggled more or less openly by New England contractors across from Vermont and northern New York.

Available British land forces consisted of some 7,000 men, of whom the majority were volunteer militia, similar in training and efficiency to the American militia. Of regulars, Prevost had but three small one-battalion regiments of foot and a detachment of artillery. In Upper Canada Major General Sir Isaac Brock, a most efficient British regular, had some 1,600 men immediately available; Major General Francis, Baron de Rottenburg, had about 5,500 in Lower Canada. On the Great Lakes Captain Robert H. Barclay, RN, commanded 6 small naval vessels, manned mainly by local sailors with a sprinkling of Royal Navy personnel. The overall British commander was Prevost, the governor general.

Reinforcements to Britain's land strength in Canada could be expected only in driblets, for the British Army, as we have noted, was fully engaged on the European continent and would remain so until after the abdication of Napoleon in March 1814. But on the high seas things were different.

Great Britain, scarcely expecting an American war, had in American waters in 1812 an inconsiderable portion of the Royal Navy's 120 ships of the line, 116 frigates and 350 lesser craft. Based at Halifax were the *Africa,* 64 (refitting at the time), six frigates and a number of small craft. In the Caribbean were two more ships of the line: the *Dragon,* 74, and the *Polyphemus,* 64. Another ship of the line and a 50-gun frigate, lying at Halifax, were not in active service. But sea power is flexible, and the Royal Navy soon increased its Western Atlantic strength.

Such was the line-up when the wheels of the war chariot began to turn.

In Washington, President Madison, War Secretary William Eustis and General Dearborn put their heads together, plotted out increases in Army personnel and planned to invade Upper Canada by way of Detroit. They also gave serious thought to the amazing proposal of Secretary of the Navy Paul Hamilton that the United States fleet be immured in harbor for the duration of the war as floating batteries for defense. Hamilton, former governor of South Carolina, was, it seems, an executive of ability but lacked completely both naval background and any concept of the application of sea power.

Happily for the American cause, Commodore William Bainbridge arrived in Washington while the plan was being debated. Bainbridge, who had quit the Navy after the Tripolitan War to enter the more lucrative merchant marine service, had been ice-locked in St. Petersburg, Russia, during the winter of 1811–1812 when he heard of the engagement between the *President* and the *Little Belt.* Convinced that war was imminent, he did not await the spring thaw but traveled through subzero weather across Finland and Sweden by dog sled to ship back home.

Bainbridge and Captain Charles Stewart, old companions of Tripolitan days, learning of Hamilton's plan, made violent protest. They appealed directly to the President, who, it appeared, had been pushed to acquiesce in Hamilton's proposal by Treasury

Secretary Gallatin, himself a disciple of Jeffersonian disinterest in a high seas, combat navy.

Amazingly enough, the two naval men carried their case. President Madison, overruling his Cabinet, ordered the fleet to sea to protect American commerce; this order was tantamount to telling it to fight.

2

The Navy Opens the Ball

On June 21, 1812, Commodore John Rodgers, senior officer of the U.S. Navy, cleared New York harbor in a hurry with his squadron. Unleashed by the presidential order, received only that morning, Rodgers, in his flagship, the USS *President*, 44, had with him the *United States*, 44, and the *Congress*, 38, the *Hornet*, 18, and the *Argus*, 16. Fortunately, Rodgers, a veteran of the Mediterranean wars with the Barbary pirates, in his eagerness to put to sea in search of a British merchant convoy known to be en route home from Jamaica, narrowly escaped a later timid Navy Department directive to establish merely a coastwise patrol.

Two days out, HMS *Belvidera*, 38, under Captain Richard Byron, was sighted off Nantucket Shoals, and the squadron gave chase. But Byron, a resourceful officer, crowded on sail. The *President*, leading the hunt, closed until within gunshot range —less than half a mile—and Rodgers in person aimed and fired the first shot of the war, from the *President*'s starboard forward 24-pounder. It scored a hit, as did the next two rounds fired. Then a gun blew up, wounding Rodgers and fifteen others and knocking out the other forward gun.

Byron, throwing away supplies to lighten his ship, got four of his guns aft to fire through stern ports. One of his rounds scored a hit, killing a midshipman and two seamen on the *President.* Then Byron jettisoned his anchors, his boats and more stores, while the *President,* lacking any bow chasers, was several times forced to yaw to get broadside guns to bear, losing ground each time. Reluctantly, Rodgers abandoned the chase the next morning and took off again after the elusive Jamaica convoy. He never caught it, although several times he overhauled orange peels, coconuts and other flotsam left in its wake. A seventy-day cruise all the way to the English Channel, then along the Portuguese coast and back to Boston netted seven prizes and the recapture of one American merchantman. Tactically this first cruise was sterile; but strategically it bore fruit, as we shall see.

The *Belvidera's* arrival at Halifax startled Rear Admiral Herbert Sawyer, station commander, into action. Commodore Philip Bowes Vere Broke, RN, one of the ablest as well as youngest post captains on the North American station, put out with the *Africa,* 64, hastily refitted, frigates *Shannon* and *Belvidera,* both 38s, and *Aeolus,* 32, to protect the convoy and hunt and destroy the impudent American squadron. Off Nantucket, HMS *Guerrière,* 38, joined the squadron.

By early July Broke's squadron was off New York, where it captured the little U.S. brig *Nautilus,* 14. Knowing neither the strength nor the whereabouts of the American squadron, Broke decided to keep his ships together. As a result all other American ports were open to incoming American merchantmen and exiting American warships.

While Rodgers had been putting to sea in June, the USS *Constitution,* 44, under Captain Isaac Hull, just returned from a Mediterranean cruise, was shipping a new crew at Annapolis, Maryland. On July 12 he cleared the Virginia Capes, under orders to join Rodgers. Off Egg Harbor, New Jersey, five sail were sighted, warships all, including one ship of the line. He was running smack into Broke's squadron. Hauling off to the southeast, Hull crowded on sail. The British vessels changed course on his heels, and Hull was in for one of the most amazing stern chases in American naval history.

At daylight on July 18, Hull saw the leading enemy frigate five or six miles astern, followed by the line-of-battle ship *Africa* and other craft. The lead vessel proved to be Broke's flagship, the swift *Shannon,* which momentarily had the advantage of a fresh breeze, while the *Constitution* moved slowly in near calm. After sunrise the breeze left the *Constitution* altogether. The enemy, having some favorable gusts, gained rapidly, and the escape of the *Constitution* seemed unlikely. Hull ran heavy guns astern, determined that, although hopelessly outclassed, he would fight to the finish. By 7 A.M. the *Shannon,* still the nearest enemy vessel, was within gunshot range. Hull began the action, but the shots from the *Constitution*'s stern guns fell slightly short.

At 8 A.M., "it now appeared," wrote Hull in his report, "that we must be taken, and that our escape was impossible—four heavy ships nearly within gunshot, and coming up fast, and not the least hope of a breeze."

But Hull had recourse other than long-range firing. He manned all the ship's boats and with them towed the vessel forward. Then Hull took soundings and found himself in no more than twenty-four fathoms of water. The shallowness of the water caused him to accept the suggestion of Charles Morris, first lieutenant of the *Constitution,* to warp the ship ahead by kedging; that is, carrying a small anchor, or kedge, ahead by rowboat, dropping it and pulling the vessel to it by the attached cable.

The *Constitution* clawed along, using two anchors alternately and some 300–400 fathoms of cable (1,800–2,400 feet). While the crew hauled away on a dropped kedge, the other anchor was rowed ahead. The British, watching, adopted the same plan; in fact, they went Hull one better, using most of the squadron's small boats to bring a single ship, the *Shannon,* within range.

But by sweat and perseverance the *Constitution* was holding her own, and her hard-laboring crew began to see hope. Occasionally in a breeze the kedging and rowing were abandoned. On the morning of the 19th, the second day of the chase, Hull witnessed astern, strung out in the clear summer freshness, moving under a gentle breeze, six beautiful enemy ships with all their sails spread, straining every cord and timber to reach him.

Late that afternoon the wind freshened. Then a squall darkened the waters. Hull, with consummate seamanship, picked up his boats on the run before pursuers and pursued were lost to one another in blinding rain and murky half-darkness. When the storm subsided, the *Constitution,* more than six miles ahead of her pursuers, was gaining every moment, at an eleven-knot clip.

At midnight the British fired two guns, signals, apparently, which the Americans did not understand. Could they presage an abandonment of the chase? On the morning of the 20th, the third day, only three of the British vessels could be seen from the *Constitution*'s masthead, their white topsails showing, their hulls below the horizon. At about 8 A.M. the British called off the futile pursuit.

Although the crew of the *Constitution* was new, it had proved itself heroic. For sixty-four hours men and officers endured steadfastly the tense strain of grueling work and constant vigilance. Hull remained sleepless, watching constantly the efforts and progress of his pursuers. He studied the surface of the ocean to detect at a distance the ripples indicating an oncoming breeze. He went among his men, encouraging them in their exertions. His skill and attentiveness, perhaps more than any other factor, enabled him to escape.

The chase had taken the *Constitution* up the New England coast; so Hull, anxious to recondition his ship, put into Boston on July 27. The episode, though trying, was indeed happy for him. Had he been able to reach New York as ordered, he would have found Rodgers gone and would have had to wait there unemployed for further orders. As it was, he could depart from Boston at will, and since the *Constitution* had suffered no damage, he was able to sail on August 2, before a Navy Department order transferring the *Constitution* to Captain Bainbridge's command could reach him. In the ears of captain and crew was ringing a waterfront ditty born of Boston's joy:

> 'Neath Hull's command, with a tough band,
> And naught beside to back her,
> Upon a day, as log books say,
> A fleet bore down to thwack her.
>
> A fleet, you know, is odds, or so,
> Against a single ship, sirs;
> So 'cross the tide her legs she tried,
> And gave the rogues the slip, sirs.

As for Broke, he turned his attention to the Jamaica convoy again. On July 29, he found it intact, 250 miles southeast of Halifax. After escorting it for 500 miles, Broke received word that the American squadron was on its way home. Leaving the *Africa* to continue with the merchantmen for a while and ordering the *Guerrière* back to Halifax for needed repairs, Broke returned to New York waters, where he arrived September 10 to resume a long-delayed blockade.

3

Dearborn Takes Command

in the North

The plan for invasion of Canada, as concocted several months before the outbreak of war by President Madison's Secretary of War, former military doctor William Eustis, envisioned a main effort from Lake Champlain against Montreal supported by thrusts into Upper Canada directed from Sackets Harbor, Niagara and Detroit. The principal planners were gouty General Dearborn—sixty-one years old and so fat he could not mount a horse and had to do his active campaigning from a buckboard—and William Hull, governor of Michigan Territory, uncle of Navy Captain Isaac Hull. Hull, fifty-nine, with a Revolutionary War record, had just been given a brigadier general's commission and was slated to lead the Detroit thrust. He had urged the creation of a naval force on Lake Erie to ensure a line of communications for the advance, but that suggestion was shelved.

Dearborn—"Granny" to his troops—conferred vaguely with New York's Governor Tompkins at the end of April and then returned to Boston. Tompkins, ready to cooperate, found himself up a dead-end street in Albany. Equipment for the militia was lacking, but no one could or would act to provide it. Superannuated regular

24

Brigadier General Peter Gansevoort, sixty-three, was in titular command at Albany but was entirely incapable of transacting affairs. Mercifully for all concerned, he died July 2.

News of the outbreak of hostilities reached Dearborn at Boston on June 22, but it seemed not to quicken his thought or action. Eustis also continued to be indecisive and procrastinating. Although he had already ordered Hull to invade western Canada, he advised Dearborn on June 26 to take his time in making the seacoast secure and in preparing troops for moving on Montreal, Kingston and Niagara. Bitterly opposed to the war, Governors Caleb Strong of Massachusetts and Roger Griswold of Connecticut now refused to honor Dearborn's request for militia in the name of the federal government. His request, they declared, was entirely unconstitutional because their states were not threatened by invasion.

Dearborn had many reasons for anxiety. Congress had lagged in creating a body of volunteers, recruiting was far behind expectations, gunboats were lacking, coast defenses needed men and supplies and there was no other general officer north of New York City to share his labors and his fears. Beset with these and other difficulties and making little progress in solving them, Dearborn remained in Boston for a month. After an exchange of vague admonitions on Eustis' part and equally vague excuses, "Granny" Dearborn lifted his 250 pounds of wheezing flesh to Albany on July 26. There he received orders to take over the militia in the Niagara sector and ensure cooperation along the entire front. More quibbling followed, to be ended on August 1 by a direct order from Eustis. The Secretary of War enclosed disquieting word from Hull and directed Dearborn "to make a diversion in his favor at Niagara and at Kingston as soon as may be practicable."

Meanwhile, Governor Tompkins had taken measures on his own to prepare New York's quota of 13,500 militia for active service. While those in the New York City area were being mustered in under Brigadier General John Armstrong, newly appointed regular, New York Major General Benjamin Mooers with three brigades was put in command of the border defense from the St. Regis River opposite Cornwall on the St. Lawrence to the Vermont border. On July 13 Major General Stephen Van

Rensselaer, with five brigades, took over the rest of the state's northern border.

The first clash along the border, a naval engagement, occurred July 19, at Sackets Harbor in Van Rensselaer's sector. Sackets Harbor lies on Lake Ontario, some twenty miles southeast of Canada's Kingston, across the St. Lawrence River mouth. Five vessels under Canadian Commodore Earle dared the harbor's ancient fort in order to capture the USS *Oneida,* the one American warship on the lake—a little brig carrying eighteen 24-pounders —commanded by Lieutenant M. T. Woolsey, USN. The whole affair had a touch of opéra bouffe. Woolsey had moored his brig with one broadside bearing on the harbor mouth; he had transferred the guns of the other side to the old fort. Also, an old iron 32-pounder long gun found lying in mud had been fished out, cleaned and mounted. Unfortunately, there were no balls to fit the "Old Sow," as the gun was named, and 24-pounder rounds wrapped in carpet were extemporized.

The Canadian ships, mounting more than seventy guns between them, ran in to exchange shots with Woolsey's defenses in a cannonade harmless to both sides, until—so the story goes— American gunners retrieved a spent 32-pounder British ball, loaded it into the "Old Sow" and scored a perfect hit on the *Royal George,* the Canadian flagship, killing 14 sailors and wounding 118 others. In any event, after a two-hour cannonade, Earle hauled off and sailed back to Kingston.

This ended active combat in Van Rensselaer's sector for the remainder of the year. Naval plans for putting fleets in the water on Lakes Erie, Ontario and Champlain were in the making, while both Dearborn and Van Rensselaer pondered the extent to which British control of Lake Ontario would hinder supply of men, rations and equipment to the New York frontier. Meanwhile, along the Niagara, American troops, regulars and militia, were short of clothing and far behind in their pay.

Understandably, under these conditions Dearborn was in a mood to listen to Colonel Edward Baynes, an emissary from Sir George Prevost, who arrived at Albany in early August singing an attractive song of an armistice. Following a tentative agreement on August 9, Van Rensselaer and Major General Roger H. Sheaffe, commanding the British garrison at Fort George, by

August 21 had worked out the details, allowing each to move troops, stores and matériel "unshackled and free" below Fort Erie; Sheaffe was also to refrain from sending reinforcements westward to General Brock, then marching rapidly on Detroit with 300 men. Hull, if he chose, was to be included in the armistice.

Unfortunately, Hull would never know about all this until too late. The shockingly inefficient and dilatory Dearborn, forwarding him the information by ordinary mail, would thus become accessory before the fact to a tragic disaster to American arms.

4

Disaster in the West

During the spring of 1812, General Hull had slowly moved from Dayton, Ohio, toward Detroit, gathering on the way three Ohio volunteer regiments and a few other troops he found waiting for him. By June 10, he had progressed to Urbana, Ohio, where the U.S. 4th Infantry joined him, completing his command. Detroit lay approximately 200 miles to the north, through mostly an unsettled and roadless wilderness, but Hull kept the wagons and caissons rolling along.

Colonel Duncan McArthur was sent ahead with his regiment to clear the way and bridge the streams. By the 16th he had gotten as far as Denton, Ohio, and had built a fort nearby that was named in his honor. On the 19th the rest of the army joined him. A small garrison was left at Fort McArthur, together with some of the sick, and Colonel James Findlay and his organization were detailed to march ahead and open a route to the Maumee River.

Hull and his men followed on June 21. Indians lurked in the surrounding forests, heavy rains were falling, the way was deep in mud and swarms of black flies and mosquitoes pestered those who wearily sloshed along. After covering sixteen miles, the army halted and built a fort well christened Fort Necessity. There Hull received news that the Wyandots were hostile, the other tribes were restive and the British were courting their allegiance.

The army slogged on. In three days it reached Fort Findlay—a small work only fifty yards square with a blockhouse in each corner, which Findlay and his men had just erected. There, on June 26, Hull received word from Eustis by special messenger. It had apparently left Washington on the morning of the day that war was declared but gave no hint of the happening. Among other things, it merely stated, "Circumstances have recently occurred which render it necessary you should pursue your march to Detroit with all possible expedition. The highest confidence is reposed in your discretion, zeal, and perseverance." It remains an enigma and a heavy indictment against Eustis that while he was expressing his confidence in Hull he failed completely to keep him abreast of the situation.

Hull, uncertain as to the meaning of this cryptic letter, promptly resumed his march, arriving at the Maumee River in a few days and camping on the site of old British Fort Miami. Having reached navigable water, he shifted some of the burden of transportation to boats. Nearby at the foot of the rapids, the schooner *Cuyahoga* was riding at anchor. Hospital stores, entrenching tools, officers' baggage and most of Hull's personal and official papers were loaded aboard. Three officers' wives traveled as passengers, as well as some thirty soldiers to act as guards and helpers of the crew. A smaller vessel accompanied the *Cuyahoga,* carrying a number of Army invalids. Both vessels set sail for Detroit on July 1.

On the same day Hull resumed his march. On July 2, approaching Frenchtown (Monroe, Michigan), he received another War Department letter, dated, like the previous one, June 18. It stated that war had been declared and directed him to hasten to Detroit, do what was necessary and wait for further orders. The letter had come through ordinary mail as far as Cleveland, Ohio, and from there the enterprising postmaster had forwarded it by special messenger.

In striking contrast, senior British officials learned of the declaration of war more quickly and used it to distinct advantage. In some cases agents of the Northwestern Fur Company carried the news. Prevost was informed on June 24, General Brock on the 25th, Lieutenant Colonel Thomas B. St. George at Fort Malden on the Detroit River by the 28th and Captain Charles Roberts at St. Joseph on July 8. Consequently, despite Hull's frantic effort to recall the *Cuyahoga,* the schooner was fired upon and captured as she passed Fort Malden July 2. Hull's papers on board disclosed his plans, his strength and his supply line—invaluable information to the enemy.

On July 5 Hull reached Spring Wells, just below Detroit and directly opposite Sandwich (Windsor) on the east bank of the Detroit River, where a British detachment was stationed. There the Americans could plainly see the enemy strengthening their defenses. The next day Hull announced to his troops the declaration of war but made no attempt to warn his exposed American outposts far to the north at Fort Michilimackinac on the Mackinac Straits and to the west at Fort Dearborn (Chicago), where large quantities of valuable furs were stored.

Detroit, a huddle of frontier houses with about 700 inhabitants, was enclosed by a high stockade surrounded by cleared ground. Behind the settlement rose the fort, a conventional earthwork with a normal garrison of 94 men. From this base Hull now began operations. While artillery sporadically blazed away at Sandwich, he openly massed his troops at Spring Wells on July 11, then brought them back at night to Bloody Bridge, north of Detroit —a clever feint that, as it turned out, was the only clever highlight of his campaign.

Next day, a bright Sunday morning, the Americans ferried across the river in detachments and completely surprised the British force massed to repel a crossing below. And there at Sandwich Hull sat, issuing proclamations of friendship to Canadians, timidly skirmishing with bands of Tecumseh's Shawnee Indians and entrenching against assault. No effort was made to attack Fort Malden, which should have been the initial objective of his invasion. All the while, able General Brock, with 300 men —mostly militia with a sprinkling of British regulars—was coming west from Fort George on the Niagara River by forced marches and lake boats, arousing the countryside with appeals to Canadian patriotism and stirring the Indians to greater effort.

Hull's indecision was aggravated on July 28 by word that Fort Michilimackinac, garrisoned only by a small detachment of regular artillerymen unaware of the outbreak of war, had been captured by a force of Canadian militia and a few British regulars from nearby St. Joseph, under Captain Charles Roberts. A rich haul of furs rewarded the victors, who treated the little garrison and the few civilian inhabitants with the utmost courtesy; Roberts took special care to see that they were protected from Indian outrage.

Still Hull dallied, despite the rising indignation of his officers. Only with difficulty could he be persuaded to assist a reinforcing detachment of volunteers convoying beef cattle and other supplies that had been attacked by Tecumseh's Indians along the Raisin River, thirty-five miles south of Detroit. And when he did, it was too late. His rescuing force was ambushed and driven back with serious loss, while the volunteers were scattered. Angry field officers on August 7 berated Hull, who then aroused himself sufficiently to announce an advance in force on Fort Malden. Instead, however, when word was received that Brock was approaching Malden, Hull hurried his entire command back across the river and into Detroit.

Attempts to keep open the supply line back to Ohio resulted only in futile thrusts by small detachments, frittered away in combat with superior forces of Indians and Canadian militia.

Brock reached Malden on August 13, conferred with Tecumseh and prepared for immediate attack on Detroit. On August 19, after erecting batteries that commanded the American position, he called on Hull to surrender immediately. The senile American commander, a trembling old man now, raised the white flag.

More than 2,000 men, including the U.S. 4th Infantry, detachments of the 1st and 3rd Infantry and artillery detachments, laid down their arms. Thirty-six guns and large quantities of powder, provisions and other matériel fell into enemy hands, including one small vessel, the brig *Adams*. (Rechristened the *Detroit,* this vessel added to the British strength on Lake Erie.) Brock permitted the militia and volunteers to return home under parole but kept the regulars as prisoners of war.

To add to the shame, Hull had included Fort Dearborn in his surrender. He sent orders to the small garrison to evacuate the post immediately. Some fifty-five regulars of the U.S. 1st Infantry, some militiamen, some friendly Miami Indians and a group of noncombatants, women and children, marched out into an ambush of hostile Indians. Most were butchered.

News of the pusillanimous surrender of Detroit rocked the United States, up to now basking in the valor of ignorance. When Hull was later returned from captivity by exchange in 1814, he was tried by general court-martial at Philadelphia. The charges included treason, cowardice, neglect of duty and unofficerlike conduct. The court did not consider the charge of treason but found him guilty on the other charges and sentenced him to be shot and to have his name stricken from Army rolls. However, the court added a recommendation for mercy on account of Hull's age and his Revolutionary War service. Madison remitted the sentence simply to cashierment from the Army.

All this, of course, was water long since over the dam. What mattered in the autumn of 1812 was that the Northwest frontier of the United States lay wide open to British invasion, while any American invasion of Canada had been badly compromised.

5

Victories at Sea

"OLD IRONSIDES'" FINEST HOUR

Stout Isaac Hull cleared Boston harbor just two weeks before his
doddering uncle William wrecked American hopes at Detroit.
Northbound to intercept any British ships coming down from
Halifax, he also desired especially to encounter HMS *Guerrière*,
whose boastful captain, James Richard Dacres, had been quoted
as belittling the Americans and warning them that his frigate was
no *Little Belt*.

> On her sails, in letters red,
> To our captains were displayed
> Words of warning, words of dread:
> "All who meet me have a care!
> I am England's *Guerrière*."

Hull scoured the Bay of Fundy, scanned the seas off Halifax
and headed east from Nova Scotia to the Gulf of St. Lawrence.
Disappointed, he turned south again. On August 19, 1812, two
hundred miles off the Maine coast, he sighted a remote sail. It
was indeed the *Guerrière*.

Hull had met the personable Dacres, whose father had commanded the schooner *Carleton* against Benedict Arnold in the
battle of Valcour Island, Lake Champlain, in 1776. In social con-
versation ashore, not long before hostilities began, when the *Constitution* ("Old Ironsides") and the *Guerrière* lay in the Delaware
Roads, Hull had jokingly warned Dacres—so the story goes—to be-
ware should their ships ever join battle. Dacres at once offered to
wager that his ship would win and Hull suggested that a cocked
hat to the victor would be appropriate. On that they had struck
hands.

Eager to fight, both captains maneuvered skillfully. After an
hour and a half of long-range firing, the two ships closed to within
fifty yards at 6:05 P.M., in the softening light of a windy August
evening. Thin clouds raced across the sky; the sea was choppy
and the well-matched frigates tossed, adding to the difficulties of
firing. Hull took some punishment as he came in, but he had his
battle planned.

At what he judged to be precisely the right moment, Hull
leaned excitedly over the railing and shouted his order to the
gunners. "Now, boys, pour it into them!" The forward guns
belched double shots of grape, riddling the *Guerrière*'s sails and
rigging. The starboard battery spoke in unison. Hull skillfully
went about, and almost before the British were aware of it, the
port battery poured in another broadside. So intent was the ship's
captain on the firing that he did not notice he had split his
breeches down the seam when he leaned over the rail to shout
his order and that he was fighting the battle with his rear exposed.

Rarely was rapid American gunnery employed with such devastating effect. Ten minutes brought rigging and spars crashing
down on the *Guerrière*'s maindeck. As the *Constitution* wore and
crossed the enemy's bow, she raked the hostile decks with grapeshot and roundshot. The *Guerrière*'s mizzenmast went by the
board. The *Constitution*, closing, became entangled in the *Guerrière*'s bowsprit. As the two captains called for boarders, both
ships suffered casualties. The British musketeers in the rigging
had easy targets on the *Constitution*'s crowded maindeck. First
Lieutenant Charles Morris fell wounded. Lieutenant William S.
Bush, commander of the *Constitution*'s fifty marines, formed them
to board but dropped from the taffrail, a bullet through his head,

just as the wind billowed the ship's sails and pulled her free of her adversary.

Dacres had his Royal Marines ready, but while he hesitated the frigates parted. The *Guerrière,* like the *Constitution,* had suffered from the topmen's musket fire. Dacres' second in command, Lieutenant Henry Ready, was killed, and Dacres himself was wounded. Pulling away, Hull resumed his deadly cannonade.

Twenty minutes after the battle began, the *Guerrière's* foremast came crashing down, carrying with it the mainmast, leaving the riddled frigate wallowing helplessly in the trough of the sea. At 6:30 P.M., twenty-five minutes after the battle began, Dacres signaled his surrender with a shot to leeward, then hauled down the British flag from the stump of the mainmast.

> The *Guerrière's* a wreck in the trough of the sea;
> Her laurels are withered. Her boasting is done.
> Submissive, to leeward, she fires her last gun.

Hull sent a boarding party under Third Lieutenant George C. Read, who found the *Guerrière* a worthless wreck. He returned after an hour, bringing Dacres with him. The Englishman, wordless, extended his sword to Hull, but it was thrust back into his hand.

"No, no, Captain," quoth Hull. "I'll take no sword from one who knows so well how to use it. But I will trouble you for that hat!"

Hull extended every courtesy to his defeated antagonist, who in his report to the British Admiralty showed that the traditional chivalry that was being lost in much warfare on land still obtained on the high seas:

> I feel it my duty to state that the conduct of Captain Hull and his officers to our men has been that of a brave enemy, the greatest care being taken to prevent our men losing the smallest trifle, and the greatest attention being paid to the wounded.

After he was exchanged, Dacres was tried by court-martial in Halifax for surrendering his ship but was acquitted unanimously.

He rose later to high rank and distinguished service in the Royal
Navy.

The defeated frigate had received her death wounds. As soon
as Hull made the *Constitution* secure, he began the work of
transferring the *Guerrière*'s crew. Through the night his boats
plied between the two vessels, but dawn came with the rescue
work uncompleted. From the *Guerrière*'s littered deck the boarding party signaled that the hold held four feet of water and the
ship was in danger of going down. She wallowed about on the
surface until the last man was taken off, each with his personal
property in his possession. Not until 3 P.M., with the last British
tar rescued, did Hull order the prize crew back to their own vessel.
The hulk was set on fire and in fifteen minutes the air was rent
by a great explosion as the flames reached her powder magazines.
Of her complement, fifteen had been killed, sixty-two wounded.

Hull came into Boston harbor again, this time in even greater
triumph. His losses had been light—seven killed and seven
wounded. Although the battle could not be measured as decisive in its bearing on the war, it did have high significance
when viewed against the background of other events. The victory
counterbalanced the dismal shock of his uncle William Hull's
Detroit disaster, and Boston went wild with joy. The *Constitution*
was surrounded by bunting-decked boats loaded with festive cele-
brators. When Hull landed he was greeted by a great throng,
cheers, speeches and artillery salutes. For days the festivities rocked
the town; a splendid banquet tendered Hull and his officers
capped the festivities.

Congress voted a gold medal for Hull and distributed $50,000
among the crew in compensation for the prize money they would
have won had the enemy vessel not been pommeled into sinking
condition. New York and Philadelphia honored the captain with
swords and silver plate, and the gifts were no more than a modest
suggestion of the nation's deep gratitude.

The victory had, indeed, much broader bearing than a mere
revival of national pride after the humiliation at Detroit. The
United States became a naval power, challenging Britannia's long
rule of the waves in a half-hour battle between two fairly matched
ships that left the British vessel a shattered wreck. The confidence

gained by the American Navy from that half-hour has abided ever since.

British public opinion appreciated this deeper significance of the battle. When news of the disaster reached London on October 6, what was described as a funereal silence seemed to descend on the waterfront. The London *Times* next day commented:

> The loss of the *Guerrière* spread a degree of gloom through the town which it was painful to observe. The superior weight of metal possessed by the enemy—the greater number of men —the sinister accident at the commencement of the action [the loss of the mizzenmast], were all urged; yet people looked only to the triumph of the Americans.

The *Constitution* did have a heavier broadside, 736 pounds to 570, and more men, 476 to 244, by the London *Times* account. She had 56 guns (12 more than her original allowance) to 46. But these odds were far from conclusive, and the crushing nature of the victory was out of all proportion to the relatively small discrepancy in firepower. Often smaller ships won victories by more skillful handling, and Dacres himself did not consider that his ship had been outmatched. Rather, he attributed his loss to bad luck. At his court-martial he said with spirit: "I am so well aware that the success of my opponent was owing to fortune, that it is my earnest wish to be once more opposed to the *Constitution*, with the same officers and crew under my command, in a frigate of similar force to the *Guerrière*." His comment shows that he did not fully comprehend Hull's tactical and technical superiority as a commander.

After the passing of more than 150 years, the victory of the *Constitution* over the *Guerrière* remains one of the most glorious events of American naval history.

THE ESSEX

Captain Hull's prize—and he did have the wreck of the *Guerrière* in his possession for nearly twenty-four hours—was not the first

British warship taken in 1812. An even earlier prize was indeed important, because it marked the beginning of one of the most remarkable operations of the war, the cruise of the small U.S. frigate *Essex*.

The *Essex* was at New York when Commodore Rodgers took his little fleet out at the beginning of hostilities, but she was so stripped down and dismantled that she was not ready to sail. Captain David Porter, who commanded her, had appeared first in naval history serving as a midshipman on the *Constellation* when Captain Thomas Truxtun defeated the *Insurgente* in the quasi-war with France on February 1, 1800. Hardly more than a boy, Porter had won fame in that battle by running up the ratlines under enemy fire and cutting loose a shattered spar that menaced the ship. After gallant service in the Mediterranean, he was a leading naval officer of the War of 1812; his son of the same name was to have an even more distinguished naval career, including high command, in the Civil War.

Porter's vigor was what made the *Essex* a doughty participant in the War of 1812. He hurried about New York to recruit a crew, equip his ship, mend her hull, procure arms and ammunition and get her to sea before restrictions could be issued by Washington or before the ship could be hemmed in by British blockaders. Of the recruited seamen, the least consequential for his cruise might seem to be the cabin boy, eleven years old, a Tennessee lad named David G. Farragut, whom Porter had taken under his care and fortune had adopted for her smiles.

The *Essex* had had as noble a beginning as she would have an honorable career. When the new republic needed ships to battle the Barbary pirates, the patriotic citizens of Essex County, Massachusetts, joined in felling and hauling the timber and building the neat little frigate of 866 tons, the smallest frigate in the Navy, and presented her to the federal government. Her decks had been trodden by the great Edward Preble, who had taken her to the Far East by way of the Cape of Good Hope, the first American warship in the East Indies. She was therefore a link between three of the most dauntless officers of the nineteenth-century Navy— Preble, Porter and Farragut.

Porter scarcely was out of New York when he began to sight British merchant ships, a number of which he captured and sent back as prizes. He met a fleet being convoyed by a British frigate but was able to cut off the rear ship. Soon afterward he encountered and captured a British sloop of war, the *Alert*. This was the first British warship taken by the Americans.

Porter took other prizes off the Grand Banks, then headed south. Judging that Boston and New York would be blockaded, he entered the Delaware River. Here he learned about an unusual challenge.

Porter had been charged in a newspaper story, printed just after the declaration of war, with mistreating a British seaman who claimed to be a British deserter but who refused to fight his countrymen. The man, John Irvin, had indeed been tarred and feathered in New York by some petty officers, but Porter had had nothing to do with the incident. Soon afterward the British minister, August J. Foster, then in New York en route home after diplomatic relations had been severed, rescued Irvin and took him to England.

Meanwhile, Captain Sir James Lucas Yeo, commanding HM frigate *Southampton,* had learned of the incident from the New York newspapers, which told how Irvin had run down Pearl Street in his tar and feathers. Yeo blamed Porter for Irvin's mistreatment and sent him a public letter by a paroled civilian. As printed in the Philadelphia *Democratic Press,* Yeo's letter invited Porter to a tête-à-tête any place between the Delaware and Havana, "where he would have the pleasure to break his own sword over his damned head, and put him down forward in irons."

Porter promptly accepted the challenge and sent a message to Yeo. He gave preference to a meeting near the Delaware and promised that no other American warship would interfere. To be sure that Yeo would recognize him and his ship, Porter added: "The *Essex* may be known by a flag bearing the motto, FREE TRADE AND SAILORS' RIGHTS, and when that is struck to the *Southampton* Captain P. will deserve the treatment promised by Sir James."

The incident was important only to the extent that it confirmed in the public mind the words "Free Trade and Sailors' Rights" as the motto of the war. This gave as good an explanation as any of why the conflict was being fought. But the tête-à-tête never took place. Yeo was assigned later to command the British squadron on

Lake Ontario, while Porter was ordered to join Captain Bainbridge cruising off South America; from there he later passed
around Cape Horn.

Meanwhile there had been other dramatic encounters at sea.

THE WASP AND THE FROLIC

The brilliant victory of the *Constitution* and the lesser battle
of the *Essex* with the *Alert* were followed by another spectacular
clash between two well-matched sloops of war, USS *Wasp*, ship-
rigged, and HMS *Frolic*, brig-rigged, on October 18, 1812, off the
southern coast. Never did warships fight with greater spirit.
Though they were small—the *Wasp* with 18 guns and the *Frolic*
with 19—both ships reflected the greatest credit on their navies.
The battle was joined on a raging sea at the tail of a West Indies
hurricane that had damaged both vessels. The Americans tri-
umphed in an engagement as desperately fought as it was quickly
won.

Master Commandant Jacob Jones, who commanded the *Wasp*,
did not have the usual naval officer's background of previous
merchant marine service. Born in Smyrna, Delaware, in comfortable circumstances, he attended Lewes Academy and was gradu-
ated by the University of Pennsylvania Medical School, then had
further training under an eminent doctor at Dover, Delaware.
Evidently he was disappointed when he did not immediately accu-
mulate a large practice. He shifted to become a clerk of the Delaware Supreme Court. In 1799, when he was thirty-one, the quasi-
war with France broke out. The thirty-one-year-old Jones suddenly
dropped his scalpels and court records and enlisted as a midshipman. Within two years, after a cruise under John Barry, he was a
second lieutenant under William Bainbridge on the *Philadelphia*.
After Bainbridge surrendered the grounded *Philadelphia* to the
Tripolitans, Jones passed twenty months in the Tripoli prison.

Following the Barbary wars Jones became master commandant,
commanding the sloop *Argus*. In the spring of 1812, in the *Wasp*,
he carried new envoys being sent to Great Britain and France and
was in European waters when war came. Returning, he headed for

the British shipping lanes from the West Indies. There he encountered a tropical October hurricane, in which the *Wasp* lost
her jib boom and two sailors. In the tail of the storm, he discovered a British merchant fleet of six ships being convoyed from
Honduras by the *Frolic*. Since the merchant ships appeared to be
well armed, Jones fell in alongside them until the next morning,
when he might choose his odds. The hurricane had battered the
Frolic also, and she was setting new topsails. Nevertheless, she
stood out unhesitatingly to meet her pursuer.

At 11:30 A.M., with the skies clear blue and the storm abating,
the two vessels ran alongside at sixty yards' distance, the waves at
times dashing over their bows. Battling the elements as well as
each other, they emitted broadsides that called for the best in gunnery. The tossing of the ships, like bark canoes pitching about on
a wind-swept river, was so severe that the muzzles of the guns
would at one instant be submerged beneath the waves and the
next pointing toward the heavens. That meant the loading had to
be done rapidly so that the gun could be fired before another roll
of the vessel wetted the powder.

In the exchange of broadsides under these conditions the skill
of the better-trained American gunners had a marked effect. They
judged their opportunities better in the tossing of the waves than
the British. The Americans fired while the *Wasp* was rolling down
and, when possible, while the *Frolic* was coming up with the roll,
whereas the *Frolic* usually fired when on the crest and while the
Wasp was in the trough. The *Frolic*'s shots went largely overhead
or into the American's rigging; the *Wasp*'s swept the Briton's deck
or hit the hull.

As the vessels rolled and wallowed, they drew so close together
that the American gunners in loading at times found the ends of
their ramrods protruding through the portholes of the *Frolic* and
even striking the British sailors at their gun stations. At such close
quarters the vessels soon fouled each other, mainly because neither
vessel was any longer under adequate control.

As they came together one of the American sailors went berserk
—AB (Able-Bodied Seaman) Jack Lang, who had once been impressed on the *Frolic* and nursed a seething hatred. He drew his
cutlass, jumped on a gun and prepared to spring to the British

deck. Jones shouted him back, but the impetuous seaman, bent on retaliation, defied his commander and leaped to the *Frolic*. Several of the *Wasp*'s sailors, wild with excitement, followed him. Yielding to the inevitable, Jones "called away" his boarders, sending them to the *Frolic*'s deck. The Americans, led by Lieutenant James Biddle, surged en masse onto the British vessel.

The boarding party found resistance feeble. The last American broadside had virtually swept the enemy away. One single veteran seaman had kept his post at the wheel, while three officers lay nearby, bloody with wounds. When a check was made it was discovered that 90 of the *Frolic*'s crew had been killed or wounded; only 17 of the 107 men she carried into action were unscathed, an exceedingly high casualty rate even in the days of wooden ships.

Honor was due the British for persevering so resolutely and to the victors for their skill under the very worst conditions for good gunnery. Surprisingly, the *Wasp*'s casualties were but five killed and five wounded. However, the *Wasp*'s rigging was so torn that she was virtually unmanageable, and Captain Jones' first task was to recondition her. Her gaff and main top-gallant mast were down; her sails were in ribbons. The *Frolic* had been hulled so frequently that she was a virtual wreck.

Jones nevertheless put a prize crew aboard the *Frolic*, headed by Lieutenant Biddle. For two hours the crews bent every effort to make both ships seaworthy. The action had indeed been a naval classic—perhaps the fiercest, most sanguinary and most evenly matched encounter of the war.

Then it was that HM ship of the line *Poictiers*, 74, commanded by Captain John Poer Beresford, hove in sight. She was too powerful for Jones to dream of battling, even had his battered little sloop been in prime condition. The *Poictiers* came alongside, and Jones was forced to surrender his own vessel and his prize. Both were taken by Beresford into Bermuda.

There Jones and his crew were exchanged. When the gallant captain reached New York, he wrote his report, which when published, stirred the American public with pride and enthusiasm approaching that aroused by the capture of the *Guerrière*. Newspapers published enraptured accounts, and poets scribbled doggerel rhymes that were sung in barroom, parlor and street. One of them ended:

And long shall John Bull rue the terrible day
He met the American *Wasp* on a *Frolic*.

Congress reacted to the public rejoicing by ordering a medal
struck for Jones and $25,000 distributed to him and his crew in
lieu of the prize money they would have been awarded had not
the *Poictiers* made her untimely appearance. Delaware honored
Jones, and cities celebrated when he appeared. The Pennsylvania
legislature voted Lieutenant Biddle a sword, and his native city,
Philadelphia, gave him a silver urn. Jones was promoted and given
command of the frigate *Macedonian,* which Captain Stephen Decatur had captured from the British seven days after the affair of
the *Wasp* and the *Frolic*.

THE UNITED STATES AND THE MACEDONIAN

Decatur, commander of the *United States,* 44, sister frigate of
the *Constitution,* had been the young hero of the Tripolitan war.
He had distinguished himself in desperate hand-to-hand fighting
with the crews of the enemy gunboats but had gained his greatest
fame by commanding the little party that stole into Tripoli harbor
to recapture the frigate *Philadelphia,* which the corsairs had taken
from Bainbridge. Decatur and his men had fired and destroyed
the *Philadelphia* and then got out in safety before the startled
corsair city quite understood what was taking place.

Decature was undoubtedly the most admired and respected officer in the Navy. His gallant conduct in the Barbary wars had
caused him to be jumped to the grade of captain over the heads
of brother officers, some of whom were disgruntled; but his courage
and forthright conduct endeared him in the end to the public
and the Navy.

Before the outbreak of the War of 1812 Decatur met Captain
John S. Carden, RN, amiable young commander of HM frigate
Macedonian, 38, which had put into Norfolk. They bantered
pleasantly; Carden spoke of the likelihood of war and the possibility that if it came, they might meet on the high seas. Decatur,
who seems to have grown serious, as he always was in matters
respecting his country, replied that if the odds were at all equal

the fight would be desperate. But he averred solemnly that "the flag of my country on the ship I command shall never leave the staff on which it waves as long as there is a hull to support it."

Captain Carden must have had a presentiment, because chance brought about the very meeting he had talked about so lightly. Off Madeira, at dawn on Sunday morning, October 25, 1812, with the sea running high, the two ships met. The *United States*, accompanying Commodore Rodgers on a second cruise, had left Boston in company with the *President*, 44, and the neat little sloop of war *Argus*, 16. The ships separated October 12, the *United States* heading southeast into the shipping lanes from the West Indies.

The Sunday morning meeting was dramatic. Neither captain recognized the other's vessel, but both broke out their respective colors. The *United States* proved a good sailor and by 9 A.M. closed to near cannon range. The opponents were fairly well matched. The *Macedonian*, rated 38, actually carried 48 guns; the *United States*, a 44, in reality mustered 54.

Decatur's crew, disappointed with the few prizes they had taken on the long cruise from Boston, shouted and cheered as the vessels approached. Their confidence was supreme. A little cabin boy, catching the intoxication of battle and certainty of victory, approached Decatur, took off his cap and asked if now that he had become ten years old his name might be inscribed on the ship's master roll. The captain asked him why. "So I can share in the prize money when we take that Britisher, sir," the lad replied.

Carden, meantime, was walking through his ship, giving encouragement and repeating Nelson's signal at Trafalgar, "England expects every man to do his duty."

Decatur, even more than Jacob Jones, was a master of rapid and accurate gunnery. The British frigate felt severely the effectiveness of the American roundshot while the ships fought at long range for half an hour. Carden, seeing that his sails were being shredded and his hull battered and that he was losing the battle at long bowls, determined to close and board. His ship was the fleeter, and he might have shown better judgment by sailing away, but British naval captains did not have the habit of running. Also, he mistook the *United States* for the *Essex*, which he had seen on his visit to Virginia, and felt he had nothing to fear from the smaller ship. But when he tried to close he began to realize how much punishment his ship had suffered. Now the attack became more intense.

Decatur personally had trained his gunners to load with great speed and fire by divisions. The years of drilling now bore the fruit of sixty fearful minutes of performance, during which the decks of the *Macedonian* became a holocaust. The *United States* played about her, cutting her sails and rigging.

The *Macedonian* had a yellow streak painted on her hull at the gun deck level.

"Aim at the yellow streak," Decatur now told his gunners. "Her spars and rigging are going fast enough. She must have a little more hulling." The effectiveness of the response was seen after the battle, when it was found that in her hull alone the *Macedonian* had taken a hundred roundshot.

The battle had an unusual climax in that the British, worsted as they were, momentarily believed they had won it. Their ship was battered and torn, but they thought that the *United States* was on fire and in even greater distress. The story was told in another of the contemporary ditties:

> They thought they saw our ship in flame,
> Which made them all huzza, sirs,
> But when the second broadside came
> It made them hold their jaws, sirs.

Actually the American vessel, by her system of division firing, fired so rapidly and continuously that the red glare from the mouths of the guns, seen through the heavy smoke clouds, gave the impression that the ship was on fire. Then as the *United States* went about, the British sailors thought she was leaving the battle in distress. They set up a loud cheer.

Instead of burning, the *United States* was dexterously gaining a raking position. When Carden saw that he was at his enemy's mercy, with his ship's hull splintered and gashed, her sails so riddled they would not hold air, her maneuverability lost and her casualties heavy, he hauled down his flag.

More than a third of the *Macedonian*'s crew of 300 were killed or wounded. The American ship suffered only 11 casualties, 5 killed and 6 wounded. The unimaginative sailor who kept the log of the *United States* summed up the most splendid day in the frigate's history the following day in matter-of-fact language: "Moderate and pleasant. Laying to all these 24 hours the wind at up S.SE. All hands busily engaged repairing damages. Shifting prisoners and baggage from the Prize . . ."

Decatur reached Newport, Rhode Island, December 6 with his prize and threw the town into a festival of rejoicing. This was the only instance during the war when a captured British frigate was brought into an American port.

One of Decatur's lieutenants, riding posthaste to Washington, found President Madison, accompanied by his radiant wife, Dolley, attending the Naval Ball, the gala occasion of the Christmas season. The gathering was suddenly silenced, the dancing halted, as the mud-spattered envoy carrying a bundle stalked into the room. Bowing in front of Dolley, he spread at her feet the tattered, bullet-riddled colors of His Majesty's frigate *Macedonian,* a present from Decatur to the inimitable First Lady. Dolley blushed through her rouge at such a gift from so gallant an officer. The band struck up "Hail, Columbia," which then served as the national anthem, and as the news spread, the capital celebrated. Medals were struck, swords presented, testimonial dinners held.

The upsurge of joy was badly needed in a nation struck numb by a succession of dismal reverses in land warfare along the Canadian border.

6

The Battle of Queenston

By September 8, 1812, when the armistice along the northeastern front ended, both sides had strengthened their respective positions to some extent. However, General Van Rensselaer had no reason to exult. On September 1 he had at Lewiston only 691 men fit for duty along a 36-mile front; more than 100 others were on the sick list. On August 27 the sad parade of the American prisoners captured at Detroit, in plain sight across the Niagara River as they trudged toward Montreal and prison camp, had shaken his troops' morale. Medicines and hospital stores were extremely scarce; there were no surgical instruments, lint or bandages. Doctors were few and not knowledgeable. Many men were without shoes, and all were clamoring for pay.

The situation was not helped by incompetent subordinates like Lieutenant Colonel John R. Fenwick, Light Artillery, commanding Fort Niagara, who took to the bottle to drown his sorrows and pestered Van Rensselaer with mournful complaints, and Captain Daniel W. Church of the New York 15th Militia, at Ogdensburg, who was sent with a small boat party to sink British supply bateaux ascending the St. Lawrence. Church met the convoy below the town, exchanged a few shots, lost one of his two boats and fled.

Another raid, a few days later, bore fruit. During the night of September 20, Captain Benjamin Forsyth was sent by General Jacob Brown with ninety-five men to destroy British storehouses at Ganonoque. Forsyth burned the supply dump and returned home in triumph with several barrels of ammunition, sixty stands of arms and eight British regulars as prisoners. In retaliation, a British force from Prescott, some 2,000 yards away across the river, raided Ogdensburg on October 4 but was driven off.

An American militia raid on St. Regis, a village astride the boundary line, on October 22 netted, without loss, forty prisoners and considerable equipment. The colors that had flown over the British blockhouse—the first to be taken on land during the war— were later presented to the State of New York by its captor, Major G. B. Young.

All this, of course, was picayune stuff, a curious blend of an old man's caution, flickering hope and procrastination. Van Rensselaer told of mythical reinforcement to come, urged caution and at the same time insisted, "We must calculate on possessing Upper Canada before winter sets in"—certainly a rare piece of wishful thinking.

To help in this offensive, Brigadier General Alexander Smyth had been ordered to Buffalo to take command of the brigade of regular infantry assembling there. On September 29, Smith reported his arrival in a letter to Van Rensselaer. At the same time he gratuitously recommended that an offensive be initiated between Fort Erie and Chippawa.

The next day Van Rensselaer answered, doubting the desirability of beginning a neighborhood offensive like the one suggested but expressing the hope of seeing Smyth soon and adopting a plan that would be mutually agreeable. Smyth ignored not only Van Rensselaer's diplomatic answer but also a later invitation to attend a conference of senior commanders at Fort Niagara.

Van Rensselaer had been planning an offensive that provided for Smyth to march his brigade to Fort Niagara, cross the river and take Fort George, while Van Rensselaer himself invaded Canada from Lewiston and seized Queenston. By this joint operation Van Rensselaer had hoped to satisfy the public demand for immediate action, capture important points in the system of British defense

and secure for his troops better winter quarters than those available on the American side.

Now, however, he decided he could not trust Smyth. Yet he felt more keenly than ever that he must do something to offset his own lack of action for nearly two months, especially after he had learned of a brilliant and successful raid by a junior officer in Smyth's sector.

On October 9, Lieutenant Jesse D. Elliott, with approximately 124 sailors and soldiers assembled near Buffalo, had seized the British brig *Detroit* (formerly the American ship *Adams*) and the schooner *Caledonia*, carrying a rich cargo of furs and skins, while both vessels were riding peacefully at anchor under the guns of

Fort Erie. The *Caledonia* was brought safely across to Black Rock. The *Detroit*, however, got no farther than the west side of Squaw Island, where she had run aground and been twice attacked by the British. The Americans then removed her cargo and set her on fire. Elliott had lost only 2 killed and 5 wounded and had taken 46 prisoners. The event caused British General Brock deep anxiety, for he was fearful that it was the beginning of American supremacy on the lakes. In Washington, Henry Clay declared it to be a capture never surpassed in the annals of his country for "judgment, skill, and courage."

Upon learning of this exploit, General Van Rensselaer determined to attack the hostile batteries on the heights of Queenston during the night of October 10. Smyth was directed to start his brigade immediately for Lewiston; once there, it apparently was to act merely as a sort of reserve. Smyth received his orders but did nothing then or thereafter to comply, despite the fact that, as a Regular Army officer and former inspector general, he had always insisted that obedience was the essence of a soldier's creed.

Despite Smyth's inaction, Van Rensselaer decided to cross the river from the old ferry opposite the heights of Queenston at three o'clock on the morning of the 11th. Participation in the operation was optional for the militia units under his command. As reported by a contemporary, "Some companies volunteered without officers; others, officers without soldiers; and some neither officers nor soldiers. From Capt. Bristol's company about 20 volunteered, from Captain Kellogg's only one; the whole marched to the edge of the river at the hour appointed . . . for crossing."

After dark on the evening of October 10, 13 large boats were secretly hauled by wagon from Gill Creek, about two miles above Niagara Falls, and placed in the river near Lewiston. They were capable of accommodating some 26 men apiece with all their arms and equipment, or about 338 all told. Lieutenant John Simms of Niagara County, reputedly skillful in the handling of boats, was put in charge and started off in one of them to lead the way. As the story goes, he moved up the river, passed far beyond the point designated for embarkation, crossed over to the Canadian side and there deserted under cover of night and storm. By hook or crook, he seems to have taken with him most of the oars belonging to the other boats, which, thus made immobile and useless, never arrived where the would-be raiders were anxiously waiting to be carried across. Disappointed and chagrined, they stood by until nearly daylight, shelterless and cold, enduring as best they could a violent wind and chilling autumn rain.

Thus did Van Rensselaer's first attempt to invade Canada ingloriously end. Undaunted, perhaps desperate, he decided to try again during the early morning hours of October 13. Winter was close at hand, making large-scale fighting almost impossible, and the militia, about to finish their term of enlistment, would soon want to go home.

For this operation Van Rensselaer selected from the militia alone five organizations—the 16th, 17th, 18th, 19th and 20th Regiments. The first two composed the 6th Brigade, commanded by Brigadier General Daniel Miller, locally prominent in Cortland County but with few of the qualities required for a general. His regimental commanders, Lieutenant Colonels Farrand Stranahan of the 16th and Thompson Mead of the 17th, were both brave but of doubtful competence.

The 18th, 19th and 20th Regiments, forming the 7th Brigade, recruited in Seneca, Cayuga and Ontario counties, were respectively commanded by Lieutenant Colonels Hugh W. Dobbins, Henry Bloom and Peter Allen. Of these three, Bloom evinced the most energy and best soldierly qualities. Their commander, Brigadier General William Wadsworth, lived in Geneseo and had been in command of the troops along the Niagara before the arrival of Stephen Van Rensselaer on August 10. Although he lacked the professional knowledge possessed by some of his comrades in arms, he never displayed the bigotry or prejudice that commonly warped the character of most of the militia officers. Where the good of his country was concerned, he did not quibble over methods or means, whether or not his own personal interests were served.

Cooperating with these militia organizations were a number of regular troops. Smyth had been asked to take part, but he did nothing more than to allow Lieutenant Colonel Winfield Scott to take two companies of the 2nd Artillery to Lewiston. Lieutenant Colonel John Chrystie, from Four Mile Creek, was to supply 300 recently enlisted men of the 13th Infantry. Lieutenants John Gansevoort and Samuel B. Rathbone were directed to bring 40 more from Captain Luther Leonard's company of Light Artillery

at Fort Niagara. From the same place the bibulous Lieutenant
Colonel Fenwick and Major James R. Mullany, 23rd Infantry,
were to have 550 others equipped and ready. In all something like
1,000 regular troops were to join in the operation with the approximately 2,240 militia encamped in or near Lewiston.

For secrecy the movement of most units to the vicinity of Lewiston was to be made at night. Bad weather the night of October
12–13 made this march an unusually tiring one for newly enlisted
recruits. The 16th, 17th and 19th Regiments set out from Niagara
Falls respectively at 7, 8 and 9 P.M. of October 12, marching about
four hours in mud and rain before they reached the point of embarkation. Scott and his men had an even worse time. They had
completed a long daylight march and had just begun to bed down
for the night near Fort Schlosser when Scott learned that Queenston was to be attacked in a few hours. Mounting his horse, he
galloped away for Van Rensselaer's headquarters to see if the
report were true and what part he might play. Once informed of
the general's plan, he hurried back, roused his men and started
them wallowing along the road for an additional eight-mile hike.
By 4 A.M. on the 13th they had reached the high ground near the
Lewiston ferry, weary and worn but ready for battle. Chrystie and
his detachment had arrived about six hours earlier, wet and be-
draggled; they had been on the way from their camp near Fort
Niagara for about five hours. After covering about seven miles in
storm and darkness, Fenwick and his men dragged into Lewiston
about daybreak. The 18th and 20th Regiments of militia were
luckier; for they were camped at Lewiston, not far from where
they were to cross the river.

Even before all the troops had assembled on the 13th, wrangling
began among the officers. Federal law provided that regular officers
should enjoy rank and command over all others of corresponding
commissioned grades in the state militia. Scott, Chrystie and Fenwick—all lieutenant colonels in the regular service—insisted that
any one of them was legally entitled to command the forthcoming
expedition instead of Lieutenant Colonel Solomon Van Rensselaer, of the New York State militia, nephew of the commanding
general. In all his preparations, General Stephen Van Rensselaer
had clearly shown that he wanted his militia troops to dominate
the enterprise. He had given them the leading and most important

assignments. At so late an hour he naturally did not want to transfer the execution of his plans to officers who were unfamiliar with those plans. He therefore declared that no change would be made. Under the circumstances, Fenwick agreed to waive his rank in case he were allowed to go along. Chrystie proved somewhat less pliant. With inscrutable ambiguity he declared that he would hold to his rank but accept orders from Van Rensselaer. Scott was uncompromising in strongly insisting on what he thought was militarily correct. In consequence, he found himself temporarily relegated to a minor role: that of bringing up his men and his guns merely to cover the crossing of others.

Solomon Van Rensselaer had hoped that 300 militia and 40 men from the Light Artillery would be the first of the attackers across the river. But when he approached the point of embarkation, he found the way jammed with regulars who had arrived during the night, and he ruefully set out with them instead. In fact, only about 60 of the militia accompanied him, the rest being from the 13th Infantry companies of John E. Wool, Richard M. Malcolm and Henry B. Armstrong, along with a detachment of Light Artillery from Fort Niagara.

Thus loaded with a majority of recently recruited regulars, 13 boats started across the 300 yards of the foreboding Niagara at about four o'clock on the morning of October 13. The night was extremely dark, the wind blew hard and a cold rain fell heavily upon the huddling men. After a crossing of about 10 minutes only 10 of the boats, averaging about 25 raiders apiece, reached the intended landing place (near the point where the Lewiston bridge would later reach the Canadian shore). Chrystie's boat had to turn back, as he later explained, because an oarlock was lost and his pilot failed him. Captain William D. Lawrence, who appeared to have lost his bearings, returned with Chrystie. Another boat, in the charge of a subaltern, went completely astray and reached land north of Queenston, where he and all his men quickly fell into the hands of the British. Thus Van Rensselaer found himself with a mixed detachment about 250 strong with which to carry out the planned attack.

The British were not entirely unready. On the 12th, Major Thomas Evans had visited the American side of the river under a flag of truce. He returned with the news that an attack was imminent. Brock immediately took steps to meet it. Captain James B. Dennis with his company of the 49th Foot, Captain Samuel Hatt and his organization of York volunteers, a small body of Indians and a 3-pounder detachment took posts on the sloping ground not far from where Van Rensselaer's troops first landed. There they waited.

Even before the raiders reached shore, a few British field pieces opened fire on them, quickly followed by volleys of musketry. Lieutenant Samuel B. Rathbone, close to Solomon Van Rensselaer, fell mortally wounded. Scrambling hurriedly out of the boats and up the banks, the Americans moved rapidly forward, pushing the British back to the outskirts of Queenston. Captain Wool was among the leaders, urging them on. While halting a moment to reconnoiter and reorganize, he received an order to storm the heights. As he organized his company for the assault, a little south of Queenston, the order was revoked. Wool halted, now uncertain what to do. In the meantime, Captain John Williams, some British light infantry and a company of York militia had reinforced the heights, from where they vigorously fired upon the Americans' front while Dennis flung his company upon their right flank.

To meet this counterattack, Wool shifted most of his men to the right while the militia protected his left. Although Dennis and his men were pushed back, the harassing fire from the heights continued. Both sides were fighting with valor and spirit, but the Americans were suffering far more. Lieutenant John Valleau and Ensign Robert Morris were both killed; Solomon Van Rensselaer received six wounds; Captains Armstrong, Malcolm and Wool and Ensign James W. Lent were all wounded less severely. Those in the ranks fared no better. With casualties mounting, Van Rensselaer ordered his detachment to fall back and seek cover under the riverbank. Once there he turned over the command to the twenty-three-year-old Wool, who, though shot in both thighs, was not as critically wounded as he was.

As they regrouped under the protection of the riverbank, the Americans were reinforced by Captain Peter Ogilvie and some men from the 13th Infantry and the militia. Wool's little force rose again to a strength of about 250 men fit for battle. A hasty reconnaissance discovered a steep and seldom-used path ascending from the river, and by hard climbing they managed to reach the heights unmolested and undiscovered by the British, who were now occupied by a new American assault wave on the river. From their new position, Wool's troops could look down the slope and see the flashing of an 18-pounder that had caused them much trouble a little while before and was doing likewise to those now trying to cross over from Lewiston. Wool decided to attack immediately. Just as General Brock, recently arrived from Fort George, was directing a gunner to make a correction in sighting, Wool and his men came charging upon the one-gun battery from the rear. The routed defenders fled toward Queenston. Wool triumphantly seized the position, quickly raising the Stars and Stripes so that his comrades across the river might see where he was and what had been done.

Brock soon halted the British retreat. He concluded that the main American attack was to center around Queenston, not Fort George, as he had previously thought. He accordingly sent word to Sheaffe to reinforce him immediately with every man available at Fort George. Then, rallying the fugitives and part of his own 49th with the cry "Follow me!" the general personally led an attack up the slope to retake the abandoned guns. At the same time, he directed a small detachment to turn Wool's left.

Though painfully wounded in the wrist, Brock pushed sturdily on, animating his "green tigers" with encouraging words and heartening action. In the opening dawn he made a conspicuous target, for he was well toward the front, taller than most of his men and dressed in the dazzling regalia of a British general. A rifle bullet fired by one of Wool's frontiersmen struck Brock in the right breast and penetrated to his left side. Carried to a farmer's house nearby, he lived only a little while. Thus died a great soldier in mid-career and in keeping with the finest traditions of the British Army.

Lieutenant Colonel John Macdonnell assumed command of the British troops. By then it was full daylight and the wind and rain had ceased. Under his direction, the men of the 49th and some York volunteers, 190 strong, moved forward to seize the heights and avenge their general. The American fire was again heavy and accurate. Macdonnell soon fell, mortally wounded, and Dennis and Williams were also hit. With the loss of these leaders, the

British again fell back in confusion to the environs of Queenston.

Wool took advantage of the lull to regroup his men on the heights. He set some of them to repairing the 18-pounder that somebody, in a moment of despair during the British assault, had just finished spiking. It was needed badly to help silence the Vrooman's Point battery of 24-pounders, a little north of Queenston. These guns were interfering with the crossing of much-needed reinforcements from Lewiston.

With the coming of daylight, boats on the river became easy targets for the British gunners. Nevertheless, a number of Americans took the risk and landed safely, bringing strength and encouragement to Wool's hard-pressed command. Among them were Lieutenant Colonels Farr, Stranahan and Thompson Mead, with detachments from their respective militia regiments; they had been scheduled to arrive with the first contingents but had been delayed until after seven o'clock because of a lack of ammunition. Lieutenant Colonel Fenwick also arrived with some regulars from the Light Artillery, bringing a single 6-pounder.

Brigadier General William Wadsworth of the militia crossed over too, without orders. He hoped that his example and that of some in his brigade would induce others to do likewise. Wadsworth now assumed command of the American troops on the Canadian side of the river.

Learning that the enemy was advancing from both Chippawa and Fort George, Wadsworth dispatched Chrystie to tell General Van Rensselaer the critical situation of his troops. Chrystie soon found the general about half a mile from the river on the American side. Wishing to show his own spirit and to learn the situation for himself, General Van Rensselaer decided to cross back over the river with Chrystie. Both of them accordingly started for the ferry, where they found about a company of militiamen who refused to enter the waiting boats. Despite all orders and threats of the general, they still refused. Disgusted, he and Chrystie embarked.

It was around noon of the 13th when Chrystie and General Van Rensselaer arrived on the heights, where they found about 350 regulars and 250 volunteers. There they learned that Brigadier General Wadsworth had waived his right to command in favor of Scott, who had brought his command across the river during the

morning. Wadsworth thought the regular officer was better fitted
for the task of command. This was a heartening example of unity
at a critical hour.

Suddenly, a force of partisan Indian warriors recruited from
along the Grand River in Canada swept along the brow of the
heights with a blood-curdling war whoop. The American pickets
precipitately fled toward the river. The militia in the rear, stricken
with terror, were ready to follow when Scott appeared and rallied
them with the strength of his words and example. Changing the
front of his line, Scott and his men fell upon the savages so
violently that they soon made for the woods from which they had
come. Here they lingered until Scott renewed the assault and
cleaned them from the heights.

While Scott, Wadsworth and their brave men were clinging to
the heights, satisfied General Van Rensselaer returned to the
American side in order to rush reinforcements to them. But he
found the situation on the east bank to be in hopeless confusion.
Less than half a dozen boats remained; the others had been sunk
by the British or stolen by deserters from the fighting on the
opposite shore. These cowards had abandoned the boats downstream, then spread terrifying tales of death and disaster. The
number of wounded brought back tended to confirm the wild
stories in circulation among the waiting troops. Those near the
river became even more perturbed when they looked across and
saw the Indians and the heavy hostile reinforcements advancing
from Fort George. To cross a treacherous, fire-swept river just to
share in bloody fighting appealed to only the strong-hearted and
brave, and these were few. When Van Rensselaer rode among his
militia urging them to embark, none would comply in spite of all
his orders, imprecations and pleading. Lieutenant Colonel Henry
Bloom, though wounded only a little while before, and Judge
Peck, a camp visitor of note, also exhorted and excoriated; but
both, like the general, failed to win converts for crossing.

Van Rensselaer's sole and immediate contribution consisted of
sending across some badly needed ammunition. With this shipment Van Rensselaer sent a note to Wadsworth, telling him that
no troops would come to his rescue and that he had better do
what his judgment suggested. In case he decided to retreat, Van
Rensselaer wrote, boats would be sent him and his withdrawal

would be covered with fire. These promises proved to be nothing more than expressions of hope.

The British, meanwhile, were far more efficient. General Sheaffe, at Fort George, promptly responded to Brock's order to bring on reinforcements. He left only a few artillerists at the fort under Major Thomas Evans. These gunners bombarded Fort Niagara so effectively that they stopped the dangerous American cannonading that had several times set their barracks on fire.

Meanwhile, with 400 men of the 41st Foot and about 300 militia, Sheaffe was on a six-mile hike to Queenston. At Vrooman's Point, he was joined by some of those who had dispersed when Brock and Macdonnell had been killed. With these additions to his force, he started for St. David's, a little village about three miles west of Queenston, to get beyond the range of American guns on the east bank. From here he reconnoitered the American position on the heights, where Scott and Wadsworth were trying to secure a commanding position and a covered route to the river. After completing his reconnaissance, Sheaffe decided to strike the American right, attacking from a field lying along the river road and west of the Americans. While his troops were forming for the attack, he was joined by some militia units, Indians and a grenadier company of the 41st from Chippawa. This brought the total force under Sheaffe's command to about 1,000 troops exclusive of Indians, of whom there were probably more than 100.

At this time Scott and Wadsworth had less than 300 men fit for combat, and they now knew only too well that no reinforcements would come over to help them. In sight of the assembling British and their allies, Wadsworth called the senior officers together and read them Van Rensselaer's message in order to determine what course should be followed. Scott, Wadsworth, Mead and some others were for holding their ground. Wadsworth agreed. Although a brigadier general, he again declared that Scott was in command and must be obeyed.

Scott, in full dress uniform, now spiritedly harangued his men, reminding them that there was no place to retreat and they must fight to the end for their country and cause. Wadsworth made it clear that he was of the same mind, heart and soul. Clad in ordinary civilian clothes, he went here and there, reiterating, with frequent and forceful profanity, that all must stand by and do their duty. Under these two leaders, the troops' response was immediate and convincing. Even so, they found themselves, before long, in a hopeless position.

In the meantime, Sheaffe, making good use of his four or five pieces of artillery, had begun to spray the American front with grapeshot. The Americans had only their single 6-pounder, and its ammunition was quickly exhausted. Then came the British assault on the American right led by the 41st Foot, accompanied by detachments of militia and Indians and some Negro volunteers who had fled slavery in the United States. About 100 yards from the American position they halted to fire, and then, breaking through the smoke that a strong wind blew straight in their faces, they charged with wild shouting and war whoops.

The attackers soon broke through the improvised defenses, striking down the defenders with bayonet and tomahawk. When Sheaffe swept forward with the rest of his troops, the American defense began to crumble. Some made for the river, but many of these, faltering because of desperate wounds, were quickly and cruelly killed with scalping knife and tomahawk. When some tried to escape by the Queenston–Niagara Falls road, the Indians cut them off, driving them back into the woods along the precipice above the rushing river. Other fugitives, descending along the face of the cliff, lost their footing and fell to their death on the rocks below. A few reached the shore and attempted to swim across, although they were nearly exhausted and the current was strong. Some may have succeeded, but most of them failed.

Perhaps half the Americans fell back in good order, under Scott's direction, to establish a new position nearer the river. But as the fighting mounted in fury, only the bravest maintained unbroken spirit, gathering in little groups under the shelter of the riverbank and ardently trying to hold their ground. Wadsworth, Scott and Chrystie grimly recognized that the hour of their annihilation was swiftly approaching unless they surrendered. Scott dispatched a messenger to the British commander to ask for terms; but the Indians killed him. When this messenger failed to return, Scott sent another, and he, too, was killed.

Without hesitation, Scott assumed the task himself. To mark his mission as one of peace, he took a white cravat, tied it to his sword, which he held aloft, and with two others he started for the

British lines. When they emerged from the cover of the riverbank, they were fired on several times. Two Indians rushed toward them with raised tomahawks, but just then some British regulars appeared and escorted them safely to Sheaffe.

Terms were quickly arranged. British bugles sounded the cease-fire, and soon the thunder of artillery and the crack of musketry dwindled away. Only the Indians continued for a little while to snipe at any unfortunate American who exposed himself.

With this exception, the agreement became quickly effective. Approximately 600 Americans who had slunk away from the active fighting came out of gullies, caves and underbrush and laid down their arms beside those of the handful who had heroically done a soldier's part. The seriously wounded reputedly filled every spare room in Queenston. Some of these Sheaffe permitted to be carried across the river to Lewiston for nursing and medical care. Others were taken to Newark, where they were bedded down in a church because the hospital at Fort George was also overflowing with patients. There were 120 of these wounded Americans, and, in spite of all efforts, 30 of them died within a few days.

The toll of American dead and wounded was undeniably heavy. Captain Thomas Gist declared that he had only 17 of his 100 men left and that he himself managed to escape only because he was able to get on a boat engaged in carrying back wounded. Henry Armstrong, the twenty-year-old son of the man who would later become Eustis' successor, stated that of the 36 men with him, 14 were killed and 16 wounded. He himself was wounded once by a musket ball and three times by buckshot. A reputed eyewitness asserted that British artillery sank one boat with about 50 men aboard and that two others did not succeed in landing more than a dozen alive on the Canadian shore. Some estimates of the American dead alone ranged as high as 500. On October 27, the Quebec *Mercury* declared that the American killed and wounded amounted to about 350. General Van Rensselaer reported 60 killed, 170 wounded and 764 prisoners—figures that are obviously too low. He made no mention of many others unaccounted for. Undoubtedly a large number deserted, several organizations completely disintegrating a few days after the battle. On October 24, Alexander Smyth wrote that Queenston cost the Army 200 men, one-half of these being deserters and the rest made up of those who were killed, wounded or prisoners. Poor as Smyth's judgment proved to be later, he seems, in his figure for total American casualties, to have come closer to the truth than most others.

The British suffered far less. In the early hours of battle a very few seem to have been taken prisoners and sent over to Lewiston, where they were later exchanged. For militia and regulars only, an official return states that 14 were killed, 77 wounded and 21 missing. These, plus 6 Indians reported killed, make about 120 casualties all told—a figure that seems entirely trustworthy. The fewer losses of the British may be largely ascribed to the fact that they had fewer troops engaged—although more at the critical time and place —more skillful leaders, troops under better control and a generally defensive posture.

Although British casualties were few, the victory was costly. They could ill afford to lose a general as loyal and able as Brock, who had proved so energetic in promoting the growing interests of the Empire. Brock was interred with full military honors at Newark on the 16th. The British minute guns were echoed by American salutes from across the river in final tribute to the memory of a man whom Americans had fought but deeply honored. In after years, the body of Brock was reburied upon the Heights of Queenston, where he had bravely died.

Besides lacking the cooperation of Smyth, General Van Rensselaer failed to get support from the militia when he needed it most. Although entirely familiar with the militia's shortcomings, he favored them as his chosen instruments for a highly perilous and difficult operation, apparently expecting more from them than they had recently demonstrated when the raid on Prescott from Ogdensburg was undertaken. Participation was put on a voluntary basis. When victory seemed likely, some crossed over; when defeat appeared imminent and the wounded began to arrive, few would follow. They were acting in character and in keeping with a law that protected them in their cowardice. Reinforcements of regulars might have saved the day; but General Van Rensselaer did not ask for them, possibly because he either considered it too late or believed that Smyth, their commander, would refuse to send them.

The American failure at Queenston must be attributed largely to the Van Rensselaers, uncle and nephew. Yielding to political pressure, they assumed responsibility for an operation to which they were not equal. To overcome the obvious difficulties in using mostly militia for invading Canada required a high degree of professional skill and human understanding. Stephen Van Rensselaer was almost entirely ignorant of the technical aspects of military art. Solomon Van Rensselaer, as his aide or chief of staff, had not the competence to supply this deficiency.

7

Inertia, Incompetence
and Failure

After the Queenston defeat, General Van Rensselaer appropriately resigned, turning over command to Brigadier General Alexander Smyth. A thoroughly demoralized army thus fell into the hands of a general without the capacity to regenerate it. Death and desertion, both in wholesale lots, were thinning ranks already riddled by disease. The camp at Lewiston was broken up and all the militia moved to Schlosser except a few who manned the battery opposite Queenston. Some regular organizations were consolidated; all of them were stationed in or around Buffalo except the 14th Infantry at Fort Niagara.

Scarcely had Smyth fallen into this evil inheritance when he received directions from General Dearborn at Greenbush, New York, 44 hours distant by express, to be prepared to cross over into Canada at once with 3,000 men. Smyth after querulous argumentation, promised to advance with 2,270 men, exclusive of militia, before November 30, as part of Dearborn's proposed invasion. This advance was to be made simultaneously with Captain Isaac Chauncey's naval force on Lake Ontario, General William Henry Harrison's command near Detroit and the troops under Dearborn himself along Lake Champlain.

Dearborn, although tortured by rheumatism, hied himself to Plattsburg and on November 16 accompanied Brigadier General Joseph Bloomfield's troops moving for the Canadian border. Bloomfield, who had succeeded General Mooers of the militia, mustered 3,000 regulars and 2,000 militia, the best units selected from the motley assemblage in the area. On the nearby waters of Lake Champlain, war vessels based at Plattsburg sailed parallel to the army. Before the day ended, Dearborn and his men were encamped near the village of Champlain, about a half-mile south of the boundary line. In the next few days they pushed on until they had reached Odell Town in Lower Canada. This place was defended by a mixed British force of voltigeurs, chasseurs, militia and Indians under the command of the daring and resourceful Lieutenant Colonel Charles de Salaberry.

In the lead were American Colonel Zebulon M. Pike and about 600 men, moving along the Lacolle River. They opened fire in error on approaching New York militia. Having no more than corrected this error, Pike discovered de Salaberry and a strong force advancing against him from the north. After a volley or two, the Americans precipitately fled, leaving their dead and wounded where they had fallen. On the day following this unfortunate venture, Dearborn, who had taken over field command from the ailing Bloomfield, after ordering a three days' march, suddenly directed the troops to face about and return to Plattsburg, when they arrived on November 23.

Dearborn's decision made some sense. He himself was physically unfit to command in a winter campaign. The militia, for the most part, would not serve beyond the boundaries of the United States. Regulars and others who might have done so were ill equipped for the move. Even if they could have been supplied with the necessary food, clothing and ammunition along the way, such matériel could not have been gotten to Montreal without barges and war vessels, which had not been provided for.

Clearly essential to a major invasion of Canada was naval supremacy on Lakes Ontario and Erie. The Navy Department in September 1812, in a move to build up the lake fleets, had transferred Captain Isaac Chauncey from command of the New York Navy Yard to command American forces on the lakes. Showing the industry and resourcefulness that had made him an outstanding young officer in the Mediterranean, Chauncey at once began assembling a fleet by building and purchase. The British squadron meantime retired to its base at Kingston, where it was frozen in during much of the winter.

Chauncey's problem was men as much as ships. The small lake shipping industry offered no surplus of seamen; consequently these had to be obtained from the coast, where they were already in sharp demand for the lucrative privateer service and for the high-seas Navy. However, by paying bounties and promising prize money, Chauncey lured several hundred men away from the coast.

The winter of 1812–1813 was used for sledding materials, supplies and men across New York State from the Atlantic ports. The picturesque event of the winter for the upstate New York towns was the passage of the great sleds, each pulled by two or more teams of horses, carrying twenty men or more to a sled. The rollicking sled parties, each bearing a large American flag and warmed by ample supplies of grog, were the object of excitement and admiration in every town, for the glory of the Navy had already been established, as we have seen. In one group a sled was occupied by a brass band, to add to the gaiety and excitement.

Meanwhile, on cold and blustery November 6, Chauncey, in his flagship, the brig *Oneida*, 18, put out from Sackets Harbor with six other small vessels. His objective was to check British dominance on Lake Ontario. On the 8th, off the False Duck Islands, he fell in with and chased the *Royal George*, 21, into the Bay of Quinte, under the shore batteries of Kingston. Here Chauncey had the best of a long-range cannonading duel until approaching darkness and increasingly strong head winds obliged him to haul off to open water. Foul weather followed, and the flotilla returned to Sackets Harbor, having lost a half-dozen men and taken some small merchant vessels.

On November 10 the American vessels *Tompkins*, *Hamilton* and *Julia* pursued and shattered the *Simcoe*, a British schooner carrying eight guns. About the same time, the *Hamilton* captured another schooner from Niagara, and Chauncey tried unsuccessfully to use her for luring the damaged *Royal George* to come out from Kingston and fight. Despite autumn gales and heavy snows, Chauncey continued to patrol the lake, hoping to eliminate the *Earl of Moira*, 14, still at large. He failed to catch her but did pick up another schooner accompanying her. In five days of cruising he had captured three merchant vessels, destroyed an armed schooner and temporarily disabled the *Royal George*. Returning again to Sackets Harbor with his flotilla reinforced by these prizes, Chauncey declared himself "so completely master" of Lake Ontario that other additions to his force would be "useless"—unless, of course, the British should unexpectedly increase their power. And that, as it turned out, was the last serious combat action on the part of a once-daring sailor.

Meanwhile, bombastic Smyth began his share in the campaign with a paper barrage along the Niagara. He mingled fiery threats against the enemy with mawkish appeals to New Yorkers to join the colors. His final soap-box blast, on November 17, ended with this gem: "Come on, my heroes! And when you attack the enemy's batteries let your rallying word be 'The cannon lost at Detroit or Death!'"

Smyth's turgid rabble-rousing fell on deaf American ears, but it did succeed in broadcasting the fact that he was hoping soon to carry the war into Canada. Accordingly, the efficient Canadian General Roger H. Sheaffe, now in charge of both civil and military administration in Upper Canada, took steps to resist the anticipated invasion.

On the 18th, some 2,000 Pennsylvania volunteers under Brigadier General Adamson Tannehill joined Smyth's command. With this timely reinforcement and the hope of an additional 3,000-odd New York militia, Smyth prepared to move across the river against the enemy at Fort Erie. On November 20 he ended the armistice that had been effective since the Queenston disaster. This brought about an almost immediate British bombardment of Fort Niagara. From dawn to dusk on November 21 the opponents exchanged a warm but relatively ineffective fire.

On the 25th Smyth ordered the whole army to be ready for marching "at a moment's warning." The tents were to remain standing, officers were to carry their knapsacks and baggage was to be left behind. Each organization was assigned its place in line of battle before reaching the Canadian shore, and the tactical task categorically defined as follows:

1. The artillery will spend some of their first shot on the

enemy's artillery, and then aim at the infantry, raking them where it is practicable. 2. The firing of musketry by wings or companies will begin at the distance of two hundred yards, aiming at the middle and firing deliberately. 3. At twenty yards distance the soldiers will be ordered to trail arms, advance with shouts, fire at five paces distance, and charge with bayonets. 4. The soldiers will be *silent* above all things, attentive to the word of command, load quick and well, and *aim low.*

By dusk on November 27, troops were to have two days' rations cooked and packed in their haversacks. At reveille on the 28th, they marched to the Buffalo Navy Yard to embark. As mental preparation, they were bidden to "Think on your country's honor lost, her rights trampled on, her sons enslaved, her infants perishing by the hatchet."

A preliminary night raid from the American shore—fantastically mismanaged by Colonel William H. Winder, prominent Baltimore lawyer-turned-amateur-soldier—ended in stalemate. Two parties, leaving Black Rock shortly after midnight, reached the Canadian shore, spiked a few cannon and captured a few prisoners. Meanwhile, most of their boats had hurriedly put back. Hastening to return before dawn as ordered, the raiders found themselves marooned while British troops swarmed about them. Some escaped, but many others were captured. Winder, who had thoughtfully remained on the American shore, was now prodded by an irate Smyth. The bumbling colonel thereupon attempted a daylight rescue, but his force of 350 men, in 18 boats, was so warmly received by the aroused British that Winder speedily turned back to safety after suffering some loss.

In the Buffalo Navy Yard, meanwhile, the milling troops awaited orders from Smyth. Their boats, although ample in number, had not been prepared. The British artillery in Fort Erie was roaring, and British troops were assembling in plain view along the opposite bank to repel invasion. Smyth, having breakfasted, rode into the yard, and remarked dourly that "we are now in confusion." Nevertheless, he sent a messenger across the river under a flag of truce to call on the British commander of Fort Erie to surrender, "to spare the effusion of blood," since the American troops

were increasing in number. Not unnaturally, the British comm'an-
der, Lieutenant Colonel Cecil Bisshop, categorically refused. So
Smyth, after conferring with his commanders, ordered his men
back into camp.

Two days later the troops once more assembled. This time, it
seemed, the boats were ready, and the bands were standing by
prepared to play "Yankee Doodle" as the signal for shoving off.
Rations were ample and liquor flowed. Only one thing was missing: a leader. Smyth never showed up. Late in the afternoon the
disgusted troops were ordered to bivouac under arms. Smyth,
it seemed, had spent the morning with his commanders, working
out another scheme: a night embarkation and a move five miles
downriver to a place where landing would be easier.

At 3:30 A.M., December 1, the shivering soldiers were once
again ordered into their boats. But by daylight only 1,500 men had
embarked, and after much argument the entire attempt was abandoned. The result was near-mutiny. Large numbers of volunteers
packed up their meager belongings and trudged away home. In a
carnival of defiance, militia and regulars alike hooted and howled,
pulling down their tents, smashing their muskets, looting government supplies and jeering at those who tried to restrain them.
Here and there officers wandered about, breaking their swords and
damning Smyth and their country. One group buried the general
in effigy, finishing it off with a unique funeral oration. Others, firing their pieces, nearly hit Smyth as he rode by with his aide. The
owner of the tavern where Smyth stayed became so disturbed that
he induced the general to move elsewhere. When he was in camp
his bodyguard was doubled in order to prevent any injury to his
person and to thwart miscreants from pulling his marquee down
around his ears.

Among those who were thoroughly disgusted was Brigadier General Peter B. Porter, erstwhile quartermaster general of New York
State, on whom Smyth had conferred the task of leading the
aborted invasion. Porter publicly denounced Smyth as a coward.
In turn, Smyth challenged Porter to a duel. On December 12 the
duelists, facing each other at twelve paces, fired their pistols at each
other. Neither was scratched; mutual honor was satisfied, valor
proved. The duelists then shook hands and spent a convivial evening dining together. The colorless and ineffectual Dearborn took

no notice of the fact that both generals had blatantly violated regulations, but in compliance with instructions from the Secretary of War, he relieved Smyth from command. Before December ended, Smyth was on his way to Washington, where Madison, after considering the case, ordered him dropped from the rolls of the Army.

There was an ironic postscript to all this futile wind and thunder along the Niagara River. On the morning of the first attempt at invasion three American sailors took off from Buffalo for the Canadian shore on their own. For two hours they wandered over the countryside without molestation, slaughtering some livestock, looting a store and setting two homes on fire. Then they returned unscathed.

With Smyth no longer encumbering the army, Colonel Moses Porter, an artillery officer of considerable experience but not of striking ability, assumed command along the Niagara. Before long he saw the militia discharged and on their way home. Since neither he nor the British contemplated any immediate offensive, his chief concern was to keep 2,600 or more regulars healthy and comfortable and ready for battle.

Navigation of Lake Ontario and the St. Lawrence River closed on November 26, 1812, when both were solidly frozen over. Chauncey kept his flotilla snugly in harbor until spring. When the St. Lawrence was covered from shore to shore with thick ice, however, the crossing by foot troops became easy, and the prospect of successful raids was inviting. Major Benjamin Forsyth, in command of the corps of American riflemen on the St. Lawrence, seized the opportunity. Crossing the river with two companies of the rifle corps, he marched to Elizabethtown (Brockville) on February 6, 1813. Meeting only token resistance, he liberated sixteen British deserters awaiting execution in the jail and some American prisoners, and captured the little garrison of about fifty men, including a major, three captains and two lieutenants. The spoils included 140 muskets and a plentiful supply of ammunition. For this exploit, in which not a single American was lost, Forsyth was rewarded with the brevet rank of lieutenant colonel.

The British were highly displeased when their friendly relations with many people across the river near Ogdensburg were thus rudely interrupted by raids. Many of their officers in uniform were in the habit of patronizing the store of millionaire David Parrish or wined and dined at his magnificent home, surrounded by beautiful gardens and a rose-covered stone wall. Parrish desired no part in "Mr. Madison's war"; he and a few other local citizens wanted peace and profitable trade with Canada. They bitterly resented having a garrison in Ogdensburg to prevent customary friendly crossing of the river whenever they or others chose. However, the garrison soon conformed to local customs. Both Americans and British drilled on the frozen river in sight of each other without an unfriendly incident.

This undeclared truce seemed to please Dearborn. He warned Forsyth against further raids, advising that they would only provoke the British into retaliation. Risk nothing, do nothing, frequently seemed to be his philosophy. When Forsyth learned of British plans to attack Ogdensburg, he immediately asked for more troops. The general replied that he had none to spare. Characteristically, he added that if they were necessary Forsyth had better retreat, abandoning Ogdensburg. A disaster such as the loss of the town might, Dearborn suggested, even stir the north country into patriotic action.

The British, about 500 strong, did cross on the river ice, arriving at Ogdensburg so early on the morning of February 22 that most of the inhabitants still lay in their beds. The raiders—regulars, militia and Indians commanded by Lieutenant Colonel John Macdonnell—advanced through deep snow near Fort Oswegatchie, met little resistance and occupied the village. Some 300 of the British under Captain John Jenkins attacked Forsyth at Fort Presentation. After a short but stubborn resistance, Forsyth struck out with his men for Thurber's Tavern, eight miles distant, leaving Ogdensburg in the hands of the British, their Indian allies and their camp followers. For several hours the invaders remained in the place, enjoying themselves at the expense of the helpless inhabitants. The homes of David Parrish and Judge Nathan were the only ones reputed to have escaped being plundered.

8

Tall Ships and Bold Sailors

A far cry from the dismal doings of American generals along the Canadian border during the first year of the war was the glorious record of the United States Navy on blue water. Before 1812 had ended, American naval captains had scored four notable victories in hard-fought single-ship actions and had captured forty-six enemy merchantmen. In addition, there were many successful privateer actions.

Isaac Hull, returning to Boston after his victory in August over the *Guerrière*, complied with orders and turned his *Constitution* over to Captain William Bainbridge, who put to sea October 26, 1812, in company with the sloop of war *Hornet*, 18, Master Commandant James Lawrence commanding. Both vessels were bound for the South Atlantic, to operate against British commerce. They would be joined there by Captain David Porter's USS *Essex*, 32, for a projected Pacific Ocean cruise. However, affairs turned out differently for both the *Constitution* and the *Hornet*. The epic cruise of the *Essex* in the Pacific Ocean will be related later.

After rounding the hump of Brazil, Bainbridge and Lawrence found the British sloop of war *Bonne Citoyenne*, 20, loaded with

71

specie, lying in neutral São Salvador (Bahia). British Captain Pitt Barnaby Greene, although slightly superior in firepower to the *Hornet,* declined to accept Lawrence's challenge submitted through the American consul. With the *Constitution* still in the area Greene prudently felt that his first responsibility was to safeguard his shipment of treasure.

Bainbridge consequently detached the *Hornet* to blockade the *Bonne Citoyenne* while he cruised in the *Constitution* farther south along the Brazilian coast.

Three days later, December 29, Bainbridge encountered HMS *Java,* 38, off the coast of Brazil. The *Java,* which had a reputation as one of the stellar British frigates, was transporting the newly appointed governor general of Bombay and his staff, about 100 passengers in all, to India. Both ships at once accepted battle, but Bainbridge at first refused to close, desiring to get away from the shoreline and deprive the enemy of the shelter of neutral waters should the battle go against him.

The two frigates were of approximately equal strength, with a slight advantage to the American. The *Constitution* was a slightly larger ship, 1,576 tons to the *Java*'s 1,340. The *Java* actually carried 49 guns to the *Constitution*'s 44. The weight of the *Constitution*'s broadside fire was the heavier, being 654 pounds to 576. The *Java* had a complement of 426 men, the *Constitution,* 475.

The *Java* was commanded by Captain Henry Lambert, whom Bainbridge characterized as "a distinguished, gallant and worthy man." Still the *Java* was not as well prepared as she should have been. She had a green crew, and although she had been at sea six weeks, her commander had been derelict in gunnery exercises. Her crew had fired only six blank broadsides, whereas the Americans on the *Constitution* were now veterans, with the victory over the *Guerrière* behind them to give them confidence. The Americans constantly practiced gunnery, the British, rarely.

The *Java* had hauled down her ensign as she approached, leaving only the Union Jack flying at the bowsprit. Bainbridge, uncertain as to why the ensign had been lowered, fired a shot across her bow and was immediately answered by a broadside. In the light wind the *Java* proved slightly the better sailer, but Bainbridge by dexterous maneuvers prevented her from crossing the *Constitution*'s bow and raking her. Bainbridge had already been hit by a bullet entering his hip when a roundshot carried away the *Constitution*'s wheel and drove a copper bolt deep into his thigh.

The plight of the *Constitution* at this moment was serious, for her rudder was out of control. She began to lose speed and position, while the *Java*, anxious for the kill, came boldly on again seeking to rake. Bainbridge, resourceful in the emergency even when crippled, had the tiller manned below decks and formed a line of midshipmen to relay orders. Despite this disadvantage, Bainbridge was able to outmaneuver his opponent and was able at length to rake her, causing appalling destruction along the *Java*'s gundeck. Now the vessels came together with the wind, exchanging broadsides at half a pistol shot. Seeing that he was being outgunned, Lambert decided to board. The *Java* struck the *Constitution* a quartering blow and ran her jibboom through the American's rigging. But as the vessels came together the *Java*'s mizzenmast crashed on her main deck and through her forecastle, hurling into the sea the men who had been on the top and crushing others caught on the deck when it fell. During the confusion on the British deck, the *Constitution* drew loose from the crippled Britisher and pounded her relentlessly through the smoke of battle.

Nothing was left for the *Java* but another attempt at boarding. Bugles sounded and musketeers on the tops of the *Constitution* saw the boarding party form. But this effort was as futile as the first. A broadside again swept the Java's main deck, while from the rigging of the *Constitution* marksmen kept up a destructive fire on the groups of boarders assembling in the gangways and on the forecastle. At this juncture Captain Lambert fell, mortally wounded. Lieutenant H. D. Chadds, his second in command, also wounded, but less severely, continued the fight. Rarely had a green crew put up a better battle, but the *Java*'s foremast now went by the board, and her guns fell silent. The *Constitution* hauled off to care for her own wounds, which were inconsiderable, and prepared to pound her stricken opponent at long range. As the American drew away, the *Java*'s mainmast tumbled into the sea, and the British frigate, now a hopeless wreck, struck her colors.

The *Java* was too far gone to save. Her captain, 5 midshipmen and 42 of her crew were killed and 105 others wounded. Thirteen of the *Java*'s passengers were killed. The *Constitution* had 5 killed and 20 wounded. One bit of salvage proved handy; the *Java*'s wheel replaced that of the *Constitution*, which the early roundshot had destroyed.

Of the boats of the two ships, only two remained serviceable. With these the difficult work of transferring to the *Constitution* first the wounded and then the other prisoners—about 500 in all —was carried on. For three days the two small boats plied back and forth. When the last man was safe the *Java* was set on fire. As the flames mounted she exploded, scattering splinters and bits of the once handsome frigate over the southern ocean.

Bainbridge put his prisoners ashore at Bahia, on parole. He then made it back to Boston, leaving the *Hornet* still blockading the *Bonne Citoyenne*. "Old Ironsides" came bowling home on February 15, 1813, to be saluted for the second time in six months by artillery and acclaimed by thousands in official welcoming ceremonies. Congress ordered a medal struck to honor the victory, and various cities showered gifts on captain and crew.

Thus closed the war at sea for 1812. The new year would dawn as brightly for James Lawrence and his *Hornet* in the South Atlantic.

This thirty-year-old man from Burlington, New Jersey, who had deserted for the sea the legal career charted for him by his lawyer father, had been one of "Preble's Boys" in the Mediterranean, second in command to Decatur in the daring raid on the captured *Philadelphia* in Tripoli harbor and later commander of a gunboat off Tripoli. Now his ship-rigged *Hornet*, one of the splendid sloops of war of the 1812 Navy, was a taut vessel under a splendid leader whose modesty and personal courage had endeared him to fellow officers and to his men.

Bainbridge had given Lawrence wide latitude to lift the blockade of the *Bonne Citoyenne* should he consider it advisable. The condition arose with the appearance on January 24, 1813, of HM ship of the line *Montagu*, 74. Lawrence eluded her under cover of darkness and, in compliance with his orders, began a return voyage to the United States.

He soon captured a rich prize, the brig *Resolution*, with $23,000 in specie, and progressed north along the coast, past the Amazon River delta. Near the mouth of the Demarara River, off Georgetown, British Guiana, he sighted the *Peacock*, 16, a show boat of the British Navy. Her fittings were so elegant that crowds came to visit her decks when she was in British ports. Captain William Peake, who commanded the brig, kept her brass polished, her decks scrubbed, her paint fresh, the discipline of her crew exemplary. She was evenly matched with the *Hornet* in personnel, carrying 134 men to the *Hornet*'s 135; the weight of the metal they threw slightly favored the *Hornet*, but not sufficiently to foredoom the *Peacock* to defeat.

About four miles from where the *Peacock* was first sighted, another British brig was anchored, the *Espiegle*, 18. But the *Peacock*, showing no desire to await her consort, came on with colors flying. As she passed the *Hornet*, they exchanged broadsides. The American's was devastating; the *Peacock*'s had little effect. The maneuvering for position was not protracted. Lawrence, by expert handling of his little ship, prevented the *Peacock* from raking, then drew near for close action. For fourteen minutes the ships blazed away at each other, until the *Peacock*'s rigging was shredded, her mainmast fractured and her hull riddled, and she was in such distress that she not only struck her colors but displayed her flag upside down in the fore rigging, a call for help.

Lieutenant John T. Shubrick and his boarding party from the *Hornet* found the vessel truly in distress. Captain Peake had been killed, and more than half her crew had been killed or wounded. She had six feet of water in her hold and was in immediate danger of sinking. Shortly after the surrender her tottering mainmast fell into the sea.

Lawrence's first thought was the rescue of the survivors. A detail under Lieutenant David Connor and Midshipman Benjamin Cooper began bringing off the wounded, then tried to save the ship. The holes in her sides were plugged, and all who could be spared from handling the wounded worked the pumps and even resorted to bailing. The guns were tossed overboard, but to no avail; the *Peacock* had been mortally wounded. When darkness came on, all the wounded and most of the crew had been removed. Then suddenly, almost unexpectedly, the *Peacock* went down, carrying with her nine of her crew and three of the American relief party. The remaining men on board narrowly escaped—some by climbing to the foretop, for the *Peacock* had sunk in only thirty feet of water, and the foretop happily remained above the surface.

Never were prisoners given more cordial and generous treatment than were those who fell into the hands of the chivalrous Lawrence, whom Theodore Roosevelt would later term "a very Bayard of the seas." The *Hornet* remained in good condition after the fight, her rigging and sails tattered but her masts standing and her hull scarcely dented. She was suddenly called on to accommodate not only her own crew and the survivors of the *Peacock* but also the prisoners Lawrence had taken aboard when he captured the *Resolution,* plus the recaptured crew of the American brig *Hunter,* which the *Peacock* had taken. The *Hornet* had suffered but one man killed and two wounded in the battle and three lost when the *Peacock* went down. In all, 277 men were packed into the 400-ton craft, making it imperative for Lawrence to sail home at once even had his orders not directed it.

The *Peacock's* survivors had lost most of their clothing, having been stripped down during the action, but the Americans shared their clothing and hammocks, rationed the water that was in short supply for so many, divided the food equally and, what seemed just as important, offered their companionship. When the British officers reached New York they handed to Lawrence an unusual testimonial to his consideration, voluntarily drafted and signed by the lieutenants, shipmaster, surgeon and purser:

> So much was done to alleviate the uncomfortable and distressing situation in which we were placed when received on board the ship you command, that we cannot better express our feelings than by saying we ceased to consider ourselves prisoners; and everything that friendship could dictate was adopted by you and the officers of the *Hornet* to remedy the inconvenience we otherwise should have experienced from the unavoidable loss of the whole of our property and clothes by the sudden sinking of the *Peacock.*

Lawrence took the *Hornet* into Holmes Hole, Martha's Vineyard, on March 19, 1813, and again the country was thrown into rejoicing over an American victory in a duel between ships of the same class. Already the Senate had confirmed his nomination to be captain, the third name on the new list, though it might have been first had his victory been known when the nominations were made. New York tendered a reception to the *Hornet's* crew. President Madison dwelled on the battle in a message to Congress, saying that Lawrence and his companions "destroyed a British sloop of war with a celerity so unexampled and with a slaughter of the enemy so disproportionate to the loss of the *Hornet* as to claim for the conquerors the highest praise . . ."

Unfortunately Lady Luck's favors were not to last for Lawrence. The beautiful *Chesapeake*—her long-time reputation as an unlucky ship enhanced by losing a mast in a gale as she entered Boston harbor from an uneventful cruise—lay waiting a new commander. To her Lawrence was rushed, with orders to sail again when her time-expired crew had been replaced. Arriving May 20, Lawrence took her out June 1, after ten days of hectic recruiting, found HMS *Shannon* on blockade duty awaiting him and steered into battle.

Lawrence was crowding Lady Luck too far. His heterogeneous crew of 379 men included some 40 Britishers, a goodly number of Portuguese and a sprinkling of other nationalities. They did not know their ship; there had been no opportunity for a "shakedown" cruise or drill. Already one troublemaker, a Portuguese bosun's mate, had stirred up a near-mutiny. But worst of all, perhaps, for the *Chesapeake* and her people, was the fact that the daring and impetuous Lawrence was pitting them against a magnificently trained fighting machine commanded by an equally bold perfectionist.

Philip Bowes Vere Broke, whom Isaac Hull in the *Constitution* had encountered the year before, was the best of the British fighting captains in American waters. He had commanded the *Shannon* for seven years and knew her every whim and habit. He was not only one of the best seamen, but also among the best artillerists of the British service. Where most others of His Majesty's post captains, smugly content, rarely exercised the guns with powder and ball, Broke held daily gunnery drill and semiweekly target practice. Sharpshooting gun crews were rewarded by an extra pound of tobacco ration.

Statistically, the ships were evenly matched. Rated as a 38, the *Shannon* mounted 52 guns, while the *Chesapeake*, officially a 38, mounted 50. The *Shannon's* complement was 347, 52 fewer than the *Cheasapeake*'s. The combined weight of the *Shannon*'s broadsides was 550 pounds, the *Chesapeake*'s, 542 pounds.

Fate and circumstance led to the meeting off Boston Light. The city was restive at seeing the *Shannon* patrolling the near waters in impudent defiance. Broke, informed about the refitting of the *Chesapeake*, challenged Lawrence to a test, ship to ship. He told the strength of his own vessel and the location of other British ships and said he would send the others beyond the possibility of interference. He suggested an appropriate meeting place.

The challenge and its frank disclosures took warfare back to more chivalrous days, before subterfuge and deception came to be commendatory attributes. Lawrence, like-minded, had already decided to remove the hostile frigate's taunt. He wrote a note to the Secretary of the Navy, June 1, his last, saying he hoped to give a good account of the enemy before nightfall.

A flotilla of small craft accompanied the *Chesapeake* down the harbor. At 1 P.M., while passing the lightship, Lawrence broke out a banner on his mainmast with the motto "FREE TRADE AND SAILORS' RIGHTS."

Lawrence's consummate skill in handling a sailing ship was now brought into play as he approached the *Shannon*. Enthusiastic James Fenimore Cooper, historian of the early Navy, would write: "The history of naval warfare does not contain an instance of a ship's being more gallantly conducted than the *Chesapeake* was now handled."

Instead of passing the *Shannon*'s stern and raking her, a maneuver Broke feared he would attempt, Lawrence steered for her starboard side and came abreast, then answered the *Shannon*'s first fire, at 5:50 P.M., with a broadside. The *Shannon* replied with a devastating broadside at close range, which swept a hundred men from the deck. Lawrence took a bullet wound in the leg but paid no heed to it. At an unhappy moment a British hand grenade exploded one of the *Chesapeake*'s powder chests. The frightful concussion shivered the ship, unnerved the gunners; bits of human flesh flew through the air; wreckage, splinters, hammocks, rigging were driven across the *Chesapeake*'s decks.

The combat reached its decisive stage in ten minutes. At 6 P.M. the *Shannon* shot away the *Chesapeake*'s jibstay, which slowed her and caused her to fall against her antagonist's side and entangle her mizzen rigging. The *Shannon*'s anchor caught in the *Chesa-peake*'s side chains. All the while the British vessel gave punishment with carronades and picked off men with musketry from the *Shannon*'s tops. With the ships fouled, Lawrence called for boarders to form, but the frightened bugler failed to blow the call. In keeping with his courage and high spirit, and perhaps his rashness, Lawrence stood the while on his quarterdeck in dress uniform—a splendid target to marksmen in the *Shannon*'s rigging. One caught him in the chest with a musket ball, pitching him into the arms of his men, who carried him to the wardroom. There he gave his last command, words that have since rung through the years as the watchword of every American naval vessel: "Don't give up the ship. Fight her till she sinks."

Above decks, meanwhile, the *Shannon*'s boarders, led by Captain Broke, swept through the shambles and beat down the last disorganized resistance. Broke was severely wounded—struck by a gun butt and slashed across the head by a cutlass. Every American officer above midshipman's grade was a casualty. *Shannon*'s First Lieutenant Watts, hauling down the *Chesapeake*'s colors, was killed by grapeshot from his own ship's carronades as unwitting gunners continued their devastating fire.

For a battle that lasted only fifteen minutes, the casualties on both ships were indeed heavy. The *Chesapeake*'s nondescript crew had given a good account of itself, suffering forty-eight killed and ninety-eight wounded. The Marine Corps detachment had fought nobly. Its commander, Lieutenant James Broome, was killed, and of his forty-four men, thirty-two were killed or wounded. The British loss was twenty-six killed and fifty-eight wounded.

The *Shannon* escorted her prize to Halifax, where rejoicing was mingled with respect for a gallant foe, whose generosity to the prisoners of the *Peacock* was well remembered. Lawrence and his First Lieutenant Augustus C. Ludlow, who died of his wounds on arrival, were given a joint funeral in Halifax in the most appropriate manner the town could offer. In the cortege were British officers of the Halifax station, leading townspeople and six companies of the 64th Foot.

No hero in victory ever received a nation's sincere affection and gratitude in greater measure than did Lawrence and Ludlow in defeat. A truce was negotiated to bring both Lawrence and Ludlow home, and large public funerals were held—the first at Salem, Massachusetts, the second in New York City, where Lawrence's body now rests in Old Trinity Churchyard on lower Broadway.

In England the victory of the *Shannon* was celebrated as if it had been a second Trafalgar. Broke—who at the moment of triumph had become delirious from his wounds, then fainted from loss of blood—recovered to become the hero of the realm. Bonfires lighted the towns, leaders in Parliament declaimed, London extended its freedom and voted a handsome sword worth a hundred guineas and Broke's native Suffolk gave him a magnificent plate of silver forty-four inches in diameter, in the center of which was pictured the duel. Finally, the Prince Regent knighted him, a well-deserved recognition.

Coming as it did after a series of defeats on the high seas, the British victory was significant. It dispelled the bogy, first expressed by the *Times of London* after the defeat of the *Macedonian* by the *United States*, that Yankee frigates were ships of the line in disguise. Above all, both the Admiralty and the public could sleep easier in the promise that Britannia would resume her rule of the waves, for the blockade, which in early 1813 exempted the New England coast, was now established tightly from Maine to Florida.

As we shall see, the blockade was not airtight, but the days of glory for the American frigates seemed to be coming to an end. By February 1813, Vice-Admiral John Borlase Warren, RN, had seventeen ships of the line, twenty-nine frigates and some fifty smaller craft off the eastern littoral of the United States. But American Navy men still dared to face the odds. Commodore John Rodgers in the *President*, 44, in company with the *Congress*, 38, slipped through the blockade from Boston April 30. Separating, Rodgers took the *President* to Europe, while the *Congress*, under Captain Moses Smith, went to the West Indies. Both cruises were barren; by September 27 Rodgers had stolen his way back into Newport, and by the end of December Smith had safely regained Portsmouth, New Hampshire.

On June 1, the very day that Lawrence cleared Boston for his fatal bout with the *Shannon*, Decatur with the *United States, Macedonian* and *Hornet* dared the blockaders off New London, but he was almost immediately chased back and all three ships bottled up in Long Island Sound.

On June 18, 1813, the little brig-sloop *Argus*, 16, flitted out of blockaded New York, carrying William H. Crawford of Georgia, newly appointed minister to France. Captain William Henry Allen who commanded the *Argus*, although only twenty-nine years old, had already participated in great moments in American history. He was a midshipman seventeen years old when he accompanied Bainbridge aboard the frigate *George Washington* to Constantinople in 1800 on the first voyage made by an American warship to the seat of Ottoman power. He had served in the squadron off Tripoli; he was the intrepid lieutenant who had taken a live coal in his fingers and rushed to one of the *Chesapeake*'s guns to fire a shot at the British frigate *Leopard* as Captain James Barron ingloriously hauled down the flag in 1807. He became a master of gunnery as first officer when Decatur's *United States* captured the *Macedonian,* and he had sailed the prize back into Newport. Now he was commanding his own ship, small but already historic as the sea power element in Eaton's near freakish capture of Derna during the Tripolitan war.

Allen's orders gave him latitude after he safely deposited Minister Crawford at Lorient. There he learned that Britain's home waters were not being well guarded while her great Navy roamed the far seas. Not since John Paul Jones and the *Bonhomme Richard* had British shipping been ravaged along Britain's own coasts. Allen was so anxious to raid into British home waters that he tarried only three days in Lorient. Then he impudently roved the English Channel, and then the Irish Sea. He virtually stopped commerce, for the insurance rates shot up to 60 percent—when insurance was obtainable at all. The British press was filled with accounts of his depredations. Sailings were canceled, cargoes withheld. In thirty days of audacious commerce raiding, Allen captured twenty vessels and cargoes valued at $2 million. The ships he burned; the prisoners he set ashore.

All went well until the night of August 13, 1813, when Allen captured a merchantman from Oporto, Portugal, loaded with choice wine, a goodly portion of which was stealthily transferred to the *Argus* by thirsty bluejackets before the wine craft was fired. That night, while the flames of the wine ship lighted the waters, Allen's men celebrated.

The Admiralty by this time had fitted out and dispatched a

small navy of frigates, cruisers and brigs to hunt down the saucy
Argus. HMS *Pelican,* 18, under Captain Maples, like the *Argus*
a brig-sloop, sighted the red sky and sailed toward the burning
ship. At dawn she confronted the *Argus.*

The *Pelican* was a larger vessel, 467 tons to 298, with a crew of
116 to the 104 on the *Argus.* In firepower the *Pelican* also had an
advantage, throwing 280 pounds to 210.

At 6 A.M. the *Pelican* came on with spirit, flying her colors, as
the *Argus* did hers, and the *Argus* met her with a broadside of
grape. The reply of the *Pelican* probably determined the result at
the very outset of the battle. A roundshot hit Allen's leg and tore
it off. He insisted on remaining at his station, but soon the loss
of blood required that he be carried to the cockpit. He died the
next day in Plymouth. First Lieutenant J. M. Watson held the
command briefly until hit on the head by a grapeshot. He too was
carried below. Lieutenant William Howard Allen, not related to
the captain, was the ship's remaining officer, and he fought well,
at a great disadvantage from loss of effective manpower. The
gunnery was not up to American standards, due no doubt to the
wine. An excuse was made that the powder on the *Argus* was of
poor quality, having been taken from one of the merchantmen.
A better explanation was that of an officer who said, "The gunners
seemed to be nodding over their guns."

Rigging and spars suffered so much that the *Argus* soon was
scarcely manageable. The *Pelican* had virtually free play to cross
her stern and deliver raking broadsides. Still, the *Argus* battled
gallantly for forty-three minutes. Lieutenant Watson recovered
sufficiently to return to the deck. By this time the American fire
slackened. Watson wanted to board but was incapable of undertaking it. Another British warship, the *Seahorse,* was coming up,
but she was not needed. The embattled brigs came together.
Pelican boarders swarmed over the side and the *Argus'* colors came
down.

Nineteen days later another American war brig, also daring the
blockade, avenged the *Argus.*

On September 1 the little *Enterprise,* 14, cleared Portsmouth,
New Hampshire, under Lieutenant William Burrows. The *Enterprise* had been a schooner when she made history in the Mediterranean against Tripolitan pirates in 1804 but now was brig-

rigged. Four days out she met HM brig *Boxer,* 14, under Lieutenant Samuel Blyth, RN. Evenly matched in armament, numbers and spirit, the two vessels clashed like a pair of Kilkenny cats.

Burrows, maneuvering for the weather gage, crossed the Britisher's bow and raked her with a precisely aimed and decisive broadside. Blyth of the *Boxer,* who had nailed his colors to his mizzenmast before the action, was instantly killed by an 18-pounder solid shot, which tore his body apart. Burrows, soon mortally wounded by canister or a musket shot, sprawled on his quarterdeck, refusing to go below, and Lieutenant Edward R. McCall took command. For forty minutes the two brigs blazed away, with the *Enterprise*'s superior gunnery dominant. Then the *Boxer* struck; at least she surrendered, for it was impossible to get her nailed-on colors down. Burrows received his adversary's sword with the remark: "I am satisfied, I die contented."

The *Enterprise* had suffered little: two men killed and ten wounded. The *Boxer*'s losses are uncertain; it seemed that several of her dead had been thrown overboard during the fight, but thirty are listed as killed in action and seventeen others wounded.

Both vessels made Portland safely, where the fallen captains were buried side by side, after public funerals and ceremonies honoring both men. Everyone, it seemed, remembered that only a few months previous at Halifax Blyth had marched in the British funeral procession honoring James Lawrence.

Such chivalrous gestures had been sadly lacking along the Atlantic coast. On April 6, 1813, Captain John Poer Beresford, commanding the *Poictiers,* 74, rudely announced the blockade of the Delaware River and Philadelphia shipping by bombarding the town of Lewes, Delaware, because the town mayor and others defiantly declined to give him supplies. The resourceful volunteer defenders of Lewes picked up the spent British cannon balls and fired them back with some Revolutionary War cannon so effectively that Beresford drew off and sailed for Bermuda. Powder the local militia had in plenty; the Duponts, their powder factory set up in nearby Wilmington, were already working at full tilt.

The blockade of the Chesapeake Bay was already known to the country through the narrow escape of the USS *Constellation,* which had been undergoing extensive repairs in the Washington Navy Yard when war was declared. The repairs had been completed on November 26, 1812, and Captain Charles Stewart, dropping down to the lower Chesapeake, found to his horror Admiral Sir George Cockburn's squadron riding at anchor off Lynnhaven Bay. Cockburn had two 74s—the *Marlborough* and the *Poictiers*—three frigates and a number of smaller warships and carried a landing force of 1,800 marines. Captain Stewart, recognizing that flight alone could save his frigate, came about and by kedging took refuge behind Craney Island, five miles from Norfolk, where fortifications were being prepared.

Several cutting-out attempts were made by Cockburn, but the *Constellation*, snugly protected by booms, boarding nets and, a protective ring of fourteen gunboats, could not be taken or damaged. However, Chesapeake Bay had been sealed and the main artery of north-south traffic along the Atlantic coast sadly disrupted. Cockburn now began a spasmodic campaign of harassment along the coastal area. Elkton was raided on April 29, 1813, and its warehouses burned. Havre de Grace, on the Susquehanna, was the next place to feel the British scourge.

With a force of 400 marines, Cockburn overran the one battery defending Havre de Grace before anyone except a watchman knew he was approaching; then he burned and sacked the town. Forty of its sixty houses were put to the torch, plus sawmills, ferry boats and much equipment. Cockburn himself came ashore after the burning was well underway and was met by some women headed by Mrs. John Rodgers, whose husband was at sea commanding the *President*. In deference to her request Cockburn agreed to suspend the burning, but it was too late for most of the householders.

It was at Havre de Grace that Cockburn made the first combat use of the Congreve rocket, a weapon whose "red glare" would be given fame by Francis Scott Key in "The Star-Spangled Banner." He threw two or three rockets into the town before he entered it. A civilian named Webster was killed by one of them. As far as is known he was the only rocket fatality of the war.

Cockburn followed the attack on Havre de Grace by a raid up the Sassafras River, destroying provisions, transportation, shipping and warehouses at Fredericktown and Georgetown, Maryland. Then he dropped down Chesapeake Bay to meet Vice-Admiral

John Borlase Warren, vice-president of the Halifax Bible Society but also a good hand with the torch, overall British commander in American waters. Warren entered the Chesapeake June 1 with his main fleet and a land force of 1,500 soldiers and marines commanded by Sir Sidney Beckwith: a brigade of Royal Marines, the 102nd Foot and two companies of Chasseurs Britanniques, French prisoners of war who had volunteered to fight in North America. The British now had in the bay eight ships of the line, twelve frigates and many smaller craft, a force much larger and stronger than all the vessels of the U.S. Navy combined.

Warren made the capture of the *Constellation* his initial objective, and to that end Beckwith led an attack in force on Craney Island.

Brigadier General Robert B. Taylor, a Virginia lawyer, commanded the defenses on the island. Taylor had about 700 men. They were aided by 100 seamen and gunners from the *Constellation,* who brought over some of the frigate's guns. Beckwith's force landed on the west side of the Elizabeth River and approached, but merely demonstrated, mainly with Congreve rockets.

Warren attacked more directly and more vigorously with his marines in fifty barges. The assault was led by a party in the *Centipede,* Warren's own elaborate barge, painted green with a figurehead of gilt. The barge was thirty feet long, was pulled by twenty-four oars and carried a brass 3-pounder in her bow. As the wave of gunboats and barges approached the island, the *Constellation's* guns, firing grape, canister and roundshot, did frightful havoc among them and so disorganized their line that the confused officers ordered a retreat. The *Centipede,* hulled by a roundshot, was captured by an American boarding party headed by Midshipman Josiah Tattnall.[1]

That ended the effort to take the *Constellation,* which remained blockaded for the rest of the war. The thwarted Warren then attacked Hampton, two miles from Old Point Comfort on the north shore of the James River. While Cockburn demonstrated

[1] Forty-six years later Commodore Tattnall, commanding the United States China Squadron, would violate American neutrality to come to the aid of a hard-pressed British squadron battling China's Taku forts in 1859. "Blood is thicker than water" was fire-eating Tattnall's curt explanation. Still later he became one of the leading naval officers of the Confederacy.

in front of the town on June 25, Beckwith landed his troops behind it and took it by surprise, then raped, pillaged and burned.

After the destruction of Hampton, Warren sailed around the Chesapeake, threatening Baltimore and Annapolis. Some of his vessels pushed up the Potomac toward Washington as far as Kettle Bottom Shoals. This caused consternation in the capital, but the trench digging was suspended when Warren turned back and sailed for Bermuda and England, to be succeeded in early 1814 by Admiral Sir Alexander Cochrane.

All this while the British blockade was hurting, hurting badly. In 1813 American exports shrank from a prewar high of $130 million to $25 million. By the time peace was declared exports had dropped to less than $7 million, while import duties collected fell from $413 million to approximately $2 million. The throttling of coastwise shipping also threw inordinate strain on the poor network of land transport. The trip from South Carolina to Philadelphia became a six-week trek for wagons, which were sometimes piled up for miles at ferry bottlenecks. Retail prices soared. But, as we shall see, the blockade didn't prevent successful privateering.

9

The Northwest Boils

While William Hull and the administration were fumbling their way to defeat in 1812, the settlers in the Northwest were preparing to defend themselves and their homes against British and Indian aggression. William Henry Harrison, governor of the Indian Territory and hero of the battle of Tippecanoe, was enthusiastically chosen to lead Kentucky troops. He at once busied himself with mobilization. Shortly afterward, he was commissioned a brigadier general in the U.S. Army; following Hull's abject surrender Harrison received a War Department directive to assume command of all troops in the Northwest and to retake Detroit.

This was a tall order; the entire frontier was now aflame. Tecumseh, the great chief of the Shawnees now commissioned as a British brigadier general,[1] was in the field with a strong force of Indians, supporting British regulars and Canadian militia under Colonel Thomas Proctor. On September 3, twenty-four men, women and children were scalped at Pigeon Roost, Indiana. On the 4th, Captain Zachary Taylor, 7th Infantry, bravely re-

[1] At least so tradition says. Documentary evidence that Tecumseh actually held the King's commission is lacking.

pulsed an Indian attack at Fort Harrison, Indiana, although more than half of his fifty men were bedridden and one of his blockhouses was set on fire. At about the same time, the Indians futilely attacked Fort Madison, near St. Louis, for several days. On the night of September 6, some 600 Indians tried to capture Fort Wayne. After seeking the garrison's surrender for six days, they heard that help was coming to its aid and precipitately fled.

Only a part of the Delawares, Wyandots, Shawnees and several small tribes remained faithful to the United States; the rest of the Indians were secretly or openly hostile. Well knowing their cruelty, the frontiersman wanted to feel sure that his home and family were safe from their raids before he started marching for Canada.

Harrison, fully sympathetic with this point of view, organized several punitive expeditions. On September 14 Colonel Samuel Wells, 17th Infantry, led a detachment against the Potawatomies along the upper St. Joseph River. Brigadier General John Payne of Kentucky led some mounted troops against the Miamis. Together they succeeded in destroying nine Indian villages and the crops close at hand. On the 16th Colonel William Russell with 1,200 men of the 7th Infantry reached Fort Harrison, much to the relief of the recently attacked garrison. Soon afterward Russell returned to Vincennes with most of his troops. From there he left with two companies of United States Rangers for the neighborhood of Peoria, Illinois, during October, destroying the principal Kickapoo town with its stores of corn and chasing the Redmen into the swamps. In November Brigadier General Samuel Hopkins led a Kentucky force up the Wabash and obliterated the town of Tecumseh's brother, the Indian leader known as the Prophet, and one belonging to the Kickapoos. He then turned back, for his men were almost "shoeless and shirtless," and the streams were beginning to freeze. During December Lieutenant Colonel J. B. Campbell, 19th Infantry, raided and burned several important Delaware and Miami settlements along the Mississinewa River, a tributary of the Wabash. Much of this autumn fighting was revoltingly cruel, sparing neither life nor property. However, it accomplished its purpose. For a while, the savages were deterred from making any large-scale raids except when they were persuaded and helped by the British.

Meanwhile, Harrison was assiduously preparing to attempt the seemingly impossible task of retaking Detroit and invading Canada. He had gathered in his area some 1,800 recruits and put them under a grueling training schedule. This brought his overall strength to approximately 6,000 men, regulars and militia, fit for duty. By late September Harrison was ready to start operations by concentrating in the area of the rapids of the Maumee. On September 22 Harrison's left wing moved out from eastern Indiana under Brigadier General James Winchester, an inept Revolutionary War veteran who deserved Zebulon Pike's label of "heavy, dull, fat, uninteresting and incapable." Winchester reached the vicinity of Fort Defiance on the 30th and established a fortified camp. The Indians were hovering around it, and his men were half-starved. Fortunately a packtrain soon arrived with supplies, and the famished were fed.

The remainder of the northwestern army made slower progress. The center column, comprising Ohio militia, was to move from Urbana to Fort McArthur at Kenton, Ohio, on the Scioto River, then follow Hull's trace northward. The Pennsylvania and Virginia troops forming the right wing were to assemble at Wooster, proceed to Upper Sandusky, then make for the rapids. Harrison established his headquarters at Franklintown, in central Ohio.

By December Harrison's army held a line across northwest Ohio. The left wing was at Fort Defiance, the center at Fort McArthur and the right at Sandusky. The troops, scantily equipped, poorly clothed and plagued by sickness, were feeling the bite of a frontier winter. Harrison, however, kept up his schedule of training, at the same time making several small thrusts against Proctor's British and Indians based at Fort Miami, near the rapids. These probes finally bore fruit. In mid-December Colonel Richard W. Tupper of Ohio, with some 1,500 men, routed a mixed British-Indian aggregation near the rapids, forcing the evacuation of Fort Miami. The enemy retired to Fort Malden and Detroit.

As 1812 closed, Harrison was considering a winter campaign. The hard-frozen roads and an ice bridge over the Detroit River would facilitate invasion of Lower Canada. He began concentrating for a thrust at Detroit, but on January 22, 1813, his plans fell asunder. Winchester's command, reaching Frenchtown on the Raisin River, bivouacked without regard for security and was overrun by Colonel Proctor's 1,000 soldiers and Indians from Fort Malden, twenty miles away. Nearly 200 Americans were killed and wounded in the melee. Winchester surrendered unconditionally to Proctor, who pledged on the word of honor of a soldier that all prisoners would be safeguarded. Instead, Proctor turned the wounded and the inhabitants of the village over to his Indians. More than 200 were massacred in the resultant butchery. Proctor, praised by Sir George Prevost, Governor General of Canada, for his "gallantry" and his "humane and unwearied exertions," was promoted to major general as a reward for the massacre.

Harrison fell back on the Maumee, giving up all thought of a winter offensive. He began construction of Fort Meigs at the rapids some forty miles south of Frenchtown. There the army of the Northwest, its time-expired militia and volunteers gone home, remained through the rest of the winter.

10

New Brooms in the North

The year 1813 dawned auspiciously for the American Army. The Congress authorized the increase of Regular Army strength from 18,945 to 48,254. Although this was as yet only on paper, the future seemed rosy. Ineffective Secretary of War Eustis had resigned in December. Madison temporarily appointed Secretary of State James Monroe as acting Secretary of War while the President sought a new permanent chief for the War Department. In February, even before his second inauguration, the President appointed the new Secretary of War.

John Armstrong of Pennsylvania, the new broom, was a Revolutionary War veteran, politician and diplomat; more pugnacious than sagacious, he proved to be a self-seeker rather than a patriot. Perhaps it would be more fair to say that he wanted to do everything himself. In any event, Armstrong pressed for speedy assaults upon both Montreal and Kingston, thus threatening England's St. Lawrence River supply line to Canada.

On February 10 Armstrong directed General Dearborn to assemble 4,000 troops at Sackets Harbor and 3,000 more at Buffalo for the purpose of taking Kingston, York (Toronto) and Forts

George and Erie on the Niagara River. The timid Dearborn argued against this bold plan. He spoke of a British threat (mythical) against Sackets Harbor and pleaded Commodore Chauncey's temporary absence as an excuse for inaction.

While Dearborn delayed, another new broom arrived in the area. This was a man who would have more influence on the outcome of the war than anyone could possibly have foreseen.

Lieutenant Oliver Hazard Perry, USN, twenty-seven years old, adventurous and impulsive, had resented his dull task of commanding five gunboats in Rhode Island waters. So he wrote letters seeking a transfer. One went to his former associate in the Mediterranean service, Captain Chauncey at Sackets Harbor. At that time Chauncey was seeking a shipbuilder, and he recalled young Perry's efficient supervision of gunboat construction. Chauncey asked for Perry and got him.

Characteristically, Perry was prepared when the transfer order arrived. The day he received it he loaded fifty picked Rhode Island officers, seamen and shipwrights on bobsleds, sent them off for Lake Erie, and before nightfall he and his thirteen-year-old brother, Alexander, also jumped into a sleigh. He was en route to hard work, high adventure and imperishable glory.

Two other groups of fifty men each, recruited by Perry, followed him westward in a matter of days. They assembled at the old French post of Presqu' Isle on Lake Erie, the site of Chauncey's proposed shipyard. The peninsula of Presqu' Isle juts from the mainland where the town of Erie, Pennsylvania, already was rising.

En route from Newport, Perry met Chauncey in Albany, New York. The two discussed the situation on the lakes as they rode across the snow to Sackets Harbor. Perry was detained there for two weeks while Dearborn awaited a British attack that never came. Released by Chauncey, Perry passed through Buffalo and on the late afternoon of March 27 launched into his construction work at Presqu' Isle.

Dearborn's Niagara offensive began April 25, when Chauncey's flotilla, carrying 1,700 soldiers, left Oswego. After two days of rough weather the American flotilla cast anchor three miles west of York, then a village of 700 inhabitants. General Sheaffe's headquarters as governor of Upper Canada was at York, and he commanded its garrison, some 700 regulars and militia and 100 Indians. Two armed vessels, the *Prince Regent* and the *Duke of Gloucester,* covered its lakeside front.

Brigadier General Zebulon M. Pike commanded the American assault. Landings began on the 28th, with Colonel Forsyth's riflemen leading, covered by the ship's fire. They were checked at the beach by British grenadiers, dour Scottish Glengarry County Fencibles and Indians, but the second assault wave, regulars under Pike, drove the defenders back into town. There an ammunition dump containing 500 barrels of powder blew up, sweeping both forces with a deadly rain of timbers, stone and other debris for hundreds of yards.

In the explosion 38 Americans were killed and 222 others wounded; the British lost 40 men, with an unknown number injured. General Pike was mortally wounded, and for a moment the American attack halted. Colonel Cromwell Pearce, 16th Infantry, rallied the attackers, and the advance continued against demoralized opposition. Sheaffe, with his regulars, some 180 strong, retreated to Kingston, leaving militia officers to surrender York.

Victory had cost the Americans 320 casualties, of whom 58 had been killed. Pike died on board the *Madison,* his head resting on the British flag that he had so bravely helped to capture. The prisoners—260 British soldiers and sailors, mostly militia—were paroled in Canada. In the surrender, all government supplies and buildings were turned over to the Americans, who promised to respect private property. Unfortunately, with local authority crippled and Dearborn exerting little control, lawless soldiers and local ruffians pillaged and stole. The Parliament building, with its library and records, went up in flames. This wanton destruction was much resented by the British, who later retaliated by setting fire to the President's House and the Capitol in Washington.

On Saturday, May 1, Dearborn's men, "sickly and debilitated," evacuated York. For a week the flotilla remained becalmed in the harbor. Then it weighed anchor and sailed for Four Mile Creek, New York, not far from Fort Niagara.

For nineteen days the troops lay inactive at the mouth of Four Mile Creek while Dearborn and Commodore Chauncey hesitated. After the arrival of reinforcements from Sackets Harbor, two young regulars prodded their commanders to take action. En-

ergetic Winfield Scott—who had been exchanged after his surrender at Queenston—was now Dearborn's adjutant general; Perry
had come up from his shipbuilding at Presqu' Isle. The result of
Scott's and Perry's prodding was the first amphibious operation
of the young U.S. Army, planned and executed by the Scott-
Perry team. The two "heavy-sterned, elderly old men," Dearborn
and Chauncey, for once refrained from meddling. Brigadier General Morgan Lewis, Dearborn's second in command, had nominal
supervision.

On May 24 Perry's flotilla shepherded the assault force, crammed
into 134 boats and barges, to a landing north of Newark, near
Fort George. The force was made up of the brigades of Winder,
John Parker Boyd and newly arrived John Chandler. An odd trio,
these three: Winder, a Baltimore lawyer; Chandler, a Massachusetts politician; and Boyd, a soldier of fortune from Newbury-
port who had served in turn in the Continental Navy, in both
French and British service in India and at Tippecanoe with
Harrison as a U.S. Army regular.

It was broad daylight, with a morning fog clearing and a heavy
sea running when the first wave of assault craft came in. Winfield
Scott, acting as the assault force commander, led the way, a large
green bough marking his command boat.

There was no British naval opposition; so the American warships devoted their attention to the British batteries at Fort
George and soon silenced them. But the assault was met on the
beach by Brigadier General John Vincent's troops. Vincent himself commanded the British center, based on the fort. The right
wing was Lieutenant Colonel John Harvey's, and the left—where
the fighting was toughest—was Lieutenant Colonel Christopher
Myers'. Myers had some 500 men—the 8th Foot and the Glengarry,
Royal Newfoundland and Black Corps militia, with a sprinkling
of Indians.

The British met the first assault wave head on and hurled them
back almost to the water's edge. Scott stumbled, fell, scrambled
up again and rallied his men, who soon gained a foothold. Vincent
now committed the 49th Foot, but superiority in numbers and
firepower told. The British left began to crumble as Boyd's men
filtered through the underbrush, firing and killing in the manner

of frontier fighting. Myers was badly wounded and captured; many of his men were casualties.

After about two hours Vincent realized that the American right wing was beginning to sweep around Fort George. He ordered the fort to be evacuated, ammunition blown up, stores destroyed and guns dismantled and spiked. The troops were to hasten south along the road parallel to the Niagara to the vicinity of Queenston, then west to rally at Beaver Dam, about eighteen miles to the west. There supplies had been collected and other detachments would gather. About noon, before this action could be completed, however, Scott rushed Fort George, halted the demolitions, took a few prisoners and started after the fugitives. By then the 2nd Light Dragoons had come up, and with their help more British might have been captured, but—to Scott's annoyance—Boyd halted pursuit in accordance with orders from Major General Morgan Lewis.

Meanwhile Vincent dispatched orders for the abandonment of Chippawa and Fort Erie; their garrisons were also to march to Beaver Dam. After vigorously bombarding Black Rock, Lieutenant Colonel Cecil Bisshop collected the British troops at both places and set out for Beaver Dam, where, before long, 1,600 troops assembled. From there Vincent planned to move to the head of Lake Ontario, perhaps ultimately to York.

Dearborn, wasting precious time, delayed pursuit. On June 2 Winder took the 5th, 13th, 14th, and 16th Infantry, two companies of artillery, a detachment of dragoons and a few riflemen and started for Burlington Heights (near the present city of Hamilton) to prevent any retreat of the British around Lake Ontario to the village of York. The next day Dearborn sent Chandler to reinforce Winder with the 9th, 23rd and 25th Infantry regiments and some auxiliary troops. On the morning of June 5 Chandler overtook Winder at Forty Mile Creek and assumed command of the combined forces. The Americans, driving in several British outposts, bivouacked for the night at Stoney Creek, not far from Vincent's main body encamped on the heights.

A comedy of errors was staged that night. British patrols found the American "camp guards few and negligent." So Vincent attacked with the bayonet and drove in the American center.

Both Winder and Chandler, rushing about aimlessly in the darkness, were captured, and the Americans fled the field. But Vincent himself got lost. His second in command, Lieutenant Colonel John Harvey, not realizing that victory had been won, recalled the British troops. The only uninjured man left on the field was Vincent, who when dawn broke was found by his scouts wandering in the woods. The American force, with all their impedimenta lost, had rallied twelve miles away at Forty Mile Creek, and the British were back in their original position. To cap the comedy Harvey sent a message under flag of truce to Major James Burn, the senior American officer, to inform him that the British had captured two American generals but had lost their own!

On the evening of June 6 Dearborn ordered Lewis, at Fort George, to join and take command of the troops at Forty Mile Creek. He was then to attack the British and prevent their escape.

Moving out along the coast road, Lewis found himself threatened by a few light vessels of Sir James Lucas Yeo's British squadron on the lake and by roving Indians inshore. At the same time, he was being harassed by a flood of contradictory orders from Dearborn. To add to Lewis' dilemma, Commodore Chauncey, by now almost as timid as Dearborn, was making no effort to dispute Yeo's ships. By the time he reached Forty Mile Creek on the 8th, Lewis was completely confused and frightened. He suddenly beat a retreat, never stopping until safe under the guns of Fort George. Left to British hands were 500 tents, 200 camp kettles, 150 barrels of flour and port and a large store of other supplies. A small British force pursuing on land nabbed 40 prisoners and more equipment, while Yeo's ships captured or destroyed all the baggage bateaux.

Meanwhile back at Sackets Harbor, left unprotected by Chauncey, an affair of different character had taken place. On May 29 Sir George Prevost, taking advantage of the opportunity, moved across the lake from Kingston with some 1,200 men to land on Horn Island, near the harbor. The movement was protected by the guns of Yeo's squadron.

Sackets Harbor was defended by Brigadier General Jacob Brown, originally a New York militiaman but now a Regular Army officer. His tiny garrison consisted of two troops of light dragoons, under Captain Electus Backus, a handful of artillerymen and an extemporized battalion of militia rushed up from Albany when word of British concentration at Kingston had been received. Prevost's assault force, some 500 strong, crossed the shallows to the mainland, where they were met on the beach by the defenders. The American militia, after one volley, fled, but Backus' dismounted dragoons, supported by fire from Fort Tompkins, checked the British advance. Brown personally rallied the fleeing militia, who then fell on the attackers' flank. Unsupported by the British ships, which were unable to close within gunshot range, Prevost's infantrymen slowed, then retreated to their boats. By noon the British were back on their ships, and Prevost sailed away, leaving his dead and wounded behind him.

Early in June the ailing Dearborn, at Fort George, where Army headquarters had been established, turned over his command to Lewis, who left for Sackets Harbor. Boyd, senior officer present, learned that Vincent's forces were moving east from Forty Mile Creek. Already a British outpost had been established at the Decroue house, near Beaver Dam, west of Queenston. Accordingly, he ordered Lieutenant Charles Boerstler, 14th Infantry, with a force of 500 men and two guns, to destroy the outpost and check Vincent's advance.

Boerstler, moving through the forest without regard for security, was ambushed June 24 by a small force of Indians and a forty-six-man detachment of the 49th Foot, under Lieutenant James Fitzgibbon. After a three-hour fight, in which the Americans, most of them recruits, lost seventy men, Fitzgibbon adroitly bluffed Boerstler into surrendering his entire command. As usual, the Indians butchered most of the American wounded.

Following this latest fiasco, Dearborn's army on July 15 officially saluted his departure. Major General James Wilkinson, his replacement, was on the way north. Meanwhile, Boyd continued in interim command. Anxious to retrieve the army's reputation, Boyd, with Chauncey's cooperation, proposed an expedition against a British supply dump at Burlington Bay, at the western end of Lake Ontario. The Secretary of War, who had established himself at Albany, approved. Scott was chosen to command the raid. Lifted on Chauncey's ships, the expedition—500 strong—

reached Burlington Bay on the 29th but found the place heavily defended. Shallow water prevented any naval artillery support; so Scott decided to seek victory elsewhere.

Troops reembarked and the fleet headed for York, about forty miles distant. When he arrived on the 30th, Chauncey ran his schooners into the upper harbor with Scott's invaders, who landed unopposed. The prisoners from Boerstler's detachment were freed and a 24-pounder, twelve bateaux and several hundred barrels of hard bread and flour captured. Whatever of military value could not be taken away was destroyed. Some effects of Sheaffe and Harvey were found. Their official papers were retained, but Scott saw to it that their personal possessions were carefully returned to them. Harvey was grateful for this courtesy, especially because a lovely miniature that he prized very highly reached him safely.

On August 4, the American fleet again cast anchor off Fort George. During the week of adventure not a man had been lost. Nothing decisive had been effected, but considerable military supplies of great value to the British had been taken, and both the Army and the Navy had demonstrated ability in cooperative effort.

For the next month there were no decisive actions along the Niagara. A British reconnaissance in force probed Fort George's defense on August 24 and sheered off. Out on the lake, Yeo and Chauncey, their respective squadrons strengthened by new ships, sparred at long bowls for several days, neither of them caring to close. On August 25 General Wilkinson, the third new broom, arrived at Sackets Harbor, called a council of war and began deliberations on plans for a thrust on Montreal. On September 4 he sailed to Fort George to inspect the Niagara front. This did not result in any significant activity.

Things were far different on the northwestern frontier, where momentous happenings were about to come to a climax.

11

Two Strong Men

Tenacious William Henry Harrison had passed a winter of discontent, plagued not only by his own problems but also by the naggings of Armstrong. The Secretary of War could not understand that the basic objective—the recapture of Detroit and the invasion of Upper Canada—depended on two nonexistent factors: an adequate, trained, equipped and supplied ground force; and the control of Lake Erie.

Harrison's vast area of responsibility—Kentucky, Ohio, Virginia and Pennsylvania—was theoretically capable of supplying the needed manpower. But short-term enlisted militia and volunteers were ephemeral; they arrived untrained and left for home before they became soldiers. Regular Army recruits were few and far between. Armstrong promised additional troops but never redeemed the promises. In addition, thieving contractors shortchanged the Army's supply. It was a question of make-do; Harrison had to beg the state governors for additional drafts of militia, prod contractors, drill, guard what he could and wait. Preservation of Fort Meigs, his stronghold near Lake Erie at the Maumee rapids, was all-important to the future.

Meanwhile, British General Proctor, as soon as the ice in the Detroit River began breaking up, prepared to launch an offensive up the Maumee River. He, too, had his problems, but he hoped by firing the zeal of his Indian allies to overcome them. The offensive was to be mounted from Fort Malden, where Tecumseh soon arrived with 1,500 warriors, all ardent for loot. A large number of Canadian militia also came streaming in.

On April 12, 1813, Harrison gathered about 500 men and moved up to Fort Meigs, where some 200 Pennsylvania militia, time-expired, were still doing duty. The fort's defenses were skillfully strengthened by Captain E. D. Wood, Harrison's chief engineer, and Harrison, knowing that Governor Isaac Shelby of Kentucky had organized a force of 1,500 additional militia at Newport, under Brigadier General Green Clay, called for its speedy advance. Meanwhile he stayed at Fort Meigs to meet the expected British attack.

Proctor moved two weeks later, his 2,500 men lifted by the British squadron across the Detroit River and upper Lake Erie. By May 1 his main body was established on the left bank of the Maumee opposite the fort, while a detachment, with Tecumseh's Indians, assisted in the investment on the other bank. British batteries of artillery, emplaced on both sides of the river, opened fire, but with only slight effect; the east bank batteries were actually silenced by the fort's guns.

Not knowing how long the siege would last, Harrison ordered artillery ammunition to be conserved. He also offered a gill of whiskey, in addition to the daily liquor issue, for every British cannon ball retrieved and delivered to the magazine keeper. As the story goes, 100 extra gills were thus issued, much to the hilarious enjoyment of the ferreting soldiers. Proctor's demand for surrender, made on the 4th, was summarily refused. That same day, Harrison's messenger to Clay returned to the fort through the loose besieging lines. The Kentucky general and his men, moving down the Maumee on flatboats, were within eighteen miles of the fort.

Two of Harrison's officers sneaked through the British lines with detailed instructions to Clay. He was to disembark about a mile and a half above the fort, putting 800 men on the west bank, to attack the British guns. Meanwhile the remainder of his command was to land on the east bank. When the left bank force had taken the guns, they were to recross the river and the combined force would move against the besiegers there. A sortie from Fort Meigs would then snap a pincers grip on that portion of Proctor's command.

Like all complicated maneuvers planned for green troops, Harrison's plan came unstuck. Lieutenant Colonel William Dudley led Clay's left bank force rapidly against the British guns and captured them. But instead of then crossing the river, he chased the fleeing gunners. His confused militiamen were met by troops and Indians called from the east bank by Proctor, who assumed that this was the main attack. This force fell on the Americans, killing or capturing most of them, while the British gunners returned to their guns.

Actually, only 200 of Dudley's force ever reached the opposite shore to rejoin Clay. The prisoners were herded into nearby Old Fort Miami, where, in the presence of General Proctor, who stood idly by, the Indians suddenly began to slaughter them. Tecumseh himself, by this time also on the left bank of the river, rushed into the melee, struck down his maddened braves and restored order. Then, turning to Proctor, according to a British eyewitness, he loudly scorned him as a squaw: "You are not fit to command; go and put on petticoats!"

On the east bank things went differently. Colonel John Miller, 19th Infantry, led Harrison's sortie, 350 strong, against the British guns, took them and drove the besiegers back into Clay's advancing force. These British and Indians broke and scattered. But Miller had lost some 30 men killed and 90 wounded, and Harrison, fearing an ambush, recalled all his troops, who brought with them 43 prisoners.

Proctor, convinced that Fort Meigs would be a hard place to take, lost heart. His Indians were no longer reliable, and the Canadian militia were clamoring to go home. So after a second demand for surrender—a futile gesture—he decamped, leaving some of his guns behind him. But at the cost of 110-odd casualties, he had killed 130 Americans and carried off with him some 600 American prisoners, 185 of them wounded. Again Tecumseh's Indians began a butchery on the carelessly guarded Americans until the great chief himself once more intervened. The surviving prisoners, crowded half-naked into open boats in a cold rainstorm, finally reached British headquarters at Malden, where after a brief confinement they were given parole and allowed to return home as best they could.

With the Maumee valley now safe for a while, Harrison arranged for constant reconnaissance and the construction of several small works along the south Lake Erie shore. Leaving Clay in command at Fort Meigs, he returned to his headquarters at Cleveland, Ohio, and resumed his arduous recruiting campaign.

Sea power—more properly perhaps, lake power—remained the controlling factor for both sides. On the lake the British naval squadron assured not only the flow of supplies to Proctor's force in the Detroit area but also unimpeded lift to the southern shore if and when he decided to take the offensive. Captain Robert Heriot Barclay, RN, who had lost an arm at Trafalgar, had a tight little squadron of 6 ships manned by more than 400 men, British and Canadian seamen and British soldiers, all knit in Nelsonian discipline. The squadron was composed of the ships *Detroit* (just built) and *Queen Charlotte,* both carrying 19 guns; the brig *Hunter,* 10; the schooners *Lady Prevost,* 13, and *Chippewa,* 1; and the sloop-rigged *Little Belt,* 3. Perry's almost superhuman shipbuilding efforts since his arrival at Presqu' Isle had produced two fine brigs: the *Lawrence* and the *Niagara,* both of 20 guns. In March 1813 their timbers still had been growing in the forests, iron was still ore in the western Alleghenies, hemp was in Kentucky, canvas was in Philadelphia, pitch was in the Pennsylvania pine woods, cannon were in the Naval Gun Factory at Washington, D.C., and shipwrights were on the Atlantic coast. By early August the vessels were afloat and ready to fight. At Presqu' Isle Perry also had the schooners *Ariel,* 4, *Scorpion,* 2, and *Porcupine,* 1.

After the British evacuation of Fort Erie uncorked the Black Rock shipyard, Perry's squadron was augmented by four schooners —*Caledonia,* 3 (captured earlier in a surprise cutting-out raid on Fort Erie), *Somers,* 2, *Tigress,* 2, and *Ohio,* a supply craft—as well as the sloop-rigged *Trippe,* 1.

Full crews were still lacking; Chauncey would spare only driblets of men from his Ontario command, and able-bodied seamen were few and far between—the lure of privateering on the high

seas was too strong. Another problem was the channel into Presqu'
Isle, only a scant fathom deep. This had been Perry's major
protection against Barclay's squadron while construction was
going on. Now it prevented the exit of his two principal ships.
Perry had prepared for this contingency, however. He would
literally lift his vessels over the bar by use of "camels," a device
frequently used in Holland. Two scows were sunk alongside a
vessel, timbers resting on them were run through her portholes
and the scows were then pumped out. Once in open water, the
scows were sunk again and the vessel floated. Interesting, ingenious
and feasible, the process had one major drawback. During the
transit the helpless ship would be a sitting duck to an enemy, and
Barclay's squadron was almost continuously in the offing these
days.

It was Proctor himself, goaded by Tecumseh, who solved Perry's
dilemma in late July. Attempting to take Fort Meigs again,
Proctor called up Barclay's squadron to make the lift once more.
On July 20 British troops secretly landed near the fort, taking
shelter in a ravine just out of cannon shot from the fort. Tecumseh's Indians, having debarked farther down the Maumee, meanwhile circled wide to the Maumee–Lower Sandusky road, where
they engaged in a sham battle. The British expected Colonel
Clay to believe that reinforcements en route to him were being
ambushed. They were counting on the Americans to sally forth
quickly from the fort to rescue the new arrivals and to be trapped.
Clay, however, was not duped. Despite the vehement urging of
his officers, he kept all his men in the fort, where they did nothing
more than fire a few rounds of shot and shell in the direction
of the enemy's counterfeit racket. Proctor, foiled, reembarked his
troops and sailed eastward for Sandusky Bay, intending to attack
Fort Stephenson on the Sandusky River, thirty miles east of Fort
Meigs. Tecumseh moved overland to join him.

Fort Stephenson was a solidly constructed rectangular blockhouse complex with high picket walls and an encircling ditch.
The garrison, 160 regulars of the 17th Infantry, was commanded
by young Major George Croghan. On July 31 the British expedition lay in Sandusky Bay; the next day it moved up the Sandusky
River on the fort—some 400 men of the 41st Foot and Canadian
militia, together with some Indians, supported by several gun-

boats. Tecumseh's Indians were already loosely surrounding the post.

Proctor's demand for surrender on August 1 was indignantly refused. A cannonade followed. Croghan's single 61-bore field gun, shifted from side to side, kept up a valiant counterbattery.

Meanwhile, the Indians, losing patience as usual at any siege process, were showing signs of disinterest. The next day Proctor launched a two-pronged assault. The northern storming party actually reached the ditch, only to be thrown into disorder by enfilading grapeshot and slugs from Croghan's field piece. The southern attack got nowhere. Leaving behind twenty-eight dead and twenty-six wounded, the British receded.

Proctor accepted defeat, gathered his troops, took to the boats and withdrew downriver next day. He and his men, in Barclay's squadron, moved back to Malden.

Meanwhile, Perry had seized the opportunity presented him. As soon as the horizon had been cleared of Barclay's ships, Perry had lifted his ships over the bar. On August 12, with a fair wind, he stood westward for Put-in-Bay, north of Sandusky, where he was welcomed by a gleeful Harrison. The pair immediately went into conference. An American squadron on Lake Erie threatened the entire British situation in the Northwest. Unless Barclay could fight and win on the water, Upper Canada was open to American invasion; Proctor's troops, their supply route choked, could do nothing about it.

Perry knew that the British ships could not remain long in Malden, fifty miles to the north. They would have to sail east for supplies, passing Perry's anchorage, which commanded a view of the western approaches. While waiting, Perry drilled his men so thoroughly that those whom he described as "motley" when he first inspected them were soon whipped into efficient seamen and gunners. He was still short-handed, but, as a substitute for the marines he needed so badly, Harrison had loaned him some 150 sharpshooting Kentucky and Indiana riflemen. This raised Perry's complement to 532, of whom a scant 160 were trained sailors.

From reconnaissance and from Harrison's spies Perry received reports on the situation in the British stronghold and shipyard at Fort Malden and the nearby town of Amherstburg. From this information, and from his own prescience, on the evening of

September 9, 1813, Perry concluded that the British fleet was ready and would come out into the lake on the morrow. He called his officers to his cabin in the flagship, *Lawrence,* that night to give careful final instructions that left nothing in doubt about how he intended to fight. The *Lawrence* and *Niagara* would engage the two largest British ships. But since the Americans were weaker in long-range guns, all ships were to close on the enemy as rapidily as possible and fight the battle broadside following Nelson's aphorism: "If you lay your enemy alongside, you cannot be far out of your place."

At the end of the conference, Perry drew out a big blue flag, on which were sewed in white letters the words of the dying Lawrence, "DON'T GIVE UP THE SHIP." When that flag broke out from the mainmast of the *Lawrence,* he told his officers, it would be the signal to close for action.

The dawn of September 10, 1813, broke bright over Lake Erie, crystal clear and free from morning mists, giving promise of a rare early-autumn day. Scarcely had the half-sun shown red over the horizon when from the foretop of the *Lawrence* came the shout of "Sail, ho!" A clump of square-riggers was in the distance. Instantly Perry signaled: "Enemy in sight. Get under way."

Across the decks sounded the boatswains' whistles that seemed to shrill merrily to the sailors who had been so long awaiting this moment. The patter of feet rippled along the decks; a thudding tramp sounded around the capstans. Then, as the sails bellowed full, the trim little fleet gracefully moved through the island channels into the open lake.

Twenty-seven-year-old Master Commandant Oliver Hazard Perry, commodore by virtue of his command, was about to fight one of the most decisive fleet actions of American history. A devout man, he had prayers said aboard his flagship. The cooks brought food to the gunners and seamen at their battle stations at 10:30 A.M. By 11:45 the British fleet was near enough for the Americans to hear the bugle calls, and then the band on Barclay's flagship, *Detroit,* burst forth with the rousing strains of "Rule Britannia." At 11:50 A.M. a long gun spoke from the *Detroit,* opening the battle.

Barclay's fleet was freshly painted red and shone beautifully against the blue lake and cloudless azure sky. His line was led by the little *Chippewa*, followed by the flagship, *Detroit*, and the *Hunter, Queen Charlotte, Lady Prevost* and *Little Belt*, in that order. Perry met him with two small vessels, *Scorpion* and *Ariel*, in the van. Then came the *Lawrence*, largest ship on either side, *Caledonia* and *Niagara*, followed by the *Somers, Porcupine, Tigress* and *Trippe*. The combined tonnage of Perry's fleet was 1,671; of Barclay's, 1,469. Perry had fewer guns, 54 to Barclay's 63 guns and four howitzers; but it has been estimated that Perry's shorter-range weapons had the advantage in weight of broadsides of about 3 to 2. Barclay had 502 men to Perry's 490 on the rolls, including the sick. Perry had 9 vessels to Barclay's 6, an advantage offset by the fact that Barclay's ships were larger and if allowed to concentrate on a single American vessel could readily put her out of action.

Barclay had taken a considerable risk in coming out before the *Detroit* was fully equipped. One of her principal shortages was matches for firing her guns. But Barclay devised a scheme for firing the guns by flashing pistols at the touchholes. This proved to be effective, and in the battle the guns fired accurately and swiftly.

Barclay's plan, obvious at the outset, was to mass his guns against the *Lawrence*, then move on to the other vessels. His aim would be abetted if all Perry's vessels did not follow orders and engage at close quarters.

The *Detroit*'s first shot fell short, but a second crashed through the *Lawrence*'s bulwark and bounded across the deck without doing severe damage. Barclay had the weather gage, but Perry sacrificed no time maneuvering for position. When his first officer, Lieutenant John J. Yarnell, remonstrated, he boldly declared he was not concerned about it. "Leeward or windward, they shall fight today," he declared, and his big blue battle flag with Lawrence's words broke out. The little *Scorpion*, ahead of the *Lawrence*, fired the first American shot. Her skipper, Stephen Champlin, twenty-three years old, of Newport, was Perry's first cousin and had come at his call.

The *Lawrence* took hard punishment from the *Detroit*'s long-range 24-pounders, her one long 18, six long-range 12s and eight 9s. She was suffering severely before she got well into action. Perry's plan was for the *Lawrence, Caledonia, Scorpion* and *Ariel* to battle the *Detroit, Hunter* and *Chippewa*. Lieutenant Jesse D.

Elliott with the *Niagara* would battle the *Queen Charlotte* at close quarters. The *Somers, Tigress, Trippe* and *Porcupine* were to engage the *Lady Prevost*—a brig much larger than any of the American gunboats—and the *Little Belt,* probably the equal of any one of them.

Unfortunately, the plan went awry. Elliott's *Niagara* opened long-range fire on the *Queen Charlotte* but failed to close. Lieutenant George Irvine, RN, commanding the *Queen Charlotte,* made sail to escape his adversary's crippling blows and joined the *Detroit* to engage the *Lawrence.* The *Hunter* and *Lady Prevost* also closed in on Perry's flagship. The *Detroit* and *Queen Charlotte* were soon pounding the *Lawrence* unmercifully, shattering her timbers, repeatedly sweeping her decks.

Of the 103 effective seamen and gunners who had gone into action on the *Lawrence,* 83 were killed or wounded within the next two and a half hours, a staggering casualty rate of 80 percent. At length only one gun remained serviceable. Perry kept firing it to show that the *Lawrence* was still fighting. He personally sighted it and fired the vessel's last shot. The *Lawrence* had fought her battle and was finished. Her masts were shattered, her hull riddled, her sails slashed to ribbons. She had fought two and a half hours against four of Barclay's six ships. She was afloat and in no danger of sinking but had nothing left to fight with. As her spars and sails went, she lost her maneuverability, became unmanageable and was blown by a freshening wind.

Meantime, the smaller craft, with their scant armaments, had plunged into the inferno with the *Lawrence*'s spirit. The *Scorpion, Ariel* and *Caledonia* had aided the flagship as best they could, pounding especially at the *Lady Prevost,* which at length became helpless with the loss of her rudder.

When the *Lawrence* drifted out of action, probably not one naval officer in a thousand would have given Perry the slightest chance for victory. Perry could not know at this juncture how much damage the *Lawrence* and the gunboats had been inflicting on the British fleet. One of the most grievous British losses was Captain Barclay, who had been wounded twice, once so severely that he lost his remaining arm. Barclay was carried below and his high fighting spirit was lost to his fleet. Soon his second in command, Lieutenant Garland, was mortally wounded and carried down, leaving the command to Lieutenant George Inglis, a large responsibility for a junior officer.

Only about twenty unwounded seamen remained serviceable aboard the wallowing *Lawrence*, but Perry had noted that the *Niagara* had not been seriously engaged and had scarcely been scratched. He made a quick decision. He would board the *Niagara* and continue the fight. Only one of the *Lawrence*'s small boats remained seaworthy; he ordered four seamen to launch it. Taking with him his brother Alexander and the big blue flag with its motto from the dying *Lawrence*, he went over the side to the stern of the boat and told his men to row to the *Niagara*, leaving Lieutenant John J. Yarnell, his face swollen with a splinter that had run through his nose, to surrender the *Lawrence* at his discretion. (A little later Yarnell did haul down the flag, only to raise it again after the battle went into its final phase.)

An artist later perpetuating this dramatic incident shows Perry, wrapped in his blue battle flag, standing up in the stern of the little boat as it was tossed about between the British ships. In any event, the passage was completed successfully, despite British marksmen firing from their rigging and lining their taffrails as his rowers pulled past their sterns to reach the faltering *Niagara*. Bullets pecked at the waves, but though the range was close none hit him. Could it have been that many of the British, admiring his courage and accounting the battle won, did not aim too carefully? Still, the fire was so persistent that the oarsmen finally lifted their oars, telling Perry that if he did not sit down they would proceed no farther.

Men in both fleets watched with some awe for the fifteen minutes required for the passage, as shot and an occasional broadside churned up the near waters. At 3:15, after the battle had been joined more than three hours, the rowboat reached the side of the *Niagara* and Perry climbed aboard. The main battle of lake Erie had not ended. In truth, it was just beginning.

To the sheepish Elliott, whose motivation has never been quite clear, Perry made but one remark: "I've been sacrificed." He sent Elliott over to whip up a lagging gunboat and took command.[1]

---

[1] Elliott later argued that his failure to close was due to lack of wind—something that no other captain in the action had found lacking. In any event, Perry buried his grievances and mentioned Elliott with the other officers in dispatches; and Elliott received an equal share of prize money—$7,500.

The *Niagara,* making sail, leapt ahead toward the very center of the British fleet and passed down a double line, the *Detroit* and *Queen Charlotte* to starboard, the aimless and rudderless *Lady Prevost* and the *Chippewa* to port. The *Niagara's* guns, double-shotted, belched forth fearful broadsides. One of the first swept the *Lady Prevost* at close range and finished her as an active participant. The *Detroit,* seeking to avoid a raking fire from the *Niagara,* fouled the *Queen Charlotte,* whose captain did not know Barclay was wounded and came alongside for orders. For eight minutes Perry played the *Niagara* about them, pouring in his raking broadsides until the *Queen Charlotte,* helpless, lowered her flag.

The *Detroit,* meanwhile, had become completely unmanageable. Every brace had been cut away; her mizzen-topmast and gaff were down and all her other masts were severely damaged; her hull was badly shattered; a number of her guns were disabled. All the while, the *Niagara* was astern and raking her. Lieutenant Inglis saw that the only course was surrender, and he struck his flag. After the battle it was found that the *Detroit* has been so wounded and shattered that it was impossible for one to lay a hand on her maindeck or her sides without covering a place where one of Perry's guns had hit.

The *Lady Prevost* and the *Hunter* soon struck, but the *Little Belt* and *Chippewa* tried flight. Perry sent the *Scorpion* and *Trippe* after them and they were brought in.

Perry's first act after the victory was to bow in prayer. Then he took a lead pencil, and holding the back of an envelope against a Navy cap, he wrote to General Harrison a laconic message: "We have met the enemy and they are ours: two ships, two brigs, one schooner and one sloop."

The battle of Put-in-Bay had cost the British 41 men killed and 94 others wounded. The Americans lost 27 killed and 96 wounded —mostly on the *Lawrence.* Lake Erie had become *mare nostrum.*

Harrison, with the gateway to Canada opening wide, lost no time. His pleas and naggings had by this time brought his strength to some 7,000 men, of whom 3,500 were Kentucky volunteers led by Governor Shelby. By September 14, when Perry brought his victorious squadron to Fort Meigs and disgorged his prisoners, the pair were ready for the next step. On the 20th nearly 5,000 men, with some artillery, were embarking on the squadron and in 100 additional boats, while a fine, hard-riding regiment of Kentucky mounted riflemen, recruited and commanded by Colonel Richard M. Johnson, moved out of Fort Meigs to encircle the head of Lake Erie on a 100-mile-long overland march to Detroit. A small garrison was left at the fort. On the 27th Harrison disembarked without opposition at Hartley's Point on the Canadian mainland, three miles east of Amherstburg. The Americans' marching column then passed through the town with flags flying and the band playing "Yankee Doodle."

While a detachment under Duncan McArthur, now a brigadier general, liberated Detroit, and Perry's squadron anchored in the Detroit River beside the town, Harrison's main body bivouacked at Sandwich, on the opposite shore. Johnson's mounted riflemen came clattering through Detroit to cross the river and join the command on October 1. The next day, after stores and ammunition had been unloaded from the squadron on Lake St. Clair, Harrison pushed the pick of his ground forces, 3,500 strong, in hot pursuit of Proctor's rear guard. Paralleling them on the Thames River came Perry with three of his light craft—*Scorpion, Tigress* and *Porcupine*—for fifteen miles. There the water shoaled and Perry, furnished a horse, joined Harrison as a volunteer aide. He wanted to be in on the kill.

With Johnson's mounted rifles spearheading the advance, Harrison's hard-marching infantrymen followed close on the smoking trail of partly destroyed bridges, flaming farmhouses and wrecked boats left by the retreating British. They brought Proctor and his 2,000-man army to bay near the village of Moravian Town by noon on the 5th.

The British position was well chosen. On their right lay a large swamp that stretched roughly parallel to the Thames River for about two miles; on their left flowed the Thames itself, with high, steep banks; opposite the center was another, smaller swamp. Proctor formed his army in two wings: on his left mostly militia and regulars were posted; on the right were chiefly Indians. The Detroit road ran close to the river, and the ground, except for the swamp areas, had little or no underbrush, being mostly covered with oak, maple and beech trees.

In his original arrangements, Harrison planned an infantry attack, to be followed up with a cavalry charge. But when Major E. D. Wood brought word that the British were drawn up in open order, instructions were reversed. Johnson's frontiersmen, well versed in riding through the woods and firing mounted, opened the battle with an enveloping charge when the bugle blew, his 1st Battalion against the British left, his 2nd against their right. They were somewhat delayed by weaving in and out between the trees and crossing fallen timber. When they came within range, the American horsemen were thrown into temporary confusion by the British fire. Quickly rallying, the Americans dashed forward regardless of bullets, broke part of the British line and scattered it in all directions. In a few minutes, the British left was completely routed; most of its 800 troops threw down their arms and surrendered. Of the 41st Foot only one officer and fifty men escaped.

The Americans on the British right had harder going. Tecumseh and his Indians held their fire until the attackers were only a few paces distant. Johnson himself was severely wounded, and his men, falling back, dismounted and fought on foot. Governor Shelby ordered Lieutenant Colonel John Donaldson to bring up his regiment and Brigadier General John E. King his brigade as support. Before either had gotten well into action, however, the Indians fled. Their brave and able leader, Tecumseh, died fighting. Some say his followers carried off his body; others state that several Kentuckians found it naked and abandoned, and stripped skin from the thighs to make into razor strops.

The casualties in the battle of the Thames were remarkably small. The Americans lost 7 men killed and 22 wounded; the British, about the same. The Indians left 33 warriors dead on the field, in addition to Tecumseh. But 601 British prisoners were in Harrison's hands. Proctor, who had galloped away early in the action with his personal staff, a few dragoons and some mounted Indians, was 65 miles away from the scene within 24 hours. His carriage, sword, papers and personal effects were left behind.

No high-ranking British Army officer along the Canadian border had demonstrated worse leadership or greater cowardice. A court-martial later sentenced Proctor to public reprimand and the forfeiture of pay and rank for six months—a sentence considered much too light by most of his countrymen, including the Prince Regent.

Praises of Perry and Harrison rang high throughout the United States, which so badly needed a victory. Between them, these two strong men had shattered British power in the Northwest. All danger of an invasion from that quarter had been erased. The Indian confederacy was paralyzed by the death of Tecumseh; British forces on land and on Lake Erie were broken in defeat.

War Secretary Armstrong, in one of his master-minding moods, now ordered Harrison's militia to be disbanded, while the regulars were ordered to reinforce Wilkinson's command on the Niagara–St. Lawrence River front. Harrison, taking the troops there himself, found that there was no place for him in Armstrong's plan. He returned to Cincinnati in high dudgeon and in May 1814 resigned from the Army.[2]

[2] Twenty-seven years later William Henry Harrison would become its commander-in-chief, as the ninth President of the United States.

12

Tarnished Warriors

At Sackets Harbor on August 25, 1813, a fifteen-gun salute announced the arrival of Major General James Wilkinson, new commander of the northern army. He had taken five months and ten days to answer War Secretary Armstrong's order of March 10 to report "with the least possible delay." This unexplained delay would not have been surprising to those who knew his record.

Wilkinson's infamous career began in the Revolutionary War, when he had been an aide-de-camp to General Horatio Gates and played a still-unexplained role in the Conway Cabal, which tried to put Gates in command in place of George Washington. After the Revolution Wilkinson settled in Kentucky, where he was involved in a number of questionable deals. In 1791 he returned to the Army, and in subsequent years he became generally detested by his fellow officers. By 1805 he had become the senior brigadier and commanding general of the Army. Activities that seemed treasonable to his contemporaries caused him to spend the autumn and winter of 1811 before a general court-martial at Fredericktown, Maryland, defending himself against eight charges and twenty-five specifications alleging him to be a paid agent of Spain, an accomplice of Aaron Burr and a disobedient and incompetent officer. Cleared on all counts,[1] Wilkinson returned to duty in February 1812, but no longer as commanding general of the Army; Dearborn, with a new major general's commission, ranked him.

Ordered to New Orleans to command the southern department, Wilkinson in the spring of 1813 seized west Florida by War Department directive, forcing out the Spanish commander at Mobile in a bloodless coup. It was then that he was ordered north to command on the Niagara front.

Stopping in Washington on the way, Wilkinson was joined in his journey by Secretary Armstrong. The pair proceeded to Albany, where the Secretary made his temporary headquarters. There he took over, in effect, the direction of operations on the Niagara and St. Lawrence fronts. Armstrong wanted an immediate offensive—simultaneous converging drives on Montreal, the center of river traffic. One of these was to be launched down the river from Sackets Harbor; the other was to move north from Plattsburg on Lake Champlain.

By this time American military affairs were in chaos along the 400-mile Lake Ontario–St. Lawrence River border and east to Lake Champlain. Wilkinson found that he would share command of the proposed invasion with one of his many Army enemies, Brigadier General Wade Hampton, who was at Burlington, Vermont, on Lake Champlain. Hampton, arriving in the Champlain valley theater in early July, had concentrated all his forces—some 4,000 men—at Burlington, leaving the border unprotected. British Colonel John Murray, with 1,500 men and two armed sloops, filled the vacuum by raiding Plattsburg on the west shore of the lake. Adding insult to injury, his sloops sailed over to Sherburne, on the east shore below Burlington, and captured a vessel loaded with flour from under Hampton's nose. Then the British departed.

In response, Hampton made a half-hearted gesture at invasion in September. By the 26th he had reached Chateaugay in northern New York, midway between the St. Lawrence and Lake Champlain. Here he presented a problem to General Sheaffe, now commanding at Montreal. Was Hampton planning to cut British com-

---

[1] Modern research, which found unquestionable confirmation in the Spanish archives, has proven that Wilkinson was indeed a traitor and a paid agent of Spain.

munications on the St. Lawrence, or would he march directly against Montreal?

Sheaffe had available only some 5,800 men, British and Canadian "embodied" militia (serving ` two-year enlistments). He set Lieutenant Colonel Charles de Salaberry, his most skillful field commander, to watch Hampton.[2]

Actually, Hampton had no better idea than Sheaffe as to what his ultimate move might be. But while he was lingering in indecision at Chateaugay, there was comparable confusion at Sackets Harbor.

Armstrong had joined Wilkinson at Sackets Harbor. Argument, bickering and councils of war followed one another. Should Fort George be evacuated now that Harrison had destroyed British strength in the Northwest? Should Wilkinson's first objective be Kingston, or should he push down the St. Lawrence to Montreal and leave that British strongpoint threatening his rear? Wilkinson and Armstrong—artful dodgers both—strained for a solution that in case of failure would make the other the scapegoat. The final decision was that Wilkinson's army was to move directly down the river from Sackets Harbor, lifted and screened initially by Chauncey, himself somewhat of a reluctant dragon. Scott was left at Fort George to put the place in shape to repel an assault.

On October 16 Wilkinson's command, 7,000 strong, began moving into the St. Lawrence aboard a ramshackle conglomeration of small craft. Winter was setting in; snow, rain, cutting wind lashed the boats. Ahead of them went a courier from Armstrong to Hampton, suggesting that although Wilkinson's intentions were not clear, he had better move down the Chateaugay River prepared to meet Wilkinson on the St. Lawrence.

Whether Hampton had powers of divination or received earlier information is not clear. At any rate, he broke camp on the 21st and started down the Chateaugay for the St. Lawrence. The going was not easy. De Salaberry, who had about 1,000 soldiers and some Indians, had blocked the indifferent road with fallen trees and had posted his light troops and Indian allies in the thick woods

[2] De Salaberry, veteran British regular, had fought in the King's Royal Rifle Corps (organized at Governors Island, New York, in 1758 as the 62nd Foot Royal American), in Martinique, at Walchern Island and in other engagements. He now commanded a Canadian militia regiment, the Voltigeurs.

bordering it. To circumvent them, Brigadier General George Izard and a detachment were sent forward in one direction to seize the open country in the rear of de Salaberry's men, while the main body, taking another direction, started for the same place. The maneuver proved entirely successful, and the army went into camp at Spears, where the Outard River flows into the Chateaugay. Here Hampton remained until more supplies could be brought up and plans perfected for the next forward movement across a seven-mile stretch of open country to another wooded area that the British had defended with a blockhouse, breastworks and a few field pieces.

On October 25 Hampton sent Colonel Robert Purdy with the 4th Infantry and some light troops to cross the Chateaugay near the American camp and to follow it for about seven miles to a ford near the British position. He would recross the stream at dawn and attack the rear of the British left flank. Purdy's opening fire was to be the signal for Hampton's main body, about 3,500 men, to start a frontal attack on de Salaberry. Purdy had covered only a short distance across the Chateaugay when he found himself lost in a labyrinth of swamp and forest. Milling around in the darkness, his men, often mistaking their comrades for the enemy, frequently fired on each other. At some time during the morning, within a half-mile of the ford, Purdy called a halt to allow his men to rest.

Without news from Purdy, Hampton decided to attack. He moved forward at two o'clock in the afternoon, easily driving back de Salaberry's outpost detachments to their main line of defense. At about this time, firing was heard from across the river. Purdy was not getting in the British rear, but some Canadian militia were firing on him. Soon each was in headlong flight from the other. Purdy's men made for the river; some swam across to bring harrowing tales of a host overwhelming them. At that moment de Salaberry, fearful of his worsening plight, tried a hoary expedient. He had his buglers, spaced over an extensive front, sound the charge. Bewildered Hampton, believing that a great force was moving against him, ordered a retreat, and his troops went streaming back all the way to Chateaugay.

Meanwhile Wilkinson's armada moved slowly on. Harassing fire from British gunboats out of Kingston, which had eluded Chauncey's screen, added to their troubles. Finally clearing the Thousand Islands, the expedition moved downriver with flank guards pressing along both shores. Wilkinson had arranged his command in four brigades, under John Parker Boyd, Jacob Brown, Leonard Covington and Robert Swartwout, respectively. Moses Porter commanded the artillery, and Alexander Macomb, the reserve. These troops were all regulars—in name, at least, for the ranks were filled by raw recruits.

The going was slow, the vicissitudes of a Canadian winter, many. The fumbling, half-frozen troops reached French Creek November 4. There they halted while Jacob Brown's brigade beat off a British raid. Two days later they were at Ogdensburg, where a mud-plastered but happy Winfield Scott joined them. Scott, having completed his renovation work at Fort George, had received Wilkinson's permission to start after the main body. No boats being available, Scott started overland with his regiment. Then he left the troops to follow under his second in command and accompanied only by his adjutant had ridden all the way to join.

At Ogdensburg, while Wilkinson was pondering how best to run British batteries at Prescott, on the opposite shore, he received word of Hampton's defeat. Wilkinson was sick, and to add to his troubles, a detachment of light vessels from Commodore Yeo's squadron at Kingston under Captain William H. Mulcaster, RN, carrying 800 troops under Lieutenant Colonel Joseph W. Morrison, was following downriver but keeping out of range of Macomb's artillery. While at Ogdensburg, Wilkinson received word from Secretary Armstrong regretting that he could not join the expedition and pleading War Department business in Washington. Wilkinson was convinced that Armstrong had lost all interest—an opinion that would have been strengthened had he known that the Secretary of War, before returning to the capital, had issued orders to Hampton for construction of winter quarters for the entire northern army.

The Prescott batteries were passed successfully, but Wilkinson's worries mounted. British reinforcements from Kingston behind him appeared to have reached Prescott. Rumor spoke of 20,000 Canadian militia before him, while Montreal's garrison of 600 men was supposedly being reinforced from Quebec. To cap the climax, at Chateaugay Hampton had refused his orders to join him. On

November 8 Wilkinson called a council of war. After deliberation, the council voted to go on.

Brown's brigade, reinforced by artillery, was debarked on the Canadian side and moved ahead over rough country to spearhead the advance. Boyd's brigade followed, acting as a rear guard to check any British advance from Prescott. By sunset on the 9th Brown had pushed fifteen miles to reach the farm of John Chrisler. The remainder of the expedition, still afloat, moored for the night not far away.

The next day confusion increased. Wilkinson's illness had worsened. He took to his bed on a boat, handing command to his deputy, the aged Lewis, who was also sickly. British gunboats nibbled at the rear but were checked by artillery fire. Downriver the Sault rapids threatened further progress. Lewis landed the main command on Chrisler's farm and bivouacked for the night.

Brown pulled his advance guard out of the mud at dawn November 10 to be checked ten miles farther on by a wrecked bridge protected by British and Indian skirmishers. Scott led a detachment to turn the enemy's left, but it was too late for any further progress. The Americans bivouacked under arms.

November 11 dawned cold and drizzly. Brown reported that he had cleared the way and urged forward movement. Lewis began advance of the main body but was checked by Wilkinson. In the rear, the British gunboats had reopened fire, while Morrison's British troops disembarked and began an advance in three echelons, each supported by a 6-pounder gun. The flank companies of the 49th Foot and some Canadian militia were on the right along the river; three companies of the 89th Foot formed the center, and the remainder of both regiments composed the left column; Voltigeurs and Indians screened the advance.

Boyd, commanding the American troops on land, moved to attack the oncoming British. Swartwout and his 4th Brigade were in the lead, supported by Covington's 3rd Brigade on the left. Boyd with his 1st Brigade planned to aid them both as necessary. Colonel Eleazar W. Ripley and the 21st Infantry opened the battle when they met hostile skirmishers and forced them back upon the British main body. The rest of the 4th Brigade and part of the 1st under Colonel Isaac A. Coles, 12th Infantry, followed Ripley in spite of heavy musketry and artillery fire. Soon the Americans were driving the British center and left into the miry field of Chrisler's farm. On the other flank, Covington, mounted on a white horse, led the 3rd Brigade against the British right, which was supported by enfilading fire from the gunboats and whose defense was naturally strengthened by a series of ravines.

From about half past two o'clock, the fighting became general and severe. It was mostly close-range infantry action; only a few artillery pieces were fired. In the confused fighting one of the American guns was captured despite the heroic efforts of mortally wounded Lieutenant Wallace W. Smith. The remaining guns escaped a similar fate because of a fortuitous and gallant charge of perhaps 100 mounted dragoons under Colonel John D. Walbach. But their numbers were few, the ground was rough and the dragoons were repelled by stubborn British defense.

As the afternoon wore on, the sky darkened, the winds grew chill and sleet and snow began to fall. The British, after retreating a half-mile or more, held their ground with confidence and valor, finally halting the American offensive. Swartwout's 4th Brigade and other units operating with it started to fall back as their ammunition ran low; those on their left did likewise. At this moment gallant Covington fell, mortally wounded, just when Morrison launched a counterattack. The Americans' withdrawal now became disorderly, and if Colonel Timothy Upham had not brought up some 600 reinforcements to steady them, the Americans might have been routed. As it happened, with this reinforcement they held their ground in a section of the woods and one of the ravines facing the British. This was the situation as darkness closed in, blotting out the figures of men along the reaches of windswept field and wintry river.

Eight hundred well-led British troops had fought twice their number to a standstill. Never had so many American regulars been defeated on foreign soil by troops so numerically inferior. American losses, out of 1,600 men engaged, were 102 killed, including one general officer—Covington. They also had 237 wounded and 100 taken as prisoners. The British lost one officer and 22 men killed and 11 officers and 137 men wounded.

Wilkinson decided to call off the offensive. His army, covered by Upham's 21st Infantry, withdrew unimpeded to their boats and crossed the river to the New York shore without opposition. They went into dismal and shockingly unsanitary winter quarters shortly afterward at French Mills—victims of incompetent leadership. Of their individual courage and fighting qualities there can be no question. The Briton Morrison recognized this; he wrote Colonel Edmund Pendleton Gaines, commander of the 25th Infantry— which had put up a particularly desperate resistance—asking his name, expressing his admiration and respect and hoping that after the war they might meet as friends.[3]

While all this fumbling was taking place along the fringes of the St. Lawrence wilderness, Prevost was taking steps to mend his fences in Upper Canada after the disastrous Battle of the Thames. General Francis, Baron de Rottenburg, lieutenant governor of the province, was relieved by far abler Lieutenant General Sir Gordon Drummond. General Vincent, still at Burlington Heights and in poor health, was replaced by Major General Phineas Riall, a stout, competent soldier.

The forces at Burlington Heights were swelling as Vincent's battered command was reinforced first by the remnants of Proctor's troops and then by additional increments of regulars and militia. Drummond now turned his eyes toward the Niagara area. Fort George was held by Brigadier General George M'Clure, left in command when Wilkinson moved north. A former carpenter, M'Clure had successively become a merchant, a justice of the New York Surrogate Court and finally commander of the 8th Brigade, New York State militia. He was an uncouth poltroon whose depredations of the Canadian countryside were aided by a Canadian turncoat named Joseph Willcocks.

Expirations of short-term enlistments had drained M'Clure's strength to less than 200 men, and his pleas for replacements had gotten nowhere. Panicking, on the night of October 10–11, he sacked the little village of Newark, near Fort George. Four hundred inhabitants—mainly women and children, for most of the able-bodied men were in the Canadian militia—were turned out into the snow and icy cold on two hours' notice, and the buildings were razed. Then M'Clure decamped for Fort Niagara, on

[3] C. W. Elliott, *Winfield Scott, the Soldier and the Man* (New York: Macmillan, 1937), p. 131.

the New York side, abandoning Fort George and large stores of clothing and matériel.[4]

Lieutenant Colonel John Murray marched to the scene with 500 British regulars and occupied Fort Erie. Crossing the Niagara on the night of the 18th he stormed unready Fort Niagara. Some 60-odd Americans were massacred before surrender was accepted. (M'Clure, fortunately for him, had left the place to drum up reinforcements.) General Riall, with 1,000 more troops and a large body of Indians, crossed near Lewiston, drove out a militia force and then turned his Indians loose to scorch the countryside. The British troops pushed south through Schlosser and Black Rock to Buffalo.

At the cost of only 105 casualties the British had completed in little more than a week the reconquest of their Niagara frontier region and had devastated the opposite shore. In a tract approximately 40 miles square, American settlements were generally abandoned. At Buffalo all buildings were burned to the ground except three; at Black Rock only one was spared. The Black Rock Navy Yard and four vessels of the Lake Erie squadron were totally destroyed. All of Niagara and most of Geneseo County were almost depopulated. The roads leading east were cluttered with heavy-hearted fugitives carrying with them whatever they had salvaged from the devastation in their rear. Between LeRoy and Cayuga Creek one person counted more than 100 of these families, wretched and miserable and cold.

On New Year's Day 1814, when Riall moved back across the river laden with booty and prisoners, Buffalo's smoking cinders stood in grim testimony to payment in full for York and Newark.

---

[4] Drummond's peremptory note to M'Clure, demanding immediate statement whether "this atrocious act" at Newark had been committed on the authority of the American government or by an unauthorized individual was answered by President Madison's disavowal. The American press blazed in indignation, and M'Clure was mobbed in Buffalo. But it was too late.

13

Old Hickory Emerges

Down in the Deep South a bloody battleground took shape in 1813. The Louisiana Purchase had opened wide the Mississippi Territory (Mississippi and Alabama) to a flood of settlers from the north and east. These had trampled roughshod over the lands of the Creek nation, churning its 24,000 population into exasperation. Following the fall of Detroit, a visit from the great Tecumseh revived Creek interest in his dream of a great Indian confederacy reaching from Canada to the Gulf of Mexico, in alliance with England. One Creek chief—actually seven-eighths white—did something about it. William Weatherford, Red Eagle to his tribe, led 1,000 Creek braves of the Red Sticks tribe against a loosely garrisoned militia outpost.

This outpost was Fort Mims, forty miles north of Mobile, near the confluence of the Alabama and Tombigbee Rivers and within the area ceded to the Indians by treaty. Here a group of settlers headed by Samuel Mims had established a rectangular stockaded enclosure covering about an acre of ground. Inside it were a dozen buildings. As friction between Indians and settlers mounted in mid-1813, nearby settler families gathered in Fort Mims for protection. To garrison the place Brigadier General F. L. Claiborne of the Mississippi Territory Volunteers set a detachment of 175 men under Major Daniel Beasley, himself a half-breed Creek.

But Beasley was a nonentity and his men were undisciplined. The great gate on the east face of the stockade yawned wide and unguarded at noon on a clear and sultry August 30. People passed in and out unnoticed. Almost a hundred little children capered and played among the tents and cabins. Two Negro slaves who had brought word of Indians lurking outside had been chained to stakes, where they sagged, awaiting a flogging for their lies. Toward noon a number of the women busied themselves preparing dinner.

A drum rolled, signal for the garrison's midday meal. It was also the signal for the onrush of Weatherford's painted Red Sticks. They boiled out of the woods and brush and through the gate to fall on the unarmed soldiers and terrorized civilians with tomahawk and club. Beasley was among the first to fall, bludgeoned as he tried to close the gate. Captain Dixon Bailey managed to rally some of the soldiers and make a stand. But flaming arrows ignited buildings and drove the defenders into the Indians' hands. When the three-hour orgy of slaughter ended, some 550 men, women and children lay murdered in the burning ruins, scalped and mutilated atrociously. A few men and one Negro slave woman escaped.

The southern frontier was electrified by this ghastly massacre. Fiery, strong-willed Andrew Jackson, senior major general of the Tennessee militia, was called to command as Governor Willis Blount responded to a federal call for 5,000 militia. Rising from a sickbed (he was recuperating from wounds received in a duel), Jackson moved out of Fayetteville on October 7 to rendezvous with Brigadier General John Coffee's advance volunteer cavalry force at Huntsville, Alabama. The combined force numbered some 2,500 men—militia and volunteers. Another Tennessee force of equal strength under Major General John Cocke, recruited in eastern Tennessee, was supposed to join Jackson but never arrived. Jackson pushed south to the Coosa River and established a base at Fort Strother, not far from Ten Islands.

Jackson had already proved his mettle as a troop leader. Raising and equipping a volunteer force at the outbreak of the war, he had brought his Tennesseans by river transport down to Natchez to supplement the forces assembled by Wilkinson, only to have the reinforcement rudely refused by the War Department on March 15, 1813. He was ordered to disband his force and to return all government property. Instead of abandoning his men so far from home, he brought them back intact after a two-month-long grueling overland hike, during which his iron discipline had made soldiers out of them, thus winning him the nickname "Old Hickory." Furthermore, he had spent $1,000 of his own money to replace the subsistence refused by the federal government. His present command contained many of his former soldiers.

Without supplies, Jackson's men were now living off the country on what meager food they could obtain from Indian villages. Despite short rations, Jackson now began a lightning campaign against Weatherford's Red Sticks. His first objective was Tallasseatchee, 13 miles away. On November 3 Coffee's mounted men surrounded the village and after a short but furious fight dispersed the Creeks, who left behind them 118 warriors dead. Coffee, who had lost 5 men killed and 41 wounded, brought back 84 women and children as captives. Some 30 miles from Fort Strother, down the Coosa, the Red Sticks had surrounded Talladega, a village of friendly Creeks. Jackson, marching to their aid on November 9, found Weatherford's Red Sticks there in force. Jackson attacked in a crescent-shaped line, militia on the left and volunteers on the right, with Coffee's cavalry on both wings. An Indian charge momentarily broke the militia, but they soon were rallied, and within a half-hour the Red Sticks were in full flight. Their losses were estimated at 300 killed and an indeterminate number of wounded. Fifteen Americans had been killed and 85 wounded.

Back at Fort Strother, Jackson faced a crisis. There was not any more food. The militia, tired of fighting battles on acorns and water, decided to go home. Jackson, who also munched acorns, stopped them with his volunteers. The next day the volunteers—except for Coffee's mounted riflemen—decided that they too wanted no more; their enlistments were expiring. This time Jackson paraded the militia in the deserters' path.

Jackson then announced that they would march back together unless rations arrived in two days. Four days passed and none came. On November 17, Jackson and his troops set out for Tennessee. After marching 12 miles, they met a detachment with 150 cattle and 9 wagonloads of flour en route to them. After they had eaten their fill, Jackson ordered his men back to Fort Strother. One company insolently ignored the order, however, and headed for Tennessee instead; others prepared to do likewise. Accompanied by Brigadier General Coffee, Major John Reed and one loyal company, Jackson stood in their path with a musket raised to his shoulder. He swore that he would shoot the first man moving forward. All the malcontents then faced about and sullenly returned to Fort Strother. Jackson went with them, tossing aside a worn-out musket that no one could have fired.

Back in camp, the brigade of volunteers seethed in discontent. They argued that the time spent at home should count on their year's term of service. By such reckoning their enlistments would end on December 10. That night they planned to slip away. Much to their dismay, however, they found the route barred by two brass cannon and gunners standing ready with lighted matches. Jackson was there and demanded an "explicit answer." Officers came forward and promised that their men would remain until reinforcements arrived. Three days later Cocke appeared with 1,450 troops; but because these troops' enlistments would expire in 10 days, Jackson considered them useless and bade them keep going. With them went most of his own time-expired men.

Jackson now found himself with only 130 men. Governor Blount wrote him to abandon Fort Strother and retreat to Tennessee. Jackson replied that he would perish first; as long as he had two others with him he would hold the fort. This reply inspired Blount. On January 14, 1814, 800 recruits arrived from Tennessee.

Meanwhile, uncoordinated operations in the theater had not only confused matters but also alienated many Creeks in the so-called Hillabee towns, heretofore friendly to the United States. In November Jackson had reached an agreement with their chieftains to preserve peace. Soon afterward, however, Cocke had raided the area, murdered 60 warriors, who had put up no resistance, and captured 250 women and children. Also in November, 950 Georgia militia and 400 loyal Indians under Brigadier General John Floyd had attacked and destroyed the Creek village of Auttose on the left bank of the Tallapoosa River, 30 miles above its confluence

with the Alabama. Some 250 Creek warriors were killed. In re-
prisal, a Red Stick attack jumped Floyd's camp near the Coleebee
River on January 26, 1814, and killed 167 soldiers before they
were driven off. Floyd gave up all further offensive moves and
his command was discharged, ending Georgian activities.

During the autumn also, Brigadier General F. L. Claiborne of
the Mississippi Territory Volunteers, ordered by General Thomas
Flournoy, Regular Army commander of the 7th District, to "kill,
burn and destroy" in what is now southern Alabama, went on a
spree of destruction. His force—regulars, militia, volunteers and
Choctaw Indians—harried the Tombigbee River valley. His operations ended in late December with the destruction of Enotachopco,
a village used by the Creeks as a place of refuge. Several hundred
Creeks were killed.

Up at Fort Strother, Jackson's own little force passed the early
winter in a touch-and-go existence of indecisive skirmishes. Several
Red Stick attacks were driven off. After the arrival of the reinforcements in January, Jackson took the offensive. His initial effort was
indecisive. But in early February his shoestring force was reinforced by the 39th Infantry, by Coffee with a newly organized
brigade of mounted riflemen, by a troop of Tennessee dragoons
and by a number of friendly Choctaws. He also had several 6-
pounder guns. To this gathering host, Jackson gave spirit and
discipline. When General Cocke and Brigadier General Isaac
Roberts would not give him their support, he had them both
arrested and sent home. When Private Wood of the militia defied
the officer of the day, he was court-martialed and shot.

The Red Sticks, meanwhile, had been leaving their villages and
gathering at a place commonly known as Horse Shoe Bend, a
hundred-acre wooded peninsula formed by the Tallapoosa River.
Perhaps 800 warriors and 400 women and children were there.
They had stocked the place well with food and improved its
natural defenses. Across the neck of the peninsula strong breastworks of logs and brush were built.

Jackson resolved to take the stronghold. On March 16, 1814, his
troops marched for the Tallapoosa, while supply boats moved
down the Coosa under the direction of Colonel John Williams of
the 39th Infantry. The contingents joined at the mouth of Cedar
Creek, where they quickly built Fort Williams for the safekeeping

of stores and the easier maintenance of communications with the rear.

Then Jackson pushed eastward with his army of approximately 2,000 men. A few miles from Horse Shoe Bend he halted and began his reconnaissance. As a result of it, he sent Coffee and his detachment to cover the Tallapoosa opposite Horse Shoe Bend to prevent the escape of any Red Sticks while he and the rest of his troops prepared to attack the breastworks stretching across the peninsula.

A little after 10 A.M. on March 27 the attack began. For two hours or more Jackson's artillery pounded the savages' defenses, but with little effect. Coffee, in the meantime, was succeeding better. He and a few Cherokees crossed the river and seized some hostile canoes, enabling reinforcements to get over, strike the Red Sticks in the rear and set the village on fire. But Coffee had too few men for decisive action. Jackson, however, now stormed the breastworks, Colonel John Williams with the 39th Infantry leading the attack. Williams' senior major, L. P. Montgomery, was killed while mounting the breastworks and urging his men to follow; Sam Houston, his ranking ensign, was painfully wounded by both bullet and arrow but continued at the front undaunted. One after the other the Red Stick strongpoints were taken in desperate fighting, but none of them asked for quarter. Some, seeking to escape by swimming across the river, were brought down by Tennessee marksmen; others tried to conceal themselves in the thickets, but they were followed and slain. A number hid under the river bluffs in a tangle of fallen trees and improvised cover. Jackson tried to induce them to surrender, but they responded by shooting at his messenger bearing them a promise of safety. Volunteers vainly attempted to storm the place. The savages' last strongpoint was then set on fire, and as they rushed from the inferno they were ruthlessly shot. Not until twilight approached did the clamor and butchery of battle end.

The Red Sticks had suffered an appalling defeat. About 560 of their best warriors had been killed; many more were wounded; only a few managed to escape unharmed. Jackson's losses were 50 dead and 135 wounded.

After remaining less than a week at Fort Williams, Jackson moved to the juncture of the Coosa and the Tallapoosa Rivers.

Four miles above it, on the site of the former Fort Thoulouse, he erected Fort Jackson, named in his honor. Here numerous Indian deputations sought an end to the fighting. They were uniformly told that they must surrender Weatherford and move to the country north of Fort Williams, where conditions of peace would be given them.

At sunset on April 14 Weatherford walked into camp, alone. Among other things, he declared, "I have come now to ask peace for my people, but not for myself . . . I am in your power; do unto me as you please . . . I have done the white people all the harm I could . . . if I had an army I would yet fight, and contend to the last . . . But your people have destroyed my nation . . . You are a brave man; I rely upon your generosity."

Appreciating truth, intelligence and bravery, Jackson told Weatherford to return to his people and win them to the terms of peace. This he promised to do.[1]

The Creek war, it seemed, was over. Jackson, turning over his command to Major General Thomas Pinckney, with troops from North and South Carolina, marched his Tennesseans and himself home for discharge. But in June he was commissioned first a brigadier general and then a major general in the U.S. Army and put in command of the 7th District. In August he arranged the final treaty with the Creeks, by which they surrendered 23 million acres of their lands.

By this unprecedented appointment, President Madison showed that he recognized Andrew Jackson as one of the new breed who, in 1814, were breaking through the crust of imbecility throttling high command in the U.S. Army.

---

[1] Weatherford tried to keep his promise, but his career as a fighting leader of the Red Sticks was over. After the War of 1812, he settled in Monroe County, Alabama, and became a respected farmer.

14

"These, by God, Are Regulars!"

In Washington after the collapse of Wilkinson's thrust toward Montreal, President Madison and his Secretary of War took stock. They ordered Colonel Winfield Scott, whose reputation was unsmirched, down to Washington to relate the story in detail. To Washington also came a delegation headed by Judge John Nichols of New York demanding a new deal on the northern front.

As a result a number of things happened. Wilkinson's dilapidated and sickly troops were moved out of their foul nest at French Mills—some to Plattsburg, the others, under Jacob Brown, to Sackets Harbor. Scott, promoted to brigadier general, hurried there also, expecting to command the fresh brigade of New York militia that Governor Tompkins was raising. At Plattsburg, Wilkinson, who had passed a comfortable two months in Malone, New York, while his troops were shivering at French Mills, saw the handwriting on the wall. He decided to try another offensive before he was relieved. On March 29 he marched north up the Richelieu River valley from Plattsburg for 22 miles with 4,000 men and 11 guns. At Lacolle Mill he attacked a British stone strongpoint. The attack fizzled out like a wet match, repulsed by 600 sharpshooting Canadian militia behind stone walls from which

Wilkinson's cannon balls rebounded harmlessly. Two days later the expedition was back in Plattsburg, and on April 12 Wilkinson was summarily relieved from command.[1]

Jacob Brown, the New York militiaman who had proven his ability in combat, was promoted to major general in Wilkinson's place, and twenty-seven-year-old Scott, youngest brigadier general in the Army, received a brigade of newly organized regulars. At war-scorched Buffalo he began to train them. Here, too, came most of Brown's command, and the new commanding general put Scott in charge of revamping the entire division. While Brown was busy attempting to make sense of a welter of new instructions from Armstrong, who still insisted on masterminding, Scott tore into his chore with whirlwind efficiency; discipline, sanitation and tactical competence were the ingredients of his prescription.

For two months Scott strenuously trained his men for ten hours a day, using a well-worn copy of French regulations as a guide. As in the days of Steuben at Valley Forge, officers were first drilled and taught their duties. Parades and other ceremonies were carried out with exactness and spirit. Companies, battalions and regiments became capable of quickly deploying and maneuvering without confusion under all conditions. Morale soared as officers and men began to feel that their units could do as much as or more than corresponding ones in the British service. Scott vowed that he was going to have the best organization in the U.S. Army.

Strict camp sanitation brought sickness down to a level unprecedented in those times—less than 10 percent "unfit for duty." Typhoid fever from contaminated water was the one unlicked problem, but only two men died from the disease between April and July at Buffalo. The weather was reasonably good; rations were sufficient; the doctors were helpful. Desertion was reduced by drastic action; a few malcontents were summarily passed before firing squads in public executions. The easy-going days were ended, as officers as well as men found out. At one time nine of Scott's officers were under arrest, as compared to seventeen enlisted men in the guardhouse.

[1] Tried by general court-martial in January 1815 for his delinquencies on the northeastern front, Wilkinson squirmed out to acquittal, but his Army days were over. His greatest claim to fame, aside from the infamy of treason, was that he was a general who never won a battle and never lost a court-martial.

By May Scott, in a letter to a friend, summed up the situation in his brigade.

I have a handsome little army of about 1,700 . . . the 9th, 11th, 21st and 25th regiments and two companies 2nd artillery. . . . The men are healthy, sober, cheerful and docile. The field officers highly respectable and many of the platoon officers are decent and emulous of improvement. If, of such materials, I do not make the best army now in service, by the 1st of June, I will agree to be dismissed from the service.[2]

By mid-June Brown was ready to take the offensive. On July 1 he arrived at Buffalo to take over the machine fashioned by Scott. His plan, approved by Madison, was to capture Fort Erie preparatory to clearing the peninsula at Burlington, then move around the northern end of Lake Ontario and march east on York and Kingston. Izard, now a major general, would cooperate from the Lake Champlain area by threatening Montreal with a revamped force. Chauncey was expected to defeat or immobilize British Commodore Yeo on Lake Ontario.

Brown's army consisted of 159 officers and 3,344 men fit for duty. It was organized in three brigades supported by four batteries of the U.S. 2nd Artillery: Scott's 1st; now Brigadier General Eleazar W. Ripley's 2nd, consisting of the 21st and 23rd Infantry; and Peter B. Porter's Pennsylvania militia, nearly 800 strong, together with an additional 600 Six Nations Indians. Ripley had proven himself to be a good regimental commander. Porter, jealous of Scott, had never yet been under fire.

Over on the Canadian side, Prevost and Drummond differed in their interpretations of American intentions. By March Drummond had concluded that any American offensive would come via Fort Erie and Burlington Heights, which was exactly Brown's intention. Prevost, however, believed Lake Champlain to be the danger spot. Riall, the field commander most concerned, governed himself in accord with Drummond's estimate.

From York on the left to Fort Erie on the right, Riall had a 200-mile horseshoe front to cover and only about 4,600 men for

---

[2] Scott was writing of his own brigade, but his training had permeated the entire division.

the job—part British regulars and part Canadian militia. Additional Indians might be available, but they could not be counted on. On the Niagara front, in particular, his strength was about 3,000, including the garrisons of Forts Erie, George and Niagara.

Brown moved on July 2; Scott's brigade crossed the Niagara north of Fort Erie and Ripley's brigade, to the south. The next day Erie's commander, Major Thomas Buck, 8th Foot, who had only about 130 men of the 8th and 100th Foot, complied immediately to a surrender demand. While this was going on, Riall began concentrating his mobile troops along the north bank of the Chippewa River, in a strong position not far from its confluence with the Niagara. From there he sent out the Marquis of Tweeddale, commanding the 100th Regiment, and Lieutenant Colonel Thomas Pearson with some Indians to reconnoiter and delay the approaching Americans. The wretched roads had already been worsened by British demolitions—fallen trees and broken bridges crossing the numerous creeks.

On July 4 Scott's brigade, leading the American advance, brushed aside the delaying skirmishers to reach the south bank of Street's Creek, about two miles below Riall's entrenchments across the Chippewa, which he considered too strong for immediate attack. He was joined by Brown and the main body before dark. The command bivouacked for the night, while preparations were made for bridging the Chippewa west of the British position. The next morning as Scott and his staff were breakfasting by invitation at the Street home, Indians were discovered creeping up. Scott upset his chair, dashed for the door, cleared the porch and hit the path that led back to his troops. Few soldiers have surpassed Scott and his aides for their burst of speed in their bare-headed, cross-country sprint on that summer day. They made the bridge in safety and rejoiced to be back with their own men.

The Indians did not follow. Apparently they were few in number and were bent on reconnaissance more than on decisive combat. General Brown sent Porter's brigade westward to prevent any infiltration, and the army settled to comparative calm. No offensive move by Riall was expected, since he was known to be inferior in strength.

By afternoon Scott's men had enjoyed the good dinner customarily accorded them on the Fourth of July, which necessarily had been postponed for twenty-four hours. Scott decided to hold a formal parade honoring the day in the field just across Street's Creek.

This field, some two miles long from south to north and a half-mile wide, lay along the Niagara River, with a dense forest on its western flank. Along the Chippewa, scattered trees partially concealed troop movements to the north. A short distance from the mouth of the Chippewa River was a bridge well protected

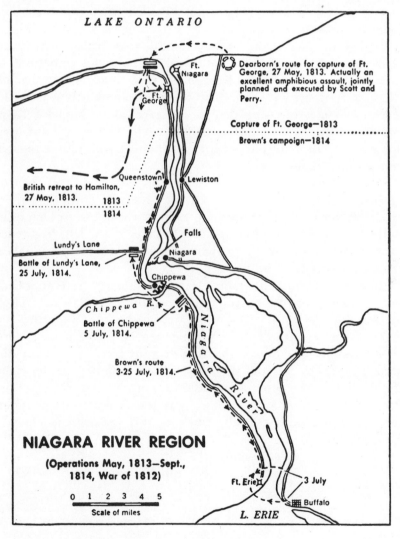

LAKE ONTARIO

Dearborn's route for capture of Ft. George, 27 May, 1813. Actually an excellent amphibious assault, jointly planned and executed by Scott and Perry.

Capture of Ft. George—1813

Brown's campaign—1814

British retreat to Hamilton, 27 May, 1813.

Lundy's Lane

Battle of Lundy's Lane, 25 July, 1814.

Battle of Chippewa 5 July, 1814.

Brown's route 3-25 July, 1814.

Ft. Niagara
Ft. George
Queenstown
Lewiston
Falls
Niagara
Chippewa
Chippewa R.
Niagara River

NIAGARA RIVER REGION

(Operations May, 1813—Sept., 1814, War of 1812)

0 1 2 3 4 5
Scale of miles

Ft. Erie
3 July
Buffalo
L. ERIE

by a battery on the south bank. Close by were a few barracks
and a navy yard. The bridge over Street's Creek was correspond-
ingly near the Niagara River and only a little distance from the
Streets' home, which Scott had left so hurriedly that morning.

About five o'clock in the afternoon, Scott was watching with
pride his well-drilled, gray-clad [3] infantry column approaching
the Street's Creek bridge when Brown and his staff came galloping
up bringing news from Porter on the left that they were immediately in for a fight. The whole British force was marching
against them.

Irish Riall, pugnacious and egotistical, took little stock in any
American valor or skill in battle—an opinion not unnatural in
that region at that time. Reinforced that morning by the 8th
(King's) Foot, weary from their long hike back from York, he
had abandoned his snug defenses to cross the Chippewa River
and give battle. He had some 2,000 men—1,300 regular infantry,
300 men of the Lincoln militia, a troop of the 19th Dragoons
and about 300 Indians—and 6 guns.

Scott, hustling his infantry across the Street's Creek bridge,
deployed on the field beyond; Captain Nathan Towson's battery
of the 2nd Artillery galloped up behind them. At this moment
Porter's small brigade of militia and Indians on the left, frightened
by the appearance of three light companies of British regulars,
came tumbling back in disorder.

Riall, noting now that more American infantry were appearing
on his front, pushed his artillery forward to disperse them. "These
are but Buffalo militia!" he cried, noting the gray uniforms. But
Scott's brigade, instead of dispersing, moved into line with pre-
cision, despite the fire of the British guns now only about 400
yards away. The 9th and part of the 22nd Infantry on the right,
the 11th in the center and the 25th on the left bolstered up
Porter's disordered units. On the right, too, Towson's 12-pounders
came into action. And Riall, watching this deployment, changed
his opinion.

"These, by God, are regulars!"

Two British 24-pounders were quickly put out of action, a

[3] Their uniforms were gray because the Army contractors had no regulation blue
cloth when impetuous Scott had insisted that his brigade have new uniforms. West
Point cadets today are clad in this uniform in commemoration of the battle of
Chippewa.

tumbril of much-needed ammunition was hit and blew up, while the advancing American line threatened to take Riall's remaining guns. Hurriedly the British commander formed two assault col-umns—six companies of the Royal Scots in one, five of the 8th Foot in the other—and personally led them against Scott's center. Three light field pieces supported the British attackers. Taking heavy losses, the columns moved in against the American line, now slightly concave. At 200 yards' distance Riall's bugler sounded the charge, but the columns were disorganized by the rough, uneven ground, while American artillery and small-arms fire raked them. Most of the British officers went down under sharpshooter fire, and the charge collapsed.[4]

In spite of all orders and his own reckless exposure of himself, Riall could not halt the headlong rush to the rear. His artillery pieces were saved only through the gallantry of the 19th Dragoons, who used their mounts to haul the guns away. The remainder of the 8th Foot, which had been acting as reserve, came up to cover the retreat. There was no immediate pursuit; American losses, too, had been heavy, and the British position along the Chippewa would have been hard to take.

The battle of Chippewa cost Riall perhaps 500 in killed, wounded and missing; according to Drummond, his force had been diminished by more than a third. Most of the British wounded and dead were left on the field; toward evening the sky clouded, and a gentle rain fell softly upon them.

American losses were officially given as 328, but they may have been greater. Ripley's brigade, slow in getting into the fight, accomplished little and suffered only 8 casualties. Porter's volun-teers and Indians lost 35; other detachments lost about the same number. It was Scott's brigade, with its 251 killed and wounded, that bore the brunt of battle and established a new record for competence and bravery.[5]

Fearful now of envelopment, Riall abandoned his entrench-ments and started his whole force retreating north along the

[4] "It mouldered away like a rope of sand" was Scott's own comment.
[5] Historian Henry Adams' summation is: "The battle of Chippewa was the only occasion during the war when equal bodies of regular troops met face to face, in extended lines on an open plain in broad daylight, without advantage of position; and never again after that combat was an army of American regulars beaten by British troops."

Portage Road. By the morning of the 8th nearly all Brown's troops had crossed the Chippewa near the old British camp. Before the sun set the Americans were pursuing Riall down the Niagara, with Porter's brigade left behind to guard stores and rebuild the bridge at Chippewa.

By July 10 Brown was at Queenston, eight miles north of Chippewa. Here he bivouacked until the 20th. Porter's brigade, reinforced by a New York volunteer contingent, had joined him. Most of the unreliable Indians now either had deserted the American force or had been discarded.

On the British side, Sir Gordon Drummond, with reinforcements of British regulars and additional Canadian militia, had joined Riall at Fort George and taken over command. Brown, anxious to advance, urged Chauncey to cooperate in assaulting the British position, but without avail. British Commodore Yeo, who had none of Chauncey's dilatory proclivities, blocked an attempt to bring up heavy artillery to Brown by water from Sackets Harbor. Without these guns an attack on Fort George would be suicidal; so on July 22 Brown withdrew to Chippewa.

Drummond, determined to keep up pressure, sent a detachment across the river to raid Lewiston. He instructed Riall to keep Brown busy and ordered a general concentration at Lundy's Lane. The Lewiston raid was only partly successful, but Riall on the west bank of the Niagara found real action on July 25 as his 3rd Brigade pushed down to occupy a hill at the junction of Lundy's Lane and the river road opposite Niagara Falls a few miles north of the American position at Chippewa.

Riall's 1st and 4th Brigades lay at Twelve Mile Creek, with four companies of the Royal Scots and four battalions of militia behind them. Altogether there were now some 4,000 British troops within a 30-mile radius of Lundy's Lane, but they were embarrassingly scattered for any quick concentration.

During the afternoon of the 25th Drummond himself moved down the river road from Queenston with a battalion of the 89th Foot, some 800 strong, just arrived from Kingston. At about six o'clock, with almost two hours of daylight still remaining, a messenger from Riall dashed up with startling news. The Americans, advancing in great force, were forming to attack Riall's hilltop position at Lundy's Lane, and Riall was about to withdraw his brigade. Drummond sent back orders that the position was to be held. He rushed a pair of 24-pounder guns forward to Riall's support and hurried along himself with the 89th.

What had happened was that Brown, learning of the British raid on Lewiston and fearing for his communications on the east bank of the Niagara, had decided that morning to start an offensive of his own. Scott's brigade, leading the advance from Chippewa, had butted unexpectedly into Riall's position.

Scott, believing that the force in front of him was small, had at once attacked. As the British rallied to Drummond's orders and artillery fire opened from the hill they occupied, he prepared for a full assault. Time was of the essence; the sun would soon set.

The British were on a flat-topped hill, rising sharply astride Lundy's Lane, with a rail fence and an orchard skirting its southern flank. Behind this fence the British guns had unlimbered and opened up as Scott deployed the 9th, 11th and 22nd Infantry in line from left to right for a frontal attack. The 25th swung east, crossing the river road and its densely wooded area to envelop the British left. Towson's artillery opened fire from the corner of the river road and the lane. At the same time a messenger was rushed to Brown calling for reinforcement.

The British line from west to east was now composed of the Glengarry militia, the 89th Foot, part of the Royal Scots and a company of the 41st. Across the river road were a militia battalion and a detachment of the 8th Foot (King's), while a squadron of the 19th Dragoons was posted on the road in the rear. In all, the British force now numbered some 1,700 men and 5 guns, with more than 1,000 reinforcements on the way: the returning raiders from Lewiston, the 103rd Foot, and 2 more guns.

By this time both sides had opened an intensive artillery fire: Towson's guns took toll of the hilltop defenders, while the British 24-pounders tore into the 11th and 22nd Infantry as they pushed steadily up the slope toward the rail fence. On the crest, Riall, severely wounded, was led away toward the river road by a group of his staff officers. In the approaching dusk they pushed into a clump of infantry. Someone shouted, "Make way for General Riall!" and Captain Daniel Ketchum of the U.S. 25th Infantry obligingly complied long enough to bag the group. The 25th, under Major Thomas S. Jesup, had worked its way through the dense cover along the river and was actually rear of the Lundy's Lane hill.

But Scott's frontal attack battered itself to pieces against the southern slope of the hill. Scott, raging up and down the line, assembled the survivors into a provisional battalion under Major Henry Leavenworth. General Brown, now on the field with Ripley's and Porter's brigades and two batteries of artillery, ordered Ripley in front of Scott. Riding up to Colonel James Miller, commanding Ripley's 21st Infantry, Brown asked if he could take the British guns.

"I'll try, sir!" was the reply. And he did.[6]

Reinforcements were now arriving for the British, too; Colonel Hercules Scott, of the 103rd Foot, completing a 14-mile march, brought up his regiment, detachments of other regular outfits and militia—in all some 1,200 men with 4 more guns.

It was now about nine o'clock, and night was falling. As Drummond stiffened his line with the newcomers, Ripley's brigade moved through the darkness to the final assault. Miller's 21st Infantry, on the right, after delivering a volley from the rail fence, took the British gun emplacements by the bayonet and moved toward the crest. The rest of Ripley's brigade, checked once, moved on again, covered by the fire of all three American artillery companies, and the hill was won.

But Drummond, rallying his broken regulars in the night, brought them back in line, and a confused and at times hand-to-hand struggle raged on. Three times the British tried to retake their position, and three times they were repulsed. One fresh battalion on either side would have settled the issue. But there were no reserves; Drummond had expended his, and all of Brown's army was engaged; Porter's brigade was now in on the Americans' left, and the battered 25th on the right could do no more.

The crack of muskets and the roar of artillery were almost continuous. At times great clouds of smoke arose and almost blotted out the light of the moon. Often the lines were only

---

[6] "I'll try, sir!" is the present-day motto of the 5th U.S. Infantry, successor of the 21st.

twenty yards apart. On one occasion an officer, ignorant of the situation around him, yelled out orders to a hostile platoon thinking it was his own.

Once, Brown and his staff, riding close to the lines, dimly saw troops approaching. A hail of "What regiment is that?" brought the answer loud and clear: "The Royal Scots, sir!" An alert aide's shouted order to halt saved the American general from unlucky Riall's fate. Some of Ripley's men were dressed like those in the Glengarry light infantry, and several times groups of one were mistaken for the other. Once, when Americans galloped up with a howitzer, the riders were shot and killed, but the horses kept going and delivered it to the British. Seldom have men shown greater bravery and been in worse confusion. "Both armies fought with a desperation bordering on madness."

Scott, who had already had two horses shot from under him went down with a bullet-shattered shoulder while trying to get his skeleton brigade around the British left along the river road. About this time on the far left, Brown, who had already been shaken by a blow from a Congreve rocket staff, was shot in the thigh. Both men were carried from the field, and Ripley took command.

Brown, as he left the field, recognized the fact that his exhausted troops could do no more and ordered a withdrawal to the Chippewa camp. Ripley obeyed, and the firing began to die away. Over on the other side of the hill Drummond, too, was content to lick his wounds. But early the next morning his probing scouts found only dead men. Americans trying to pick up the British guns that Miller's men had captured discovered the British once more on the hill position.

Lundy's Lane was one of the most sanguinary battles of the war. The numbers engaged were almost equal: some 2,800 men each. Reported British casualties were 84 killed, 559 wounded and 235 missing. The Americans lost 171 killed, 572 wounded and 117 missing.[7]

Who won? A meeting engagement had been followed by piecemeal reinforcements, assaults and counterassaults. At the close

---

[7] One may question the accuracy of these figures, particularly the prisoners and the missing. Desertions were frequent on both sides during the northern campaigns.

of action both sides stood exhausted. Tactically, one might call
it a drawn battle. Strategically, it was a British victory, for one
more American attempt at Canadian invasion had been halted.
Ripley now drew back to the protection of Fort Erie, which
Drummond then invested.

15

Honor and Shame
and the Bladensburg Races

Fort Erie in August 1814 presented an imposing military obstacle. The original stone and earthwork fort lay on the Lake Erie shore at the western edge of the Niagara River mouth, opposite Black Rock on the New York side. Its northwestern front looked out on cleared ground with a good field of fire fringed by dense woods beyond. The Americans had enlarged the defense since its capture in 1813. A stone work mounting two guns and emplacements for two additional field batteries were linked with Snake Hill to the southwest, where a five-gun battery was now established. Altogether, the complex consisted of a 15-acre area, presenting a 1,500-yard front well protected by parapets, ditches and abatis.[1]

Inside the fortress lay Brown's army, some 3,000 effectives temporarily commanded by now Brigadier General Edmund Pendleton Gaines, summoned from Sackets Harbor by the wounded Brown, who had lost confidence in Ripley. Sir Gordon Drum-

---

[1] Two brilliant young engineer officer graduates of the recently established Military Academy at West Point—Lieutenant Colonels William McRee and Eleazar D. Wood—superintended the final hasty construction.

mond had invested the place a few days after the battle of Lundy's
Lane but for a short while frittered away time by futile stabs
across the river. A raid on Black Rock in early August was repulsed. A cutting-out party on the 12th—carried out by a detachment of Commodore Yeo's bluejackets from Lake Ontario, whose
boats had been hauled overland from the river to the lake west
of the fort—netted two American schooners anchored inshore to
protect it but had no further effect. Meanwhile, a sortie from the
fort against one of Drummond's field works had been equally
unsuccessful. Intermittent cannonades fell on the fort, while
artillery from Black Rock across the river supplemented the
American reply by harassing fire on the British river flank.

On August 15, Drummond, by now reinforced, launched an
assault in force at two o'clock in the morning. Lieutenant Colonel
Victor Fischer led 1,300 men of the 8th Foot and De Watteville
regiments against Snake Hill on the British right. Simultaneously,
Lieutenant Colonel William Drummond,[2] 104th Foot, and Colonel
Hercules Scott, 103rd Foot, led storming parties respectively against
Fort Erie itself and the sector between it and the lake on the
British left. In all, some 2,200 men took part in a bayonet assault;
flints had been removed from muskets, lest hasty firing disclose
their approach.

Discovered as it closed in, the Snake Hill assault was met by
heavy artillery and small-arms fire. The scaling ladders proved
too short to mount the works and, without flints in their muskets,
the assaulters were unable to reply to Wood's 21st Infantry manning the parapets. After five futile attempts, the assault melted
away.

Colonel Scott's attack on the left fared no better against the
fire of the 9th Infantry and the New York and Pennsylvania volunteers, supported by artillery. Scott was killed, and the survivors
of his regiment and two companies of the Royal Scots, recoiling,
joined Colonel Drummond's assault on the fort itself. This group,
though twice repulsed, finally stormed the northeast bastion,
wiping out the gunners of the 2nd Artillery opposing them.[3]

Despite Gaines' efforts to reinforce and counterattack with the
11th, 19th and 22nd Infantry and 4th Rifles, Drummond's men

---

[2] Drummond of Keltie was the British general's nephew.
[3] Colonel Drummond is said to have ordered his men to give no quarter.

hung on to their position in the fort until a powder magazine blew up, completely wrecking the bastion and killing most of the British assault party, including Drummond. The few survivors fled.

The British reported 57 men killed, 309 wounded and 539 missing. By contrast, American losses were 17 killed, 50 wounded and 7 missing. For the defenders, victory was due to the faulty planning of Drummond, the explosion of the magazine and the alertness of Gaines and his men. Gaines himself, who gave full credit to his subordinates, would later receive the brevet of a major generalcy, a gold medal and the thanks of Congress.

Presumably Sir Gordon Drummond knew that General Prevost was preparing for an advance up the Champlain valley. If successful, that classic British approach would open the road to the Hudson, and the entire American front from the Great Lakes to the Atlantic would have to collapse. He must have known, too, that British seapower was knocking at the mid-Atlantic coast. So, licking his wounds, Drummond settled down to a dreary siege of the fortress that had turned back his assaults.

Meanwhile, in Washington, a fatuous Secretary of War and a trusting President argued and metaphorically twiddled their thumbs while in the Northwest, with the energetic Harrison out of the picture, Brigadier General Duncan McArthur, his successor, made gestures against St. Joseph and Mackinac, both still in British hands. In July George Croghan, hero of the Fort Meigs resistance and now a lieutenant colonel, took St. Joseph with some 500 newly organized regulars and about the same number of militia. Croghan then pushed north to Mackinac but was repulsed. The area would remain in British hands until the end of the war.

For the United States all these things became but pinpricks when a British amphibious tornado swept into Chesapeake Bay, crashed an egg-shell defense, captured Washington and fired the Capitol, the President's House and other public and private buildings.

The catastrophe had been long in the making, its probability hidden only from official eyes blinded by ignorance. For aside from a handful of bluejackets and marines and another handful of newly recruited regulars, the defenses of the nation's capital had been left to a mob of ill-trained and hastily mobilized militia.

The eclipse of Napoleon in April 1814 had released the British Army from the Continent. By June British expeditionary forces were mounting for the war in America. Some of the troops were going to Canada; others were bound for the United States itself. There was no secrecy about these preparations. In fact, as a prelude, in early June blockading Admiral Sir George Cockburn had resumed his depredations along the Chesapeake Bay shores.

The only opposition was presented by Commodore Joshua Barney, USN, with some 500 bluejackets in 26 gunboats and barges—part of the 270 cockboats that economy-minded President Thomas Jefferson had provided for coast defense. These gunboats were 50 feet long, carried 2 small-boat cannon and 20 men each and eked out their sails by oars. Barney's flagship was the *Scorpion,* carrying one long gun, eight carronades and a furnace for heating shot red-hot.

Stout Joshua Barney, former fighting privateersman of the War of the Revolution and Continental Navy officer, later in the French service and now recommissioned in the U.S. Navy, grouped his peanut squadron in the Chesapeake just below the mouth of the Patuxent River. At the approach of some of Cockburn's vessels, led by the schooner *St. Lawrence,* 13, he offered battle. The British retired to the protection of HMS *Dragon,* 74. Barney prudently withdrew to the Patuxent and the shallow water of St. Leonard's Creek.

The British, from the Patuxent mouth, started a flotilla of ship's boats, loaded with marines, up after him. Barney's gunboats pushed them back. On June 10, the British tried again, with 21 barges, 2 schooners and a rocket boat. Barney forced the fight with 13 gunboats, actually coming to hand-to-hand grips, and the invaders withdrew after an hour of furious fighting. At the mouth of the Patuxent a British schooner checked his advance but was forced ashore and abandoned. Barney then established a makeshift base at Pig's Point, on the Patuxent. Outside, unable to close because of the shallow water, waited the *Dragon,* now supported by the *Albion,* 74, *Loire,* 38, *Narcissus,* 32, and *Chasseur,* 18. Barney was effectually corked up, but he was also occupying Cockburn's attention, halting further coastal raiding for the moment.

Meanwhile, President Madison, finally realizing the gravity of the situation, began to have some doubts about his Secretary of War. The President called a Cabinet meeting July 1. Armstrong seemed undisturbed, but Madison insisted that a new military district be established and troops be raised. Accordingly, the 10th District, comprising Maryland and that part of Virginia lying north of the Rappahannock River, came into being—split off from the old 5th District. To command it, Madison chose blundering William H. Winder, who had been exchanged after his capture at Stoney Point in the north and—perhaps unfortunately for his country—was available. Armstrong, it appears, had recommended Moses Porter, regular artilleryman, who had proved his worth in the Niagara campaign and was now commanding the old 5th District.

Madison, supported by his Secretary of State, James Monroe, overruled Armstrong. Winder, prominent in Maryland politics— whence the majority of the new troops must come—was also the nephew of Maryland's Governor Levin Winder, an antiwar and antiadministration man. Thus politics once more won out over military considerations.[4]

The situation was indeed serious. The only regular troops within the district were the 36th Infantry (plus one company each of the 12th and 38th), stationed at St. Mary's down on the peninsula and only 350 men strong; two troops of light dragoons, up at Carlisle Barracks, in Pennsylvania; and in Washington some 500 recruits for the 10th Infantry. In the Washington Navy Yard was one company of marines. Altogether less than 700 regulars were available. On July 4 the War Department ordered drafts of militia "for immediate service"—6,000 from Maryland and 12,000 from Virginia.

On July 6 Winder received his appointment as major general, commanding this agglomeration. From that time until July 27 he

[4] Later Armstrong would go on record as supporting the nomination because "being a native of Maryland and a relative of the governor [he would be] useful in mitigating the opposition to the war, and in giving an increased efficiency to national measures within the limits of the State." Cf. R. Ernest Dupuy and Trevor N. Dupuy, *Brave Men and Great Captains* (New York: Harper, 1959), p. 81.

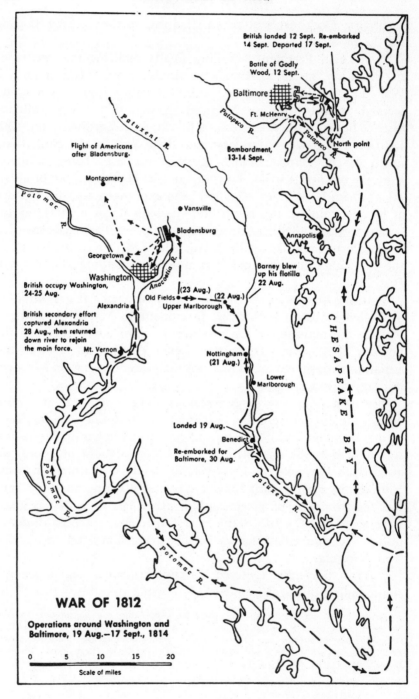

British landed 12 Sept. Re-embarked
14 Sept. Departed 17 Sept.

Battle of Godly
Wood, 12 Sept.

Baltimore

Ft. McHenry

Patapsco R.

Patapsco R.

North point

Bombardment,
13-14 Sept.

Flight of Americans
after Bladensburg.

Patuxent R.

Montgomery

Vansville

Bladensburg

Annapolis

Georgetown

Anacostia R.

Washington

Barney blew
up his flotilla
22 Aug.

British occupy Washington,
24-25 Aug.

Old Fields   (23 Aug.)   (22 Aug.)
Upper Marlborough

Alexandria

British secondary effort
captured Alexandria
28 Aug., then returned
down river to rejoin
the main force.   Mt. Vernon

Nottingham
(21 Aug.)

Lower
Marlborough

Potomac R.

C H E S A P E A K E   B A Y

Landed 19 Aug.

Benedict

Re-embarked for
Baltimore, 30 Aug.

Patuxent R.

Potomac R.

Potomac R.

WAR OF 1812

Operations around Washington and
Baltimore, 19 Aug.—17 Sept., 1814

0   5   10   15   20

Scale of miles

circulated in his area, from Annapolis to Port Tobacco, hoping to gather a force sufficient to resist invasion. Whatever his limitations, Winder at least knew what was confronting him. The British, he reported on July 9, "can proceed without dropping anchor, to within three hours rowing and marching of Baltimore, within less of Annapolis, and upon arriving off South River, can debark and be in Washington in a day and a half." Armstrong did not even reply. Impressed with his own importance and still confident of his military competence, the flood of his orders, instructions and advice became such that Madison on August 13 ordered him to desist from orders "involving necessarily and in the public understanding, a Just responsibility of the President."

Two days later Admiral Sir Alexander F. T. Cochrane swept into Chesapeake Bay with more than fifty sail—six ships of the line, twenty-one frigates, six brigs and transports bearing 3,500 British veteran troops under General Robert Ross. His orders were to destroy and lay waste such towns and districts upon the American coast as he might find desirable. Admiral Cockburn's flotilla furnished him additional marines, who were pushed in force up the Patuxent against Barney's flotilla. When they arrived they found the American gunboats destroyed, by order; Barney and his men were marching to join the Washington defense, where Winder was slowly assembling his mob of militia.

General Ross' troops debarked at Benedict on the Patuxent August 19 and marched slowly north under blazing sun and in torrid heat. A few horses were requisitioned from farms to mount the senior officers, but the sweating redcoats had to tug their guns—one 6-pounder and two small brass 3-pounders—over the dusty roads. No opposition, no demolitions, blocked the way. Reaching Upper Marlboro on the 23rd, Ross had to make a choice. Would the objective be Washington, the capital, or Baltimore, the thriving seaport?

Admiral Cockburn, accompanying the column, voted for Washington and Ross complied. Early on the morning of the 24th, after a westward feint toward the Eastern Branch (Anacostia River) and the bridge to the Washington Navy Yard, Ross thrust directly up the road to Bladensburg, where the river crossing would be easier and where he knew the Americans were in some force.

Colonel William Thornton's Light Brigade led, with the Bucks Volunteers as advance guard. Behind came Colonel Arthur Brooke's 2nd Brigade, the 4th and 44th Foot. Colonel William Patterson's 3rd Brigade—the 21st Foot, a battalion of marines and bluejackets and a rocket battery—brought up the rear, with an improvised baggage train of farm carts. In all, Ross' force amounted to some 4,500 men; practically all his officers and most of his infantry were seasoned veterans of the Peninsular War. It was almost noon when the advance guard sighted Bladensburg village and a confused mass of American troops moving in the fields across the shallow Anacostia River.

Washington had been in a state of panic since word of the British landings had been received. Winder, uncertain of the enemy's destination, had lathered himself into frenzy trying to organize his 7,000 troops, with their 27 guns of various calibers. He had no staff; but advisers he had in plenty, it seemed. The President and the members of his Cabinet arrived on horseback; metaphorically they hung about his neck, vocative in their amateur, conflicting guidance.

Up from their billets at the Washington Navy Yard had come the Maryland and District of Columbia militia, the 36th Infantry, light dragoons and the one disciplined force in the neighborhood: Barney and his sailors, to whom had been added the one company of marines at the Navy Yard. The conglomeration numbered about 2,000 men and a few guns.

Down from Baltimore had come Brigadier General Tobias E. Stansbury's militia brigade, little more than a mob haphazardly drawn from "paper" regiments and only partially armed and equipped. To this force now was added the 5th Maryland, elite volunteer militia under Lieutenant Colonel Joseph Starrett, plus a battalion of so-called riflemen and two batteries of light artillery. There were about 4,000 of these part-time soldiers from Baltimore, exhausted after a forced march of 40 miles.

After a stupid sequence of conflicting orders, of marching and countermarching, the Americans were disposed in three ragged echelons on rising ground west of Bladensburg. The town sat astride the Anacostia River, which was bridged there but was fordable to the north. Stansbury's brigade, holding earthworks

hurriedly dug by civilian volunteers from Washington, lay between the diverging roads to Washington and Georgetown. The
5th Maryland formed a second line; the third echelon was composed of the forces from Washington, with Barney's sailors and
marines its nucleus, astride the Washington road. Barney's five
guns, two 18-pounders and three 12s, were sited to sweep the
approaches from the bridge, which had strangely been left intact.

The British advance guard, probing the deserted village, found
and quickly crossed the unguarded bridge. Colonel Thornton
began pushing the Light Brigade over the river and into the
field beyond. Sporadic artillery fire and sharpshooting riflemen of
Stansbury's brigade slowed but did not stop the British. Ross'
rocket company opened fire from the east bank of the river but was
soon silenced by American artillery—probably Barney's gunners.
But the Light Brigade's skirmishers, despite a few casualties,
moved steadily up the slope. The rocket battery, displaced to a
new position, sent its screaming Congreve missiles—all noise and
no punch—over the heads of Stansbury's men. The militiamen
were unnerved by the sight of the oncoming redcoats and the
scream of the rockets. Winder's left began to crumble. Ross
hurried the 44th Foot in to support the advance, crossing on the
fords north of the bridge. Although they had suffered no casualties,
this was too much for the American militia. They broke and fled,
their artillery joining them in the retreat.

For a short time the 5th Maryland in the second line stood fast,
but the rout became contagious, and they too were soon streaming
off the field. The pursuing redcoats swept on over the entrench-
ments only to hit Barney's sailors and marines and recoil from
the blasting fire of their artillery. Re-forming, the British advanced again, only to be repelled a second time. To Barney's cry
of "Boarders away!" the bluejackets and marines charged into
the 85th and 44th, actually driving them back for a short distance.
But the British veterans quickly rallied, and the remainder of
their 2nd Brigade outflanked Barney's left.

Barney went down, seriously wounded but still conscious. Realizing that further resistance would be suicidal, he ordered his
men to abandon their guns. The road to Washington lay open.
Barney's stand had cost Ross some 250 casualties, against 26 of

Barney's men killed and 51 wounded. Barney himself, unable to flee, was captured and received the greatest consideration from both Admiral Cockburn and General Ross in person.

Far to the north and west Winder's disorganized horde was streaming—led by President Madison and his embattled Cabinet —in a sixteen-mile scurry that would go down in history as the "Bladensburg Races." The tired victors went marching into one end of Washington while Mrs. Madison, the charming Dolley, went out the other, carrying with her a few of her cherished belongings. That night British officers dined in the President's House (not yet known as the White House). By ten o'clock the Capitol, the President's House, the Library of Congress, the Navy Yard and a number of other buildings, both private and public, were in flames. Cockburn, vindictive because the *National Intelligencer* had long castigated him in its columns for his coastal raids, is said to have paid personal attention to the sacking of its office; presses and type were smashed, and its library was burned.

A tornado swept the city that night, somewhat dampening the British glee. The next day an unexplained explosion in the Greenleaf's Point Arsenal took further toll of the invaders; twelve soldiers were killed and thirty others wounded. Then Cockburn, Ross and the troops quietly evacuated the capital. By August 27, when the President and the government returned to the blackened, smoking city, the invaders were aboard their ships in the Patuxent.[5]

---

[5] Peculiarly enough, there was a tincture of humanity amid the vandalism. Cockburn spared the Patent Office and its invaluable exhibits and records because they were considered to be private property. And General Ross, who had to leave fifty seriously wounded men behind him, also left a considerable amount of cash with Dr. James Ewell, for their care.

16

Locked Doors at Baltimore and Lake Champlain

The capture and burning of Washington rocked the nation, and it brought quick house cleaning in the administration. Armstrong, hissed and mobbed on the streets, was summarily relieved, and James Monroe again temporarily assumed the duties of Secretary of War in addition to his own task at State. There was a sense of urgency in the chastened government; danger still threatened the mid-Atlantic states. There was a grim reminder of this when a detachment of Cochrane's massive squadron, coming up the Potomac to Alexandria the day after the British troops left Washington, seized ships and a large amount of merchandise.

Meanwhile, Cockburn turned his attention to Baltimore, hotbed of American privateering. On September 11 Ross' troops were landed at North Point, fourteen miles away, while the warships attacked Fort McHenry, a star-shaped brick and stone Vauban-type structure two miles southeast of the city. McHenry mounted four 32-pounders and fourteen 24s on the sea front, while a battery of 18-pounders protected the land side. Lieutenant Colonel George Armistead commanded the garrison of 1,000 regular infantrymen and gunners.

Defending the city itself were some 18,000 troops, mostly militia. Included were the now-sheepish runners of the "Bladensburg Races." When General Winder arrived to take command, doughty old militia Major General Samuel Smith (a Revolutionary War veteran and a U.S. senator in civilian life hooted him down peremptorily.[1] Smith assumed command of the city's defense. He put his troops and all available citizens and slaves to work on field fortifications to cover the main approaches to the city.

The British advance collided with a brigade of militia on the North Point road. After a sharp skirmish at Godley Wood on September 12, the militia retreated, but British General Ross had fallen, mortally wounded. His successor, Colonel Arthur Brooke, of the 44th Foot, carried on, only to be checked later by General John Stricker's brigade of regulars and militia. The British veterans finally won through but were again halted before the elaborate field fortifications with which old General Smith had ringed Baltimore's land front.

Meanwhile, the British squadron was tackling Fort McHenry, without much success. Sunken craft in the channel impeded use of large ships, while the fort's fire damaged the light vessels trying to close in. A forty-eight-hour bombardment included rockets, whose "red glare" inspired "The Star-Spangled Banner." At the end Francis Scott Key—and the Royal Navy—could both see "by the dawn's early light" the fort's flag still flying. An amphibious attempt against Fort Covington, between McHenry and Baltimore, was also repulsed. Cockburn gave up. The troops were reembarked and the squadron sailed for Halifax and later Jamaica for another momentous rendezvous.

On the northern front, meanwhile, the month of September 1814 was proving fateful. Sir George Prevost, taking the field in person, had moved down the Richelieu River to follow in Burgoyne's footsteps into the Champlain-Hudson valley. The expedition, composed mainly of more than 11,000 British regulars just shipped in from the Continent, organized in four brigades. This was the largest and best hostile force that ever crossed the northern boundary of the United States. By September 3, Prevost's army was knocking at Plattsburg's door. Prevost, meticulous in his treatment of civilians, took no Indians with him; he wanted

---

[1] To his credit, Winder participated in the defense as a brigade commander.

no atrocities. Behind this consideration lay a very valid practical reason: the British were feeding, and feeding well, on fresh beef supplied openly by New England contractors whose herds swept into Canada over an unguarded frontier.

At Plattsburg was thirty-two-year-old Brigadier General Alexander Macomb, one of the "new breed" of American general officers. He had about 3,300 regulars, 1,700 of whom were "fit for duty," plus Major General Benjamin Mooers' New York militia brigade of 1,500 men and a Vermont militia battalion that had vehemently rejected Governor Martin Chittenden's craven recall of his militia. These troops were all that was left when General Izard had been summarily ordered by Washington to move down to Sackets Harbor with 4,000 men to attempt to break the siege of Fort Erie.

Plattsburg, on the western shore of Lake Champlain, lay south of the mouth of the unfordable Saranac River. Cumberland Head to the north jutted in a southward arc to form Plattsburg Bay. American land defenses fringed the south bank of the Saranac. Here Macomb, destroying the bridges, massed his little force of about 3,500 men as Prevost's army moved down to the river. But out in the bay lay the real defense not only of Plattsburg itself but of the entire Champlain-Hudson corridor: the naval squadron of young Captain (and Commodore by courtesy) Thomas Macdonough, USN.

Like Perry on Lake Erie, Macdonough had done a remarkable job of shipbuilding since his arrival on the lake in 1813. Actually, up until Prevost's advance he had controlled the lake, the British naval forces having been far inferior. But Prevost had realized that without control of the lake he could not long maintain his large land array, based on St. Jean on the Richelieu and dependent on water transport. Under his direction, therefore, a new British naval force had been growing at St. Jean in an attempt to match Macdonough's squadron. Captain George Downie, RN, newly arrived from Yeo's squadron on Ontario, was rushing last-minute construction as Prevost's troops marched south.

Prevost's impatient needling soon brought Downie out of the Richelieu into the lake. His flagship was the *Confiance*, 38, theoretically the most powerful ship on the lake, but just built, newly manned and with a scratch crew of sailors and soldiers and cer-

tainly unready to go into action. His other vessels were the brig
Linnet, 16; the sloops *Chubb* and *Finch*, both 11; and twelve row
galleys, mounting among them 17 guns.

Against this force Macdonough had the ship *Saratoga*, 26, the
brig *Eagle*, 20, the schooner *Ticonderoga*, 17, the sloop *Preble*, 7,
and ten galleys with a total of 16 guns among them. The firepower of the opponents was almost equal except that the British
had more long guns than did the Americans, giving them an advantage in a fight of long-range maneuver. But Macdonough had
canceled out that advantage by simply anchoring his ships inside
the mouth of the bay. He knew that Downie could not afford to
by-pass the American squadron, leaving it free to harass Prevost's
supply line. But if Downie wanted a fight he would have to come
alongside to get it; there was no maneuver possible in a horseshoe bay a mile and half in diameter. To give greater flexibility in
the use of his guns, Macdonough had anchored his vessels with
spring lines out, so that if necessary they could be "wound." [2]

Downie's squadron, turning Cumberland Head at about eight
o'clock on the morning of September 11, beat into the bay against
light, puffy breezes from the northeast, the little *Finch* leading.
The anchored American squadron's line from south to north—the
ships were heading north—was *Preble, Ticonderoga*, flagship *Saratoga* and *Eagle*. The galleys, in two clusters, lay between the
Preble and the *Ticonderoga* and the *Saratoga* and the *Eagle*, respectively.

The *Finch*, with the British galleys surrounding her, fell away
from the wind, engaging the *Preble* and the *Ticonderoga*. The
Chubb, following, moved to the other end of Macdonough's line,
taking punishment, and engaged the much stronger *Eagle*. The
Linnet came up third to assist the *Chubb* and throw the odds
against the *Eagle*, and finally Downie grandly passed Cumberland
Head with his flagship. Despite a raking from the *Saratoga*, the
Confiance poached in and confidently anchored alongside the
American flagship. The broadside blast had done the *Confiance*
considerable injury, however. Macdonough had sighted and fired
the first cannon personally, and he was a good gunner. The shot
from his 24-pounder bounced and rolled along the deck of the

---

[2] Turned completely around by heaving on the spring cables, thus permitting
use of both broadsides by each vessel.

British flagship, scattering splinters and killing a number of seamen. The shot damaged the wheel, though that was not critical since the ship was soon anchored.

The *Confiance*'s first answering broadside of sixteen double-shotted 24-pounders, fired at close range, was even more devastating. The *Saratoga* shivered and shook from the fearful impact of metal crashing into and splintering the oak timbers. This single broadside killed or wounded nearly one-fifth of the *Saratoga's* crew, among them Macdonough's first lieutenant.

While the flagships slogged at one another, the fighting all along the line raged in frenzy. Rarely had such a high percentage of casualties been recorded. A British marine veteran of Nelson's battles later commented that Trafalgar "was a mere flea-bite in comparison with this."

On board the *Confiance* Commodore Downie was killed during the first fifteen minutes. Macdonough, twice knocked senseless by concussions, still kept his feet on the *Saratoga*'s deck. The *Chubb*, crippled by the *Eagle*'s superior firepower, drifted south to come under punishment from the *Saratoga*'s unengaged port battery; she soon struck. She was later boarded and towed ashore with half her crew killed or wounded. The *Finch*, crushed by the *Ticonderoga*'s heavier guns, fell out to come aground on Crabb Island, where she struck to a one-gun battery manned by American hospital convalescents.

Meanwhile the British galleys, concentrating against the *Preble*, forced her out of action. Then they turned on the *Ticonderoga*, attempting to board, but were repulsed. The *Eagle*, her starboard battery badly punished by the *Linnet* and some rounds from the *Confiance*, broke out of line to reanchor back of the *Saratoga* and *Ticonderoga*, then reopened fire with her port battery.

At the end of two hours the guns on both flagships were almost silent. The last of the *Saratoga*'s starboard guns was knocked from its carriage and sent rolling across the deck until it fell down a hatchway. Virtually all the *Confiance*'s portside guns were likewise out of action.

At this moment Macdonough wound his ship around until her port broadside bore, opening on the *Confiance* with an entirely fresh battery. Caught in a devastating fire she was unable to return, the British flagship struck her colors.

Only the *Linnet* remained of Downie's squadron. On her the *Saratoga* now concentrated her guns while the *Ticonderoga* still battled the gunboats. Outclassed and outgunned, the *Linnet* courageously held out for fifteen minutes, then struck. Following this the British gunboats, scattered and disorganized, one by one lowered their flags; the battle of Plattsburg Bay was ended. It had lasted two hours and twenty minutes. The British casualties were about 300, a heavy loss considering that the fleet carried only 937 men. The Americans suffered 200 casualties of their 882 men engaged, including a heavy loss of young officers. The gallant *Saratoga*, whose name has gone down through the Navy lists to the present day, was worthless, her career run.

Macdonough's victory, the most decisive sea or land action of the war, ended any further threat of British invasion. His flank and rear open to attack, his only supply line untenable, Prevost and his army were in grave danger. He well remembered the history of Burgoyne's ill-fated expedition. As soon as the sun set on September 11, Prevost's men began to dismantle the batteries they had just set up north of the Saranac River. During the night they began to move their baggage and artillery north. The main body followed. The rear guard, the Light Brigade, started the next day at dawn. Munitions, stores, tents and various kinds of equipment, worth a half-million dollars, were left behind. The sick and wounded were abandoned; they were generously cared for by their recent foes.

So quickly and quietly had the British departed that not until they had reached Beekmantown did Macomb realize they were hastening back to Canada. A few Americans pursued the fugitives as far as Chazy, taking several prisoners but accomplishing little more. On September 24, the last redcoat left the village of Champlain and crossed back into Canada.

On September 17, six days after Macdonough's victory on Lake Champlain, Fort Erie erupted in Drummond's face. General Brown, who had reassumed command despite his still disabling wounds, launched a sortie. Under Porter's command some 1,600 men, in three columns, led by Wood, Gibson, and militia General Daniel Davis, dashed unexpectedly from the fort. They stormed the besieger's works, overran the British batteries and sent Drummond's troops staggering in retreat. Wood, Gibson and Davis all fell in the assault, and Porter was wounded. On the 21st Drummond evacuated his remaining positions and fell back on the Chippewa position. As Sir William F. Napier, British historian, writes, this was "the only instance in history where a besieging army was entirely broken up and routed by a single sortie." [3]

General Izard's force, coming down from Sackets Harbor, joined with Brown's on the west bank of the Niagara in early October. The army moved north against the British, who had reorganized near the battlefields of July. But cautious Izard, now in command, never closed with the enemy. After a few skirmishes the American army withdrew, blowing up Fort Erie and moving back across the Niagara River into New York. Farther west, where American General McArthur had been engaged in desultory skirmishing north of Detroit, the fighting also died away. McArthur returned to Detroit in November. Canada remained inviolate.

Along the Atlantic coast all this while, British amphibious raids had harried New England from Maine to Connecticut, while the strictures of the blockade fell heavily on the civilian population of the United States. In July Admiral Sir Thomas M. Hardy, RN, had captured Eastport, Maine; he had landed troops and declared the town and all the territory in and around Passamaquoddy Bay to be a British possession. Leaving a garrison of 800 redcoats, Hardy then sailed south to join the British blockading squadron off New London, Connecticut.

Anchoring off Stonington, Connecticut on August 9, Hardy sent a raiding party ashore. The attackers met a hot reception from the local militia and their one 18-pounder cannon. In the fight that followed, the British landing parties were driven off with a loss of twenty-five killed and fifty wounded. Some forty buildings were destroyed by the British bombardment, and six Americans were wounded. No further raids were made against Connecticut towns, but up north Hardy's Eastport venture was followed up by a British invasion in force.

Rear Admiral Edward Griffith, RN, with two ships of the line, three frigates and three sloops, convoyed from Halifax a 4,000-man force under General Sir John Cope Sherbrooke, governor of

---

[3] As quoted by R. Ernest Dupuy, *Where They Have Trod* (New York: Stokes, 1940). Although the historical accuracy of the statement can be questioned, it was an effective characterization of an amazing feat.

Nova Scotia, into the mouth of the Penobscot. Castine, Belfast, Hampden, Machias and Bangor were soon occupied by the British. An unexpected victim of the expedition was the little USS *Adams*, 28, which, returning from an unproductive cruise to the British Isles, had run ashore on the Maine coast. Captain Charles Morris worked his ship off, then ran up the Penobscot River on the approach of the British squadron. Admiral Griffith sent a heavy cutting-out party after him. After a short engagement Morris set fire to the *Adams* and marched his crew overland to Portland.

The British occupation of the area between Passamaquoddy Bay and the Penobscot continued until the end of the war. British Major General Gerard Gosselin's rule was gentle, however. There were no depredations. Commerce resumed; the population made money, and so too did the invaders. Sufficient tariff and customs duties rolled in to pay for the foundation of Dalhousie University in Halifax! Conditions were different, however, elsewhere.

During 1814, officially the final year of the war, both the United States and Great Britain were experiencing economic strangulation. The commerce of the United States had been swept from the seas. The British blockade became increasingly effective in 1814, when war conditions had eased in Europe. Foodstuffs transported by wagon commanded exorbitant prices in northern cities. Flour cost $18 a barrel in Boston. A count made at a Pennsylvania ferry showed more than 800 wagons waiting at one time to be transported across the stream. Herds of animals were driven along the highways, in many instances for sale in Canada, where they commanded good prices. Transportation charges were sometimes four times the cost of producing the goods. Commodities hauled by oxen from Charleston, South Carolina, took a month and a half to reach Philadelphia. About the same time or more was required to transport dry goods from Philadelphia to South Carolina. The American economy was stagnant; the main hope of the people was for peace.

Yet Great Britain was also suffering severely. This was the result of the stoppage of American imports and of the havoc to her shipping being inflicted by the American privateers. Goods for export jammed British warehouses. The United States, one of Britain's best buyers, was out of the market. The country had passed through nearly twenty years of intermittent war with France at high cost and yearned for a reduction of taxes. Above all, the British people fervently wanted peace.

How was it that American seamen had been able to keep the British economy writhing, despite the overwhelming might of the Royal Navy?

17

Pacific Ranger
and Atlantic Sequel

David Porter stood on the quarterdeck of the frigate *Essex*, 32, in
late 1812 when she cleared the Delaware, bound on one of the
most dramatic cruises of the old sailing Navy. Porter was to join
William Bainbridge's Pacific-bound squadron at Porto Praya in
the Cape Verde Islands. Not finding the squadron there, Porter
tacked back across the Atlantic to a second scheduled rendezvous
at Fernando de Noronha, an island off the Brazilian coast. On the
way, the British armed packet *Nocton*, 10, was easily captured,
with $55,000 in specie in her hold, a most welcome prize. At
Noronha a letter was waiting from Bainbridge, disguised by pre-
arrangement as a communication addressed to British Admiral Sir
James Yeo. It advised Porter, in disappearing ink, to meet his
commodore off Cape Frio, north of Rio de Janeiro. But again no
Bainbridge appeared, and Porter, after getting a garbled account
from a Portuguese shipmaster of an encounter between American
and British warships, decided to go on alone.[1]

In the stiffest sort of weather, the *Essex* bucked her way around
Cape Horn on February 14, 1814, the first American naval vessel

[1] Bainbridge's adventures have been related in Chapter 11.

160

to make the transit.[2] After a short stop at the deserted island of Mocha off the Chilean coast to slaughter wild hogs and horses for much-needed fresh meat, she reached Valparaiso on March 14. The weather-beaten ship and her tired crew received a royal welcome; Chile had just thrown off allegiance to Spain, and the arrival of the first naval visitor from the republic of the north—another "first" for the *Essex*—was a matter for official celebration.

But Porter hastened his departure. After loading in supplies paid for from the *Nocton*'s captured specie, he made for the Galapagos Islands, 580 miles off the Ecuadoran shore and an unofficial meeting place for British whalers. There they all came, sooner or later, to stock up with succulent giant turtles and to exchange letters in the improvised, unattended but respected hutment serving all as a post office.

On the way to the Galapagos the *Essex* overhauled the Peruvian privateer *Nereyda*, which had been preying on American whalers —Peru was still a possession of Spain, Britain's ally. The *Nereyda*'s prizes, the *Barclay* and *Walker*, were freed. Porter unceremoniously dumped the privateer's guns into the Pacific; she was sent on her way with a caustic protest to the Spanish viceroy of Peru.

For six months Porter cruised the Galapagos area, bagging in all twelve prizes, approximately half of all the British whalers in the Pacific. This effectively broke up the entire British whaling traffic, for as the news of the *Essex*'s presence spread, the others fled to the protection of neutral ports. Some of the *Essex*'s prizes were sent home; two were sent into Valparaiso with prisoners under cartel, and with the remainder Porter built up a tidy little squadron. His crew during this time subsisted on supplies from the captured craft as well as on the abundant turtles.

But by now the *Essex* was a tired ship, her bottom fouled, her seams weeping, her holds swarming with rats. Her principal auxiliary—the *Atlantic*, now rechristened USS *Essex Junior*, 20, under Porter's first lieutenant, John Downes—was in almost as bad shape. Furthermore, Downes, on a visit to Valparaiso, learned from reliable sources that the British Admiralty, alarmed by this Pacific audacity and spurred by the screams of London merchants whose pocketbooks were pinched, had ordered a squadron into the Pacific

---

[2] *Essex*, under Preble, in 1800 had already been the first U.S. Navy craft to round the Cape of Good Hope.

to hunt down the *Essex*. Somewhere at sea was Captain John Hillyar, RN, with HM frigate *Phoebe*, 36, and sloops *Raccoon*, 22, and *Cherub*, 18.

What Porter craved now was a secure base to refit, overhaul and prepare for battle. But there was no such base within 10,000 miles. So Porter made one. He disappeared westward into the mid-Pacific, where he hoped to find in the Marquesas Islands safe harborage, good beaches for careening his ships, plenty of food and a friendly native population.

Porter found all three things. After making a treaty with the native chiefs on November 19, he formally annexed the islands for the United States. On Nukahiva Island he built a fort and began the major task of refitting his squadron. Almost at once unexpected difficulties rose. A hostile tribe threatened Porter's friendly natives, who called on him for help. A detachment under Lieutenant Downes was roughly handled; so Porter himself, with 200 tars and marines, subdued the recalcitrants. Then all hands turned to the ship overhaul. The job completed, the *Essex* and *Essex Junior* made sail for Valparaiso on December 12, leaving behind the other vessels and a colonizing detachment.[3]

The *Essex* and her consort arrived at Valparaiso on February 3. On the 8th Captain Hillyar followed in with the *Phoebe* and *Cherub*. Hillyar dropped anchor so near the *Essex* that the *Phoebe* was covered by the American's awesome carronade broadside as the American sailors scrambled to battle stations. Hillyar hastily hailed to say he had no hostile intent, and Porter held fire. Later, meeting ashore, the British captain thanked Porter for his restraint and assured him that he would never violate the neutrality of the port. The British ships, taking in stores, then departed, taking station outside the harbor mouth, effectively blockading the port.

The *Phoebe*, rated a 36, actually carried 46 guns, 30 of them long 18s. The *Cherub*, an 18, mounted 28, two of them long-range 9-pounders. The *Essex*, also armed beyond her rating, carried 46 guns, but only 6 of them were long 12-pounders. The remainder, 32-pounder carronades, were murderous in a close-in fight but useless in a long-range contest. As for the *Essex Junior*, her pop-

---

[3] This venture shortly afterward disintegrated; Congress never ratified Porter's treaty with the natives. Porter's men, in USS *Sir Andrew Hammond*, a prize, made Hawaii safely. In 1842 the islands were formally annexed by France.

guns would be no help in any slugging match distant or close. Hence, in a long-range fight Porter could pit only 6 guns against his opponents' 32.

Confident in the ability of his now clean-hulled ship to outsail his opponent and to close with her for decisive battle, Porter attempted several times to coax Hillyar into a duel—*Essex* versus *Phoebe*. But Hillyar, with good reason, declined; his orders were to destroy the American ships, not to indulge in nautical knight errantry. Fearing that his enemies might reenter the harbor and open fire beyond carronade range, Porter decided to run for it.

On March 28, in offshore winds of almost gale force, the *Essex*'s canvas suddenly blossomed and she made for the harbor mouth. For a time it seemed she would show her heels to Hillyar's hurried pursuit, but off the Point of Angels a sudden squall carried away her canvas-laden maintopmast, and the *Phoebe*, drawing into range, opened fire. In his crippled state Porter could not make it back to port; so, clearing his wreckage, he ran southward for neutral coastal waters three miles from Valparaiso.

Both British ships, carefully keeping out of the *Essex*'s range, now began a systematic, well-directed fire with their long guns, to murderous effect. Porter tried to run his ship ashore; but she couldn't beat in against offshore winds. An attempt to lay his crippled ship alongside the *Phoebe* and board was also futile; the *Essex*, her top-hamper maimed, just could not be maneuvered and was not fast enough. By the end of two hours most of the *Essex*'s officers were casualties; flames from her hatchways were threatening her magazines; the decks were shambles of wreckage and dead and wounded men.

Realizing that his ship was doomed, Porter told his crew that any who so wished could jump overboard and try to swim for the shore, then sadly struck his flag. As the first boat's crew of British boarders approached, twelve-year-old Midshipman David Glasgow Farragut, Porter's adopted son, destroyed the signal book. The *Essex*'s cruise was over.

The *Essex*'s casualties were enormous. Of the 230 officers and men on board only 75 remained uninjured; 58 were killed, 66 wounded and 31 missing, probably drowned as they tried to swim ashore. British casualties were negligible: 4 killed and 7 wounded on board the *Phoebe* and 1 killed and 3 wounded on the *Cherub*. The outgunned *Essex Junior* took no part in the fight. Lieutenant Downes, rowing to the *Essex* under fire for orders, was told to destroy his ship if necessary. But after the *Essex* struck, the *Essex Junior* also hauled down her colors. Captain Hillyar made her a cartel ship, took the paroles of Porter and his men and shipped them out for the United States. Off Long Island HMS *Saturn* overhauled the *Essex Junior* and, quibbling over the validity of the paroles, detained her. But Porter, escaping in a rowboat, safely made Babylon, sixty miles away.

The *Essex*, before her cruise ended in magnificent defeat at the hands of a British squadron whose sole mission was to hunt her down, had wrecked Britain's large and very prosperous whaling industry in the eastern Pacific and sent all British merchant traffic along the west coast of South America scurrying out of the area, from Cape Horn to Panama. The estimated cost to Britain's maritime pocketbook was $2.5 million.

The gallant end of the *Essex* was the first of several notable naval engagements during 1814. All the others took place in the Atlantic, where despite the blockade of the North American east coast, daring skippers clawed through with the objective of harassing the Royal Navy and roughing up Britain's merchant marine in a *guerre de course.*

By the end of 1813 American shipyards had launched new warships in feverish haste. None of the frigates built that year got to sea, but three sloops of war, all from the drafting board of one designer, William Doughty of Georgetown, D.C., made history. They were the *Frolic, Peacock* and *Wasp,* all fast ship-rigged sloops of war, each rated as an 18 but each actually carrying twenty 32-pound carronades and two long 12s.

The *Frolic,* under Master Commandant Joseph Bainbridge (younger brother of William), failed to live up to expectations. Clearing Portsmouth, New Hampshire, February 2, 1814, bound for the Caribbean, Bainbridge nabbed one large British privateer. And then luck turned against him. On April 20 he encountered HM frigate *Orpheus,* 36, and schooner *Shelburne,* 12, south of Jamaica. Despite desperate efforts, he could not get away from them.

Overboard in turn went the *Frolic's* stores, anchors and finally guns. And still the fast-footing frigate and schooner crept up. With the *Orpheus* within gunshot of the *Frolic*—18 grinning gun muzzles in her broadside—and the *Shelburne* threatening on the other flank, Bainbridge struck the *Frolic*'s colors. A naval court later exonerated captain and crew, but the seemingly abject surrender caused much comment at the time.

The *Peacock*, named in commemoration of the USS *Hornet*'s victory in 1813 over a British brig of the same name, did better. Dodging the blockade off New York, Master Commandant Lewis Warrington accomplished his first chore: landing a cargo of war stores at St. Mary's, Georgia. Cruising the Florida straits, he learned that a Jamaica convoy under heavy escort would be making for England, so he stood north into the Gulf Stream.

Off Cape Canaveral (Cape Kennedy) on April 20, four sail were sighted: three merchantmen and a British sloop of war. The sloop at once interposed herself between the Yankee ship and her flock. She was HMS *Epervier*, 18, under Captain Wales. The vessel was remarkable, it turned out, for the amazing inefficiency of her gun pointers. Both ships maneuvered for a while, seeking the weather gage, then closed, exchanging broadsides close aboard on opposite courses. Warrington, now coming smartly about, ran parallel to the British sloop, his gunners hulling the *Epervier* forty-five times, ripped away her headsails and cut her spanker boom in two. As the Britisher lay unmanageable, Warrington tried to get in raking position. But one round, the only one, it seems, of the *Epervier*'s balls to scotch *Peacock*, struck her foreyard, messing up both fore course and fore topsail and momentarily checking her way. So the slugging match continued. The *Peacock*'s carronades pounded her adversary's hull, scoring twenty holes just above the waterline, and the *Epervier* struck forty-two minutes after the action started. The booty was rich; she carried $120,000 in specie. The *Peacock*'s casualties amounted to only two men slightly wounded.

Feverishly Warrington's crew repaired damages; the damaged foreyard was fixed and new sail set in forty-five minutes, while the holes in the *Epervier*'s hull were being plugged. Victor and vanquished then ran north, hoping to pick up the three British merchantmen. The next day two sail were sighted, but these turned out to be British frigates. Ordering the *Epervier*'s prize crew to make for the Florida coast, Warrington turned south.

The Britishers turned after the *Peacock*—a fielder's choice of sorts —which was unfortunate for them, for the speedy *Peacock* soon lost them. The *Epervier* made Savannah, Georgia, safely on May 1, and Warrington followed triumphantly three days later.

After unloading the captured specie and refitting, Warrington cleared Savannah again a month later, on June 4. He made a long cruise over to the Irish coast then down to the Canaries and the Cape Verde Islands and got back to New York October 12. He had taken thirteen prizes, all of which he destroyed except two used as cartel ships to return prisoners. We shall hear of him again.

Meanwhile, the USS *Wasp*, Master Commandant Johnstone Blakely commanding, left Portsmouth on May 1, 1814. He was following in the wake of John Paul Jones and his *Ranger* of thirty years previous, to ravish the English Channel.

A taut ship, apparently, was the *Wasp*, with veteran officers and a picked crew of 173 men, all American citizens. She took one prize on the way across the Atlantic and on June 13 really went to work in the crowded Channel, taking six more prizes in two weeks. On the 29th, while chasing two other vessels, she fell in with HMS *Reindeer*, 18, a brig-sloop reputed to be one of the smartest vessels of her class in the Royal Navy. The *Reindeer*'s broadside guns were all long 24-pounders, and Captain William Manners, who held the weather gage, might have hauled away from the *Peacock* and hammered her, while outranging the American's 32-pounder carronades. Instead, Manners came flying in and Blakely held his fire until the *Reindeer* was abeam. Then the heavy carronades opened fire. Manners' attempt to rake was foiled by clever ship-handling, and as the vessels ran alongside one another again, twenty yards apart, the *Wasp*'s broadsides chopped the *Reindeer*'s flank to matchsticks along the line of gun ports.

Manners, wounded but retaining command, turned in to board, his port bow nosing the *Wasp*'s starboard quarter. But a burst of small-arms fire from the *Wasp*'s tops shot Manners out of his own forerigging and swept the *Reindeer*'s deck. The Americans in turn came pouring over the bulwarks, and the British captain's clerk, the only officer unwounded, surrendered the battered brig.

The *Reindeer*, a complete wreck, had lost sixty-seven men killed or wounded; the *Wasp*, twenty-six. The shattered prize was burned, and Blakely ran out of the Channel and down the Breton coast to Lorient. Oddly enough, although France and England were for the moment at peace, Blakely was permitted full use of the French port's maritime facilities while he openly recruited a number of American privateersmen who were for the moment "on the beach."

On August 27 the *Wasp*, tuned up again, stood out and reached again for the English Channel. She bagged and burned two prizes almost immediately. Then on September 1 along came ten merchantmen, convoyed by the stately HMS *Armada*, 74, one of whose broadsides could have blown the *Wasp* out of the water—if within range. But that was what Blakely avoided. Outfoxing, outfooting and outpointing the clumsy ship of the line, he conned the *Wasp* into her flock, cut out the brig *Mary*, with a cargo of military stores, removed the crew and burned her. Then the *Wasp* fled from an outraged post captain and a disgruntled crew of British tars. It was a masterpiece of daring ship handling.

But that wasn't all. In the later afternoon four more sail were sighted, all of them brigs and, by the cut of their rigs, sloops of war. The amazing Blakely tried his luck again.

In one of the most daring feats of naval warfare, Blakely interposed the *Wasp* between the enemy farthest to windward and her consorts, who would thus have to beat up laboriously to help her. Blakely raked her and then closed. The British brig's gaff was shot away, her mainsail too came tumbling down and finally the mainmast itself went by the board. Evidently badly punished, she finally answered Blakely's hail and surrendered. But as Blakely was about to lower a boarding boat the enemy's three consorts were discovered close by, and the *Wasp* shook free, under a parting broadside from the nearest of the newcomers. Blakely never learned who his adversary was, but distress guns in the night told that she was in serious trouble. Actually, she was HM brig-sloop *Avon*, 18, under the Honorable James Arbuthnot, and the *Wasp*'s cannonading had left her sinking, with loss of 42 men.

Free of pursuit, Blakely repaired damages to his top hamper— the *Wasp*'s hull was practically unharmed, and only three of her men had become casualties—and then cruised south. In following days he took four prizes, only one of which was worth sending in—

the brig *Atalanta*, 8, which made Savannah with the only official report of the action and of the *Wasp*'s latest exploits.

Down in the South Atlantic on October 9 the *Wasp* spoke the Swedish brig *Adonis*. Two passengers, officers from the *Essex*, were taken aboard, and the *Wasp* sailed away—never more to be heard from.

18

Letters of Marque

Privateering—in effect legalized wartime piracy long sanctioned by international law and custom—was the use in wartime of private ships to capture enemy vessels and convert the resulting profit to the captor's personal benefit. The authorizing document—a plural term for a single commission issued by a nation at war—was termed letters of marque.

War against an enemy's commerce—*guerre de course*—has always been the natural resource of a weaker against a stronger maritime power, and privateering could be a potent adjunct of such a war. The practice came into disuse only in the mid-nineteenth century; it had been of particular assistance to America in the Revolution. Now, because the United States was an active maritime and commercial nation possessing a large merchant fleet and numerous shipyards, with a reservoir of seafaring population to man its vessels, privateering bit deep into the British economy.

In consequence, when Congress authorized President Madison to issue letters of marque in 1812, the response of thrifty shipowners was eager and prompt. Shipyards from Maine to Georgia at once began refitting old vessels and building new cruisers. Almost before Great Britain was aware of the existence of the war a host of small craft was out in the Gulf Stream seeking British merchantmen that customarily followed the current home to England from the West Indies laden with rich cargoes. Soon the privateers had spread out into all the oceans. Before the war ended, letters of marque had been issued to 526 American ships, who captured or destroyed 1,334 British merchantmen.[1]

Great Britain was especially vulnerable to the privateersmen because she had the most extensive maritime commerce and largest merchant marine in the world. Although the Royal Navy tried to protect British commerce, the privateers ordinarily could outrun the warships; they were not seeking battles, merely merchandise and the cargo carriers as prizes. They were not at all interested in defeating and sinking a hostile vessel, unless it meant their own survival; rather, they were immensely concerned with getting a prize into port safely. The profit could be enormous.

For that reason the privateers usually left American ports heavily overmanned, so that prize crews could be adequate to sail their prizes home to American ports. This made it difficult for the U.S. Navy to recruit experienced crews. Seamen, who shared the profit on a privateer, preferred the prospect of greater gain at less hazard in battle. It was not unusual for a privateer to return with no more than a fifth of the crew she had sailed with in quest of quick wealth; the remainder were manning prizes.

In size the privateers ran from small schooners to large, three-masted, heavily armed vessels. The basic consideration was speed; the privateer had to be able to show her heels to ships of superior force. The average type carried amidships one "Long Tom"—an affectionate name for a long-range effective gun—and about ten lighter and shorter carronades, very effective at close range.

The fantastic story of the American privateersmen who literally ranged the seven seas during the War of 1812 is unfortunately too long for this book. But a sampling is in order. For instance, the ship-rigged *America*, out of Salem, in a sixteen-month cruise took forty-one prizes and cleared $1 million over all expenses. The brig *Yankee*, out of Bristol, earned some $300,000 off the African coast in the fall of 1812.

---

[1] The U.S. Navy's own toll of British merchantmen during the war was also respectable: 22 warships captured 165 British vessels.

Captain Thomas Boyle in the brig *Chasseur*, out of Salem, ravaged the English coasts and closed his career in an engagement with a British warship—HM schooner *St. Lawrence*, 15—off the Cuban coast. Boyle had earlier thrown overboard ten of his sixteen long 12-pounders while escaping from HM frigate *Barbarossa* but had replaced them later with eight long 9s. He now mistook the *St. Lawrence* for a merchantman and sailed toward her. Both ships were almost alongside each other when the Britisher broke out the white ensign and opened fire. So, ramming the *Chasseur* alongside, Boyle carried her by boarding, losing thirteen men to the *St. Lawrence*'s casualties.

And then there was the schooner *Rossie*, 14, out of Baltimore, Captain Joshua Barney commanding (this was two years before Barney became the sole American hero of the "Bladensburg Races"). He had been a lad of only twenty during the War of the Revolution, when his Pennsylvania Navy *Hyder Ally*, 16, captured HM sloop of war *General Monk*, 20, off Cape Delaware in a battle heralded as one of the most brilliantly fought naval actions of the War of the Revolution.

Barney, now fifty-three, was one of the first privateers to put to sea in the War of 1812. The *Rossie*, with a crew of 120 men, cleared Baltimore July 12. She fell in with a British frigate on the 30th but outsailed her. Between August 1 and 30, when Barney put back into Newport, he took no less than fifteen British ships in the Gulf Stream traffic lane, sinking nine of them. Another prize was manned by paroled prisoners and set loose for St. Johns. The remaining vessels, all carrying valuable cargo, were manned with prize crews and sent back to Baltimore.

It was not all one-sided. The armed packet *Princess Amelia* put up a fight; Barney lost his first lieutenant and a number of seamen before she struck. The ship *Jeanie*, too, which carried 12 guns, gave battle before surrendering. Later, Barney was recommissioned in the U.S. Navy in time to fight at Bladensburg.

Finally, there was the one privateer action that strategically influenced the course of events. That indeed is a tale worth the telling.

Toward mid-1814, as we have seen, Britain began deployment in America of her regular forces liberated by Napoleon's eclipse. The largest expeditionary force was to rendezvous in Jamaica, British

West Indies, before proceeding to the mouth of the Mississippi River to capture New Orleans and throttle the American West's outlet to the sea. So to Jamaica had come Admiral Cochrane with the troops of the Washington-Baltimore expedition to await the arrival of reinforcements direct from England and also an Army commander to replace General Ross, who had been killed before Baltimore.

Time, as the British leaders knew, was of the essence. In the little Flemish city of Ghent, American and British peace commissioners had been dickering since August, each side hoping for a military situation favorable to their respective causes. The British affirmed the principle of uti possidetis (retaining territory held in actual possession), while the Americans held out for a status quo ante bellum (return to prewar territorial conditions). The successful invasion of Louisiana would mean to Britain not only a prize of great riches—New Orleans—but also an inestimable bargaining point at the conference table at Ghent.

So Captain Robert Lloyd, RN, convoying from England the transports carrying not only troops but also all the artillery for the coming expedition, was in a hurry when he entered Horta harbor on Fayal in the Azores, September 26, 1814. He needed water for his transports and for his warships—the *Plantagenet*, 74, *Rota*, 38, and *Carnation*, 18. Once his hogsheads were filled there was no further need to tarry.

But up in the neutral roadstead lay an armed Yankee brigantine, evidently a privateer, and Lloyd could not resist the temptation to do something about it. Not only did the Royal Navy of that period pay little attention to a neutrality unsupported by force, but Portugal, a traditional ally of England, might also be expected to overlook a British peccadillo. So Lloyd decided to cut out the little vessel. He did not know that she was commanded by a skipper who could fight and a crew as well trained as any tars afloat.

This was the *General Armstrong*, out of New York, carrying one long 42-pounder and eight long 9s. She had made one previous successful cruise in 1813, during which she had beaten off HM sloop *Coquette* after an hour-long fight, for which the *Armstrong*'s stockholders, convened in Tammany Hall, had voted her wounded skipper, Guy R. Champlin, their thanks and presented him with a sword. The brig and her veteran crew of ninety men were now commanded by Captain Samuel C. Reid, formerly a midshipman under battling Commodore Thomas Truxtun. Reid, suspecting a British boarding attempt, prepared to defend his vessel.

That night, in bright moonlight, four armed British boats loaded with sailors and marines came slashing up to the *Armstrong*, where Reid and his men were waiting with boarding nets rigged out. The cutting-out party closed in despite a warning, but, as they came alongside, the brig's side blazed with small-arms fire, and the boats pulled away in confusion. Reid then warped his brig close under the Portuguese fort overlooking the harbor. Lloyd, enraged, mounted a serious assault despite the Portuguese governor's immediate protest. He would, he said, destroy the vessel at the expense of all Fayal; were any attempt made by the fort to protect her, he would not leave a house standing in the village.[2]

At midnight, 400 men in 14 armed boats closed in on the *General Armstrong*, to meet a furious fire as they attempted to board. A 40-minute contest ended with the loss of 4 British boats, and the attackers again drew off.

The next morning Lloyd tried again. HMS *Carnation* drew in to slug it out at close range with the privateer. The Americans had the best of the ensuing violent exchange. The *Carnation*, her top hamper tattered and her hull battered, sheered off. But the *Armstrong*'s Long Tom and several broadside guns had been dismounted; she was in no condition to withstand another attack. Accordingly Reid cut away her masts, blew a hole in her bottom and abandoned ship. He and his crew, carrying their small arms, rowed ashore to set up a defense in a small convent. Lloyd, after threatening to send a force ashore after them, thought better of it. The *Armstrong*'s battered hull was set afire, and after a delay of ten days to get water on board, repair the damage to the *Carnation* and shake down the battered personnel, the fuming Lloyd sailed on for Jamaica, where Cochrane was impatiently waiting.

Lloyd's little venture had been costly. The British official casualty count was 34 men killed, with several officers among them,

2 Holloway Halstead Frost, *We Build a Navy* (Annapolis: Naval Institute, 1929), p. 337.

and 86 wounded. Reid's account put the British loss at 120 killed and 130 wounded, against 2 Americans killed and 7 wounded. In either event, it had been a costly adventure for Lloyd. But what the ten-day delay meant strategically to Britain was something else again, as we shall see.

19

Victory at New Orleans

In late autumn of 1814, while the representatives of two tired nations were arguing at the peace table in Ghent and their respective forces along the Canadian border stood in skirmishing stalemate, American eyes turned southward. It was an open secret that the British were preparing a great invasion of the Gulf of Mexico littoral. The rumors trickled in from Europe, from Florida and from the West Indies, confirmed in September by a British thrust against Fort Bowyer at the entrance to Mobile Bay. This was only a few hours' sail from Spain's Pensacola, where British Lieutenant Colonel Edward Nicholls, serenely ensconced with a small detachment of British troops and a large force of Indians, was proclaiming his intentions to invade Louisiana and free its people from American "usurpation." [1]

On September 15, 1814, Admiral Sir William Percy, RN, with 5 ships, landed 100 marines and Nicholls' Indians on the coast near Fort Bowyer. Then he stood boldly into the bay to dare a

[1] The Pensacola situation constituted an outrageous breach of neutrality. With the open sanction of the Spanish governor, Nicholls had recruited and armed a force of 600 Indians. His proclamation of August 29, 1814, addressed to "The Southern and Western Inhabitants," was dated from "my headquarters, Pensacola."

run-by of the fort. General Jackson had garrisoned Bowyer with 130 men under Major William Lawrence, 2nd Infantry. Percy's flagship, HMS *Hermes*, 20, received such a pounding from the fort's 20 small guns that she became unmanageable and grounded. The British-Indian land party, too, was beaten off. Percy, blowing up his ship, beat a retreat back to Pensacola with his remaining 4 vessels. He had lost 232 men, whereas only 4 of the garrison had been killed and 4 more wounded.

Jackson had already begun concentrating his scanty resources at Mobile. At once he marched on Pensacola on his own volition with some 4,000 men determined to erase the British threat. He did not tarry to ask governmental permission. So far as he was concerned, the Spanish neutrality had already been compromised by permitting the British to use Pensacola as a base. On November 7 Jackson reached the defenses of Pensacola and sent a demand to the Spanish governor, Don Matteo Gonzalez Manrique, to eject the British. When the governor rejected the demand, Jackson immediately attacked St. Michael, one of the two Pensacola forts. Don Matteo promptly surrendered the town and both forts, whose British garrisons retired to Percy's ships in the harbor. Percy then put to sea. Jackson, satisfied, destroyed the defenses of Pensacola, admonished the governor and marched away. For the time being Pensacola was no longer a British base.

Down in New Orleans Governor William C. C. Claiborne of Louisiana and the townsfolk had for some time clamored for defense against invasion. But Jackson was convinced that Mobile, and not a militarily difficult thrust through the Mississippi delta, would be the first British objective if there were an invasion. But in late November, shortly after his return from Pensacola, Jackson received word that changed his estimate of the situation.

For some years past two flamboyant French émigrés, Jean Lafitte and his brother, Pierre, had established themselves in Barataria Bay, on the Gulf of Mexico just west of the Mississippi delta. Here they harbored a covey of smugglers, buccaneers and so-called privateers under the flag of New Cartagena (Venezuela). From their Barataria base this motley crew preyed on non-American commerce in the Gulf. Jean commanded the operations; Pierre was the "fence" in New Orleans. To the townspeople the Lafittes were heroes; to the governor and the United States government they were a source of annoyance and frustration even though they respected American shipping.

To Jackson in particular, they were "hellish banditti." In September 1814, Captain Daniel T. Patterson, USN, with a force of bluejackets and soldiers had swept into Barataria Bay from New Orleans, seized the buccaneers' "navy" of twelve assorted craft, confiscated large stores of loot and brought a number of the offenders back to jail in New Orleans. Jean Lafitte, who had escaped capture, promptly set about reorganizing his band, but brother Pierre languished in jail.

In November the Lafittes' attorney, Edward Livingston, a respected lawyer (he would later become President Jackson's Secretary of State), sent to Jackson at Mobile a written British offer to Jean Lafitte to ally himself and his band with a coming occupation of New Orleans. If he cooperated, Jean would receive a British commission and Pierre would be freed from jail. The alternative would be complete elimination of the buccaneers. Jean, politely promising an answer to the British in fifteen days, had put the documents in Livingston's hands.

Jackson received the message on November 22. Ten days later he came marching into New Orleans with his 39th Infantry. He found the volatile city seething in a mixture of patriotic fervor and almost abject fear, while footless Governor Claiborne and his legislature talked but did nothing. The one sane activity was a citizens' committee of defense, organized by Livingston, whom the thin, dour Jackson now commissioned as his aide. Jackson further endeared himself to the citizenry by praising the gaily uniformed volunteer militia companies and by putting one of their officers— the brilliant and capable engineer Major A. La Carriere Latour— in charge of renovating the old municipal fortifications.

New Orleans, lying on the east bank of the broad, unfordable Mississippi River, was practically invulnerable to any attack from the west. An amphibious attack up the long winding river would be logical, but Fort St. Philip, sixty-five miles downstream and garrisoned by regular artillerymen, would present a considerable obstacle. From the east, an attacker could choose between two courses. First was a preliminary attack on Mobile, which Jackson had long feared, followed by a tedious overland march. The alternative was a landing in the area of Lake Borgne, a wide, shallow

Gulf inlet whose western and northern shores were but a few miles from the city. Above Lake Borgne and connected with it by an extremely narrow strait was Lake Pontchartrain, whose southeastern edge was only two miles north of New Orleans. However, once ashore from either of these lakes, all land approaches to the city were over flat, swampy, partly wooded land, netted with bayous and almost bereft of roads.

Jackson by this time had sent appeals for troops to the governors of Tennessee and Kentucky and also had importuned Claiborne for more Louisiana militia. Some troops from Tennessee and Kentucky were already on the way south. At New Orleans, besides the city militia and the 39th Infantry was a small U.S. Navy detachment under Captain Patterson: the war sloop *Louisiana*, 16, and schooner *Carolina*, 14, on the Mississippi; and little one-gun *Seahorse*, and a flotilla of five small gunboats on Lake Borgne, where Patterson shrewdly thought the British might intrude. But until Jackson had better information about the British intentions, he refused to move the majority of his regulars from Mobile.

On December 8 Admiral Cochrane's armada, making an offing in the Gulf at the Chandeleur Islands, moved into the entrance of Lake Borgne, between Ship and Cat Islands. There were some sixty sail in all: the mighty *Tonnant*, 80, flagship; the *Royal Oak, Bedford, Norge, Ramillies,* and *Asia,* all 74s; plus numerous frigates, sloops and gunboats escorting a flock of transports. The 14,000 troops on board were the pick of the British Army. They included the four regiments of the Washington raid, another brigade of Wellington's veterans, the 93rd Highlanders, and two Negro regiments from the West Indies, together with a reasonable number of artillerymen, sappers and rocketeers with their impedimenta (Lloyd's contingent from England had finally joined). Everything necessary for establishing a new colony was aboard, including printing presses for a newspaper. All British hearts were high; capture of rich New Orleans would mean sacking, loot and prize money—"beauty and booty"—to be enjoyed in the coming Christmas holidays.

Sixty barges, each carrying a carronade in its bow and crammed with 1,200 sailors and marines, swept into the lake on December 14, under Captain Nicholas Lockyer, RN. They swarmed against the 5 American gunboats and cockle-shell *Seahorse*, all commanded by Lieutenant Thomas ap Catesby Jones, USN. But the Americans fought stoutly, and before taking these boats the British paid a toll of 300 casualties, including Lockyer, who was seriously wounded. The Americans, 182 strong, lost 6 killed and 35 wounded. With the way cleared, on December 16 Major General John Keane, temporarily commanding the expedition, began debarking his troops on Pea Island.

Jackson, learning of the British arrival off Cat Island, was faced with the fact that he must prepare for a defensive battle at New Orleans against what must be an almost overwhelming force of the best professional soldiery in Europe. He had three major problems: assembling an adequate defending force, deciding where and how to meet the invaders and coping with the panic-stricken citizenry of New Orleans. Calling up all resources, Jackson declared martial law in the city; shilly-shallying Claiborne and his legislature were temporarily set aside as the general clamped his iron control on the town.

British General Keane completed the landing of his division on the 20th. He then pushed his command westward through the swampy morasses of narrow Bayou Masant, captured a militia detachment guarding it and three days later floundered onto the Villere plantation on the plain 9 miles south of New Orleans. Actually Keane had the city within his grasp at that moment. But gabbling prisoners told of 12,000 Americans within the city and 4,000 more nearby; so hesitating Keane put his tired, muddy troops into bivouac to await reinforcements and the arrival of his commander, Major General Sir Edward Pakenham (one of Wellington's trusted subordinates, as well as the Iron Duke's son-in-law).

Now the British began to pay for that costly error of Commodore Lloyd at the Azores. Had it not been for the *General Armstrong*'s gallant stand at Horta, Keane would probably have debouched in front of New Orleans on December 13, to find as his only opposition some 300 men of the 39th Infantry.

As things now stood, Keane not only had surrendered the initiative but also had given Jackson an opportunity to choose a battlefield. Into New Orleans by now had come Coffee's brigade of Tennessee mounted riflemen and Mississippi dragoons from Baton Rouge; Major General William Carroll's division of Tennessee militia, 3,000 strong, had arrived by flatboat from Natchez. The

New Orleans militia were under arms, together with another odd assortment of volunteers—Jean Lafitte's picaresque buccaneers, experienced seagoing artillerymen. The 7th and 44th Infantry and a detachment of artillery had also arrived, force-marched from Mobile.

In all, Jackson now had 5,100 men, with a hard core of 700 regulars. A few additional Kentucky and Louisiana militiamen were also approaching, but these rabbles in arms would not increase Jackson's effective strength. Best of all, Jackson had the genesis of a defensive position made to order, complete with moat, unturnable flanks and a clear field of fire. This was the Rodríguez Canal, an abandoned millrace 20 feet wide and 3–5 feet deep, running westward to the Mississippi across the 1,000-yard-wide stretch of cultivated land that lay between the river and the dense cypress swamp that stretched westward from the tip of Lake Borgne.

Jackson received word during the afternoon of the 23rd of the British arrival at the southern edge of this plain and put things in motion. First he set Latour and an enthusiastic rallying of New Orleans citizens at work constructing defensive works on the north flank of the canal, raising embankments behind the moat. Next he moved to hit the invaders in their bivouacs that very night.

Under Jackson's personal command the 7th and 44th Infantry, two battalions of New Orleans militia, Patterson's handful of marines and a few artillery—some 1,500 men in all—moved down the levee road from the canal. Coffee's Tennesseans swung to the left to cut the British communications with Lake Borgne. The *Carolina* slipped downriver to open fire on the British left. Her first broadside was to be the signal for the attack.

The night was foggy; the British, beside their twinkling campfires, were entirely unprepared. The *Carolina*'s 12-pounders blazed on their left; the American infantry overran their pickets in front; and on the far right Coffee's dismounted Tennesseans emerged from the tangled swamps to add to the surprise. For the moment the redcoats panicked in the hand-to-hand melee. But Peninsula War veterans did not stampede easily. Their rally and counter-attack drove Jackson's men back. When the firing ceased, Keane's troops were standing on their bivouac ground, having lost 46 killed, 167 wounded and 64 taken prisoner, while the Americans, **retiring** behind the canal, had lost 24 killed, 115 wounded and 74

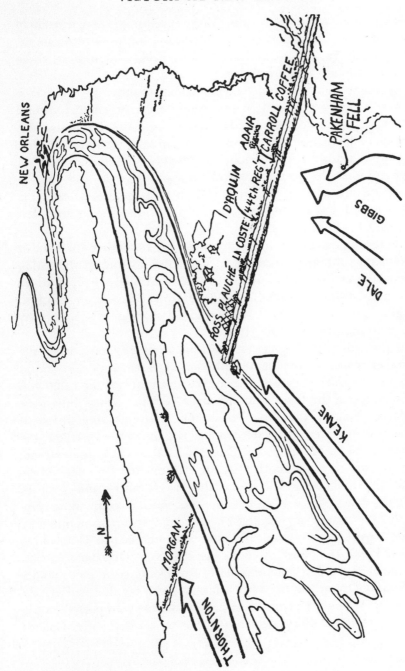

The Battle of New Orleans

taken prisoner. In the morning Keane, erecting his own entrench-
ments, decided to remain on the defensive until reinforcements
and General Pakenham arrived; it was evident that here there
would be no "Bladensburg Races."

The thirty-eight-year old Pakenham, brave and impetuous to a
dangerous degree [2] arrived on the scene on Christmas Day to find
his troops frost-chilled in mud. He made a personal reconnaissance,
from which he learned little, and so decided on a reconnaissance in
force to develop the situation. Meanwhile, he hurried several
heavy cannon through the mud from Lake Borgne to drive off the
two American craft on the river. The fire of these guns sank the
Carolina and forced the *Louisiana* to seek shelter on the west
shore, out of range.

The reconnaissance in force took place on December 28. Most of
Packenham's infantry advanced in two columns toward the canal.
But lacking artillery support, the British were sharply repulsed by
combined artillery and small-arms fire from the American position;
the guns taken from the *Carolina* added to their discomfort by
their flanking fire from the river.

All the while, the American position was being improved; the
volunteer workers raised embankments of earth, logs and cotton
bales behind the canal. An advance bastion south of the canal was
extended along the levee near the river. Twenty heavy guns were
emplaced along the ramparts. Precise unit positions were allocated;
Jackson distributed regulars among the militia to stiffen the
morale of the part-time troops. Beale's City Rifles held the extreme
right, by the river, supported by an artillery battery manned by
Mississippi dragoons. Next came the 7th Infantry and Jean B.
Plauché's battalion of Creole volunteer militia companies, supported by a battery of two long 24-pounder ship's guns manned by
Lafitte's Baratarian buccaneers, under his lieutenants Dominique
You and Beluche. East of them lay the New Orleans battalion
of "free men of color" and another of San Domingo mulatto volunteers; beside them was the 44th Infantry and a regular artillery detachment. William Carroll's Tennessee riflemen, supported by another regular artillery detachment, came next, while Coffee's

---

[2] As Wellington, according to the historian Napier, had chidingly remarked of his
daredevil assault at Salamanca in Spain during the Peninsula War.

Tennesseans, dismounted, anchored the left, knee-deep in the swampy cypress tangle.

Over on the west bank of the Mississippi Patterson's bluejackets manned a three-gun battery sited to sweep the British left flank, a battalion of militia supporting them. In addition, the *Louisiana* was prepared to resume action. Far in the rear of the main position the unreliable Kentucky militia rabble, arriving January 4, lay where the least harm would result if they did break and flee.

Packenham had accomplished one thing by his reconnaissance in force. He had discovered that maneuver was impossible. The impatient general now spurred his command in preparation for a major frontal assault. Additional troops were brought ashore behind the breastwork now covering the British front. By back-breaking labor twenty-four heavy ships' guns were rowed and portaged through the bayous and emplaced in positions within convenient range of the American lines. Boats were manhandled across the plain to the riverside in preparation for a flanking Mississippi crossing and an advance up the west bank.

To handicap the British, however, the no man's land between the opposing lines became a field of terror at night. Patrols of cat-eyed frontiersmen sneaked Indian-like up to the British lines, cut down sentinels and ambushed patrols, while sporadic artillery fire sprinkled the British camp. Daylight patrolling by Pakenham's men was out of the question; American riflemen, whose bullets carried twice as far as the British "Brown Bess" musket, picked off everything that moved near their lines. Miasmic fogs helped blanket visibility.

Meanwhile Admiral Cochrane, still thinking in terms of the easy advance on Washington, was apparently needling Pakenham by taunts that his tars were quite capable of doing what the redcoats could not do—not that the Royal Navy was doing so well itself. Cochrane had been unable to get his big ships over the delta bars. A flotilla of light craft—two war sloops, a schooner and two bomb ketches—had sailed upriver only to be definitely stopped by the guns of Fort St. Philip and forced to retire after eight days of futile bombardment.

Packenham's assault was set for January 8, 1815, before dawn. In three columns the British troops were to advance across the plain and storm the American position. At the same time an amphibious force, ferried across the Mississippi, would capture the west bank battery whose galling fire threatened the flank of the main effort. Lieutenant Colonel William Thornton commanded the crossing movement, 1,500 strong. Unfortunately, only 47 boats had been hauled up by the evening of the 7th, and an opening then had to be cut in the levee to launch them. Dawn was long gone before the first, and as it turned out the only, wave of Thornton's force, 600 men, began their ferrying across the river.

The frontal assault was also delayed by heavy fog. It was six o'clock when Pakenham's three dense columns began moving through the mist, Colonel Robert Rennie's light infantry up the levee road paralleling the river, Keane's brigade in the center and Major General Samuel Gibbs' brigade, which included the West Indian troops, pointing for the American left.

Nothing could go right, it seemed, for Pakenham that morning. The final straw was the blunder of Lieutenant Colonel Thomas Mullens' 44th Foot, scheduled to lead the right-wing stormers; they forgot their scaling ladders! By the time that stupidity had been rectified, the remainder of the assault force was already within range of the murderous fire of American artillery from front and flank.

Rennie's column reached the embankments, and its three leading companies actually got into the advanced bastion and the main position, but the sharp counterattack of the 7th Infantry across the cotton-bale ramparts drove them out.[3] Keane's brigade in the center reached the canal moat, but the leading elements melted under American fire and the column was halted; in the deadly pause that followed many redcoats crawled into the shelter of the moat itself.

Gibbs' brigade, on the British right, attacked with three regiments echeloned in depth, the 44th leading. But the men of the 44th would not need their scaling ladders after all. Carroll's sharpshooters laid them down in swathes when they got within 200-yard range, the following regiments piling up behind them. Far over on the right flank the West Indian regiment, fondly expected to work well in swampy jungles, clawed into the cypress swamp, to be met by the fire of Coffee's Tennesseans. The West Indians came out

---

[3] The 7th today bears a cotton bale on its coat of arms in token of New Orleans.

faster than they had gone in. Gibbs' entire brigade now recoiled. Pakenham, already slightly wounded—apparently by a Negro sharp- shooter—galloped up to rally it, only to be hit again; beside him the brigade commander went down, mortally wounded. At that moment a round of grapeshot finished Pakenham.

Keane, now in command, tried to rally his shaken center col- umn. He personally led the 93rd Highlanders obliquing across to bolster Gibbs but was himself wounded and carried off the field. The 93rd, which had gone into the fight 925 strong, gallantly butted its way across the moat into the Tennesseans' sector, and a handful actually mounted the breastwork beyond, only to die there. The 125 survivors went stumbling back across the ghastly corpse-strewn plain.

By this time Lambert's brigade, in reserve, was forming to ad- vance; Pakenham had ordered it into action before he fell. But by this time no reserves could save the day. The survivors of the as- sault columns were streaming back; Lambert, unexpectedly find- ing himself in command, quite properly ordered a general British withdrawal into the fortified bivouac line.

The American fire died away. Now some 500 of Keane's men who had been hugging the moat's protection raised their hands in surrender and were marched inside the defense lines. In the distance came the faint roar of musketry across the Mississippi, where Thornton's flanking effort was capturing the American bat- tery there, all too late. The battle of New Orleans was over—a forty-five-minute-long debacle to British arms that was completely senseless. For over the ocean in Ghent the treaty of peace had been signed fifteen days earlier, on December 24.

By Jackson's iron-clad order there was no counterattack. He knew better than to permit his raw troops to leave the shelter of their fortifications in pursuit of a disciplined foe. New Orleans was safe, the back of the British Army broken at the cost of 71 Ameri- cans killed and wounded, out of about 3,500 actually engaged. The British losses had been appalling. Of the 6,000-odd redcoats en- gaged on both sides of the river, more than 2,000 were killed or wounded and 500 taken prisoner.

The next day, under a flag of truce, the British dead were buried in mass graves, the discarded scaling ladders of the 44th Foot their biers. Many of the redcoat wounded were evacuated into New

Orleans, and on the 18th a general exchange of prisoners was effected. Late that night the British quietly stole away; by January 29 the expeditionary force was embarked on the waiting transports.

Off Mobile, the disgruntled British made one more gesture. Fort Bowyer was threatened and meekly surrendered without a shot fired. British troops disembarked on Dauphin Island. But on February 14 news of the peace treaty arrived, and early in March the ill-fated expedition sailed for England.

The last combat in the South occurred off Savannah, where Admiral Cockburn's squadron made its final raid, taking a fort on Petre Point at the mouth of the St. Mary's River. On Washington's Birthday, February 22, 1815, the last inconclusive skirmish between Cockburn's raiders and local militia forces occurred.

Meanwhile, Jackson held New Orleans in the iron grip of martial law until March 13, when he received official word from Washington that hostilities had ended. Until then he had rebuffed all efforts at relaxation of his control, even going to the extreme of locking up and exiling federal Judge D. A. Hall, who had issued a writ of habeas corpus for the release of a prominent Louisianian jailed by Jackson for inciting mutiny among the local militia. As Jackson's minute guns saluted the arrival of peace, the general released all military prisoners. Judge Hall, resuming his functions, ordered Jackson into court to show cause why he had refused to recognize his writ of habeas corpus. Jackson immediately appeared, respectfully accepted the judge's sentence of a fine of $1,000 and stated his belief in obedience to the civil law. At once he became a hero. He refused a public subscription to reimburse him, declaring it might better be used to assist the families of his soldiers killed in action.[4]

After the battle Jackson learned that the Army paymaster in New Orleans had held up the pay of all Negroes and Indians in his command, apparently on the assumption that they should not be reimbursed at the same rate of pay as the white troops. Jackson sternly instructed the paymaster to pay all of the men "without inquiring whether the troops are white, black, or tea." There was no further delay.

[4] Thirty years later Congress repaid Jackson's fine, with interest.

20

Finale on the High Seas

Early 1815 found four United States warships on the high seas, unaware—as of course were the British ships they encountered—of the signing of the peace treaty. The *Constitution*, under Captain Charles Stewart, had cleared Boston December 17, 1814. Running the blockade without incident, she sailed for the Bay of Biscay and began combing the coastal sea lanes southward. In mid-January Commodore Stephen Decatur's squadron—the *President*, 44, *Peacock*, 18, and *Hornet*, 18—slipped piecemeal out of New York harbor, then blockaded by a powerful frigate squadron made up of the *Majestic*, 56, *Endymion*, 40, *Pomone*, 38, and *Tenedos*, 38. Decatur was under Navy Department orders to raid British commerce in the Indian Ocean.

Decatur had gone first, on the 14th, his flag in the *President*, taking advantage of an offshore gale that blew the blockaders well to sea. But the ship grounded on the Sandy Hook bar, where she pounded for several hours. Underway again, with some damage to her hull and her masts sprung seriously, Decatur found that the wind prevented beating back into port; so he made sail to the southeast. At dawn the next day he found himself in the midst of the British squadron.

By early afternoon the *Endymion* was close enough to open with her bow chasers, and Decatur, fearing damage to his top hamper during a protracted stern chase, came about and closed, pouring in salvos of bar and chainshot that ripped the *Endymion's* canvas to shreds. Then the *President* fled again. But her weakened masts and damaged hull so slowed her that the *Pomone* and *Tenedos* overhauled her after dark, and Decatur struck his flag. It was a tame ending to a bitter fight. However, there could be but one end to a battle between a damaged 44 and two fresh 38s, with the *Majestic's* 56-gun firepower close at hand. So Decatur's later court-martial cleared him, and the verdict was confirmed. HMS *President* would sail the seas again under the British white ensign for many years to come.

The *Hornet* and *Peacock*, with a supply ship, the *Tom Bowline*, got away on January 23, knowing nothing of the *President's* fate, and made for Tristan da Cunha, the appointed rendezvous. The *Hornet*, under Captain James Biddle, who had been first lieu-tenant in the old *Wasp* under Jacob Jones, got there first, on March 23, to find no sail in sight. As she was cruising nearby, HM sloop *Penguin*, 19, under Captain Frederick Dickenson, hove in sight. Both vessels closed, running westerly on the starboard tack, on parallel courses, with a fair breeze and heavy swells. The *Penguin* held the weather gage.

A fifteen-minute slugging match began to hurt the *Penguin*; so Captain Dickenson, putting up his helm, closed to board. The *Penguin's* bowsprit rode over the *Hornet's* starboard rail amid-ships. As the ship pitched the bowsprit slammed down with a crash and snapped, parting the forestays. Down came the *Penguin's* foremast. The wreckage tangled in the *Hornet's* mizzen rigging, breaking her spanker boom. Meanwhile, the *Hornet's* marines swept the *Penguin's* deck with musketry, breaking up the boarding party.

The vessels rubbed clear, and Biddle, wearing ship, brought his port broadside to bear. After taking a few well-aimed volleys, the battered *Penguin's* ensign came down. A 22-minute action had wrecked her. Captain Dickenson and 13 others were dead and 28 more wounded out of 122 officers and men. The *Hornet*, unhulled, with only 2 killed and 9 men wounded, had some damage to her top hamper and her spanker; that was all. Two days later the *Pea-*

cock and the *Tom Bowline* arrived. The prisoners were put on board the *Bowline*, and she left for Rio de Janeiro. The *Penguin*'s stores were transferred to the *Hornet* and the British ship scuttled; the two American warships, after waiting vainly for Decatur, resumed their course for the East Indies.

The *Hornet* did not make it. On April 27 she chased a strange sail, which turned out to be HMS *Cornwallis,* 74, and the *Hornet* became the hunted. After tossing overboard all his guns but one, together with anchors, cable, spare spars and ammunition, Biddle managed to creep out of range of the big but speedy ship of the line. Making São Salvador (Bahia) on June 10, he learned that peace had been declared.

The *Peacock* alone of Decatur's squadron reached the East Indies. Still under Captain Warrington, who had commanded her when she trounced the *Epervier,* she found rich pickings—four great East Indiamen loaded with valuable cargo. Picking them off was easy; England had established no convoy system in the Indian Ocean. And then, June 30, in Sunda Strait, Warrington fell in with an East India Company's armed ship, the brig *Nautilus,* 14. The *Nautilus* hove to when ordered, but her skipper hailed that peace had been declared. Fearing a ruse, Warrington demanded unconditional surrender, enforcing the order with two broadsides. Later convinced, Warrington released the *Nautilus.*

Meanwhile, "Old Ironsides," bowling south down the Bay of Biscay, closed the naval book of the war with one last brilliant victory. On February 20, 180 miles from Madeira, she fell in with HM frigate *Cyane,* 34, and sloop *Levant,* 21, both full of fight and throwing a slightly heavier weight of metal. This firepower superiority and their maneuverability as a team should have given them an edge in the fight, which became one of maneuver. Unfortunately for them, their armament consisted of short-range carronades instead of the long 12s and 24s of the *Constitution.* And finally, Captain Stewart's "superb skill in seamanship, quickness of decision and tactical judgment"—to quote one naval historian [1]—won the day.

The opponents came within gunshot as dusk was falling, all three on parallel courses; the *Cyane* and *Levant* were in line ahead,

[1] Rear Admiral Dudley W. Knox, *A History of the United States Navy* (New York: Putnam, 1936), p. 130.

the *Constitution*, with the weather gage, was on their starboard flank. A fifteen-minute gun duel ended when the *Levant* attempted to rake the *Constitution* by luffing and passing close under her stern. But Stewart, bracing his after sails aback, turned his ship broadside to the *Levant* and pounded her, while the *Cyane* forged ahead. In a series of brilliant maneuvers Stewart now swung his fast-sailing frigate around his opponents, raking first the *Cyane* and then, for a second time, the *Levant*. The British ships separated, with the *Levant* badly damaged. Stewart, making for the *Cyane*, ranged close aboard on her starboard quarter, prepared for a stunning broadside, when she struck her colors and fired a lee gun to emphasize her surrender.

Hurriedly a prize crew was put aboard and then Stewart turned to search for the *Levant*. He did not have far to go, for plucky Captain J. E. Douglass, having made hasty repairs, came back to help his consort and almost ran the *Constitution* down. Sheering off, Douglass tried to get away, but the *Constitution*'s bow chasers came into play and by ten o'clock the *Levant* had struck.

With her prizes "Old Ironsides" on March 10 dropped anchor in Porto Praya harbor, Cape Verde Islands. Some 120 prisoners were paroled ashore, and the *Constitution*'s crew spread over all three vessels to make repairs.

The next day a picket boat came flying in to report three large British warships heading for the harbor. Stewart wasted not a second. There was a ripple of signal flags and a gunshot to warn all hands; within a quarter of an hour "Old Ironsides" and her prizes had slipped their cables and put to sea. The Britishers turned and followed. The *Cyane*, last of the fleeing Americans, lost ground and on Stewart's signal broke away. Admiral Sir George Collier, RN, commanding the British ships, let her go; he wanted the *Constitution*, it seemed. The *Cyane* reached New York safely to begin a new career in the U.S. Navy. But when Stewart later cast off the *Levant*, also a slow sailor, Sir George for some unknown reason turned also and chased her back into Porto Praya. Lieutenant Edward J. Ballard dropped anchor under the guns of a Portuguese fort hoping against hope that the British might respect neutrality. But the paroled British prisoners rushed the fort and turned its guns on the little *Levant*, while Sir George brought the *Acasta*, 40, and *Newcastle*, 50, to join in a bull-in-a-china-shop gesture.

Their broadsides never touched the *Levant* but thoroughly wrecked the innocent town. Ballard struck his colors and Sir George hurried ashore to attempt to make his peace with the governor. The British admiral never did live down his failure to capture the *Constitution*; his suicide, ten years later, is said to have been caused by remorse.

In any event, thanks to Sir George Collier as well as to her own captain and crew, "Old Ironsides," queen of the Yankee frigates, sailed triumphantly into New York harbor in the middle of May 1815. Her last war cruise was done, her permanent place in naval history assured.

The War of 1812 was at last ended. News of the peace agreement hammered out at Ghent December 24, 1814, and of its ratification by Britain's Prince Regent four days later had arrived in New York February 11, 1815. Six days later the Senate unanimously ratified the treaty, and President Madison signed it without delay. Shortly afterward he proclaimed the second Thursday in April as a day of general thanksgiving for the blessings of peace.

Actually, the treaty provided for little more than the cessation of hostilities, return of prisoners and resumption of the territorial status quo ante. Boundaries were to be adjusted by commissioners, and joint measures were to be taken in suppression of the slave trade. The ostensible purpose of the American declaration of war, preservation of freedom of the seas—discontinuance of search, impressment and blockades—went unmentioned. But—and this must be stressed—never again would any British ship attempt search and impressment against an American vessel. Worth equal stress is the fact that Americans made no further efforts to seize Canada.

Appendix

Weapons, Tactics and Uniforms

ARMY

Ordnance

The standard British infantry hand arm of the period was—as it had been for nearly a century—the "Brown Bess" or "Tower" musket (so-called because of the ordnance inspection stamp it bore, a schematic replica of the Tower of London). It was a smooth-bore, flintlock, muzzle-loader, 4'9" long and weighing, with bayonet, about 11 pounds. It threw a .71-inch-caliber spherical ball weighing a little more than an ounce, which so loosely fitted the .75-inch bore that unless the weapon was badly fouled it could be seated home by a smart tap of the musket butt on the ground (a practice quite common in the British Army). Accordingly, since the weapon carried no rear sight, accuracy in this wobbly trajectory beyond 50 yards was nil.

The British theory of musketry was the cone of fire: a spray of shots delivered by masses of men in close order; of course, any individual so unfortunate as to encounter by chance any of this spray would receive a murderous wound. Loading and firing this piece was an awkward process. Ball and powder were contained in a paper cartridge case. The soldier, standing, bit off the powder end of the cartridge, sprinkled some powder into the the flintlock pan, then poured the remainder down the muzzle, ramming home the ball and the case, now a wad, with an iron ramrod. Returning the ramrod to its socket along the barrel and putting the weapon to his shoulder, the user then pointed it in the general direction of the enemy and on order pulled the trigger. This brought down the hammer, holding a flint, onto the steel frizzen of the pan with sufficient force—hopefully—to strike a spark, igniting the loose powder in the pan. Again hopefully, this flame would flare into the touch hole and explode the powder in the bore, sending the bullet on its way. In theory, the rate of fire by well-drilled soldiers was 5 shots a minute; actually, 3 rounds would be deemed fortunate. Misfires were frequent. Success was finally dependent on the weather; rain, dampening the priming, would of course render the piece useless.

All in all, this musket was a most unreliable firearm whose principal function was to carry the 21-inch bayonet, which, in last resort, decided infantry action.

American regular infantry and such militia and volunteers as were equipped from government sources used a musket that was comparable to the Brown Bess and manufactured by the arsenals at Springfield and Harpers Ferry. This weapon was fitted with a rear sight. But the great mass of militia and volunteers from the west and southwest, who supplied their own arms, carried the so-called Kentucky rifle: a muzzle-loading flintlock with a spirally grooved bore. So, too, did the 4 small Regular Army rifle units raised hurriedly during the war.

This privately manufactured weapon, an Americanized version of the short, heavy (18-pound) rifle of the Bavarian huntsman, is worthy of note. During both the Revolutionary War and the War of 1812 American frontiersmen armed with it created havoc by their aimed fire at ranges astounding to the British regulars.

The Kentucky rifle—really the Pennsylvania rifle, since it was originally manufactured in that area by patient German gunsmith immigrants—was specifically tailored to the frontiersman's needs. No mass production here; each piece was an individual product.

Its overall length averaged 62 inches and its weight 10 pounds; its approximately .40-cal. spherical lead bullet, wrapped in a greased patch, was jammed tight into the rifle grooves of the bore by a wooden ramrod. Its comparatively high muzzle velocity sent the bullet on an almost flat trajectory for the first 50 yards, and in a marksman's hands it was deadly at 300 yards or more. A bayonet could not be fitted to this rifle.

An interesting variant in American musket loads, and one that had already drawn British ire during the Revolutionary War, was "buck and ball." The soldier simply added two buckshot to the normal charge, with devastating effect at short range.

On the British side the rifle was not used until the very end of the war, when the 95th Foot—later the Rifle Brigade—came with Pakenham's troops to New Orleans. They were armed with the Baker rifle, English-made and much lighter (9½ pounds) than its German prototype. Like the German rifle, however, its tight-fitting bullets had to be driven home by an iron ramrod and a wooden mallet—an awkward procedure.

There was very little cavalry combat in the European sense during this war. A number of mounted rifle organizations were present on the American side, but these men had little or no experience in cavalry maneuvers, and few, if any, carried sabers. They were, as their title indicated, riflemen using horse transport who went about their fighting business on foot.

Swords and flintlock pistols were normal officer equipment on both sides.

Field guns, all smooth-bore muzzle-loaders, were of four general categories: 4-, 6-, 8- and 12-pounders, according to the weight of their solid iron balls, which ranged upward to one mile. Against personnel, in the open or at close range, grapeshot (clusters of iron balls in a metal frame) or canister (musket balls in a container) were frequently used. The containers or frames of these projectiles disintegrated shortly after leaving the muzzle of the piece, permitting the balls to sweep a wide but shallow area, like buckshot fired from hand arms.

Besides solid roundshot, shell was coming into use—hollow balls filled with gunpowder and detonated by a slow fuse, presumably ignited by the powder charge in the gun, but neither accurate nor dependable. Shell was fired from howitzers, shorter and lighter pieces than guns of corresponding calibers; small howitzers were termed "cohorns." Against fortifications, shells were frequently fired from mortars; their curved trajectory, higher than that of howitzers, would lob the projectiles over walls and earthworks.

Siege ordnance was, of course, of heavier caliber—24-pounder or larger—and more cumbersome than the field artillery. Used primarily to batter down fortifications, siege pieces also flung shell for antipersonnel effect and incendiary projectiles. The "carcass," an iron shell packed with combustible material and pierced with holes from which the flame blazed, was common, but red-hot shot was also used, particularly in coast defense against naval vessels.

Tactics

The formalized concept of European infantry assault tactics of the period consisted of a line of battalions, the basic tactical unit, formed three men deep. The mass moved to the attack, delivering one or more volleys at the last moment and at the shortest possible range, then rushed to the assault with the bayonet. British infantry at the time of the War of 1812 was already in transition from the Napoleonic three-deep line to the deep line, thus adding to the firepower immediately obtainable from a given number of men— hence the expression "the thin red line."

Aggregations of battalions were gathered into larger units for command convenience: brigades, divisions, corps or wings, which actually bore little relationship to today's standardized nomenclature. British regiments were actually 10-company, 1-battalion units commanded by a major or lieutenant colonel. Some 8 of the companies, each mustering from 20 to 40 men, were "battalion" or "line" companies; the 2 remaining companies, the elite of the regiment, were the grenadier and light infantry units, commonly termed "flank" companies because in ceremonial formation they paraded on each of the flanks of the battalion. The grenadier company—theoretically the reserve unit—was composed of the largest men in the outfit and formed on the right of the line. Its title descended from the days when the largest and strongest men were chosen to throw hand grenades. The light infantry company on the left was composed of the most agile men, presumably better able to bear the active work of skirmishing and patrolling.

Normal British practice with large elements in the field was to assemble all the flank companies into provisional battalions, respectively grenadier and light infantry. It should be noted that the term "grenadier" as used here had nothing to do with the Grenadier regiment of the Royal Foot Guards, Grenadier, Coldstream and Scots.

In the American service, while the 10-company battalion was the basic tactical unit, regiments were frequently of more than 1-battalion strength. There were no special units, grenadiers or light infantry. In fact, the Regular Army infantry, mostly engaged in Indian fighting, was more accustomed to light infantry or skirmishing tactics, utilizing a single line that sought cover as it advanced through wilderness. Until Winfield Scott reorganized and drilled the troops of General Jacob Brown on the northeast frontier during the war, the Regular Army was incapable of meeting the British in formalized tactical maneuver on open ground. Neither the militia nor the volunteer organizations had any recent close-order combat experience. In brief, the average American soldier in 1812 was an individualist accustomed to loosing aimed shots, a stranger to the bayonet.

Uniforms

Regular troops of both sides wore uniforms more or less standardized by their respective regulations: a coat or coatee, swallow-tailed, gilt-buttoned, with high choker collar; trousers or overalls of white drill; leather leggings over black shoes. The British coat was red, with a variety of facings, according to regiment and arm of service; the American coat was blue, single-breasted; the facings of white, red and buff in general but not invariably denoted infantry, artillery and cavalry respectively. British headgear in general was a black leather shako; the American soldier early in the war appeared in a cockaded black high hat of civilian style, which was later replaced by the leather shako—the "tar bucket." High-ranking officers of both sides wore black chapeaux—cocked hats, plumed.

It is impractical here to detail all the niceties and variations in clothing and headgear of the period. The British blockade of American shores and the deficiencies of the U.S. Army supply department contributed, early in the war, to shocking shortages in cloth; so the traditional blue of the American uniform was frequently eked out by brown or gray cloth. Scott's vociferous demands for uniforms resulted in procurement of gray for his brigade, a color that, as we know, brought about British General Riall's embarrassing and costly initial estimate that the American regulars at Chippewa were militia from Buffalo. The drafted militia on both sides were lucky to wear clothing of any sort; the volunteer militia, however—the organized and incorporated units of both American and Canadian citizen-soldiers—took the field in uniforms as gay and variegated as Joseph's "coat of many colors."

One fact stands out: the soldiers' outer garments, which took no account of climate or comfort, were designed to make the wretched individual soldier as uncomfortable as possible. When one adds to this the existing abominable conditions of sanitation, the butchery and gross abuses of military medical care, the unscrupulous chicanery of food purveyors, the lackadaisical delays of pay departments and the appalling cruelty of the military punishment codes, the picture presented of Army life is indeed a sorry one.

NAVY

Warships of the period fell into three loosely formalized classes. Ships of the line carried from 64 to 110 guns in broadside on three decks. Frigates—faster and lighter, built for commerce destruction, escort duty and patrol—mounted from 24 to 44 guns on 2 decks (a few large English frigates were officially rated as 50s, but this was a compromise class—too light to fight in the line, too slow to catch a frigate). Ships of the line and frigates were all ships (three-masters, square-rigged). Sloops of war, carrying from 16 to 24 guns, might be ship-rigged, brigs (two-masted square-riggers), or brigantines (two-masters, square-rigged on foremast), schooner (fore and aft-rigged) in the main mast. Smaller craft were usually known by their rig—schooner, sloop or ketch.

It was customary in naval parlance to identify a warship's rating by noting, immediately after her name, the number of guns carried. This, however, was a rule of thumb; both English and American warships usually carried more guns than their official rating, and individual ship captains were allowed considerable latitude in altering their ordnance to suit their individual preferences. For instance, we find the USS *Constitution,* 44, in her fight with HMS *Guerrière,* August 19, 1812, actually mounting 52 pieces: 30 24-

pounders, 14 12-pounders and 8 32-pounder carronades. But some-time prior to December 29 of that year, when she captured HMS *Java,* the carronades had been removed.

Naval ordnance consisted of 4-, 6-, 9-, 12-, 18- and—in U.S. Navy ships only—24-pounder long guns and of 32- and 42-pounder car-ronades, shorter, lighter, less expensive pieces whose projectiles had tremendous smashing power but much shorter range. The light 4- and 6-pounder guns were used mostly by privateers; regular Navy ships carried the larger calibers.

Ammunition for these pieces consisted not only of the conven-tional solid iron roundshot but also of grape and canister (useful against personnel) and barshot and chainshot (linked projectiles that ripped canvas, rigging and spars).

Use of red-hot shot to create conflagrations had become common practice by this time afloat as well as in shore batteries. Many of the larger warships carried small furnaces in which roundshot could be heated. A wet wad was rammed home on top of the powder charge and the glowing projectile then inserted by tongs. Hot-shot furnaces with cranes to handle the shot were part of the normal equipment of coast-defense installations. Fire ships—ves-sels crammed with explosives—were sometimes used against massed enemy craft if the wind favored.

Since all the vessels carried their guns in broadside, application of firepower—gunnery—depended upon the skill and experience of the commander to handle his ship so as to train his practically rigid battery on the target, no mean feat when dependent upon wind and weather for steerage way and maneuver. Hence, it may be well to orient the unnautical reader on a few rudiments of this complicated art of sailing shipmastery and on naval procedure of the period.

A sailing vessel with the wind pushing her from astern was run-ning "before the wind." Against the wind, forward motion could be attained only by zig-zagging, with sails trimmed on a slant to catch the wind. This was termed "beating to windward"; with the wind blowing on her right (starboard) side, she was on the "star-board tack"; conversely, she was on the "port tack" when the wind blew on her left side. Heading directly into the wind, in order to bring the wind against another side, was to "luff" or "tack." Were the ship so slowed up during this operation that she lost steerage way and hung motionless, she had "missed stays" and was helpless, "in irons," until her yards had been "braced" (turned) to catch sufficient wind to start movement again. She might, in such case, for a time be moving backward ("making sternway"). A change of course that definitely took the vessel away from her objective or from combat was termed "hauling off" or "hauling out." And finally, forward movement could be checked or halted by bracing the yards so that the wind pushed against the sails—"backing" them.

A vessel anchored by a cable from her bow always swung to rest head up to wind or tide, whichever was the stronger. In this position a sailing ship, short of actually getting underway—hoisting ("weighing") the anchor or slipping the cable free and setting sail— could not change position without mechanical aid. This could be accomplished by fastening a line to the anchor chain or cable and then passing it outside the hull to the stern. By heaving in on this "spring line" the ship could be slowly pulled around by manpower to face in the opposite direction.

When becalmed, a sailing vessel in emergency might be towed by her own rowing boats or moved by "kedging." The kedge was a light anchor, with cable attached, which was carried forward by small boat and dropped. The crew on board then pulled the ship up to the kedge by heaving in on the cable; the process was repeated as needed.

As to combat, since no fleet actions at sea took place during the War of 1812, discussion will be confined to single-ship actions, duels between two individual warships.

On meeting an unidentified vessel in wartime, accepted naval procedure was to fly either a neutral or the enemy flag until within hauling range or until other identification was made. However, the naval honor code demanded that before fire was opened the authentic national colors be displayed.

The combat began usually by preliminary jockeying for the "weather gage," each vessel trying to put herself between the wind and her adversary. The weather gage was important in that it gave the holder choice of either closing or avoiding combat. The ship to leeward, while she could avoid battle, must beat against the wind— a tedious process—in order to close to cannon range. Gaining the weather gage gave opportunity also to cross the opponent's path and "rake" her: sweep her with fire from stem to stern while the majority of the target's guns could not be brought to bear. A further and most important nicety of the weather gage position, to a ship armed with long guns against a carronade-carrying opponent, was the potential ability to knock the adversary to pieces before her murderous but shorter-range battery became effective.

The final stage of all this jockeying for position found the opponents side by side, sometimes lashed together, engaged in a slugging match until one of them gave up. Often, the *coup de grâce* was given by the boarding party, sailors clambering over the enemy's bulwarks to fight it out on deck with cutlass, boarding pike and musket. Surrender was normally indicated by "striking" (hauling down) the colors or by firing a cannon on the disengaged side of the vanquished vessel.

The normal hand arms of the sailor were cutlass (a heavy saber), boarding pike or—extemporaneously—hand spike, belaying pin or any other convenient clubbing weapon. Naval officers carried swords and pistols. The marine, the "soldier of the sea," was of course equipped with the musket and bayonet.

Naval uniforms, both British and American, during this period were similar. For the enlisted men no regulations had been yet established by either nation, but by long-established custom, sailors wore blue jackets, white trousers and round tarpaulin hats on dress occasions. A black scarf protected the jacket from the greased pigtail so frequently affected in the forecastle. In action, of course, the sailor stripped to the minimum of clothing. Officers' uniforms were prescribed by regulation in both navies, but the wearer's pocketbook and personal vanity governed wide variations; excessive gold lace, epaulettes of fantasy and embroidered waistcoats frequently elaborated a basic gilt-buttoned blue coat, white knee-breeches and cocked hat.

Marines of both nations, in contrast to the tars, wore military uniforms of coatee and overalls, definitely prescribed by regulations. The British coat was red, with blue facings; the American, green, with white facings. Officers' uniforms were in theory more elaborate, with gilt buttons, lace and epaulettes of rank. The official U.S. Marine Corps officer's distinctive sword was the curved, Oriental-scimitar type, hilt without guard, emblematic of Barbary war service; it would be proudly carried as long as U.S. Marine officers wore swords.

Bibliography

Primary Sources

The contents of the books, pamphlets and articles in this list were written about the time of the War of 1812 by persons who were concerned with it.

Adams, Charles F. (ed.). *Memoirs of John Quincy Adams.* 12 vols. Philadelphia: 1874–1877.

Adams, Henry (ed.). *Documents Relating to New England Federalism.* Boston: 1877.

———. *The Writings of Albert Gallatin.* 3 vols. Boston: 1877–1879.

Aiken, S. *An Address to Federal Clergymen.* Boston: 1813. (Pamphlet.)

American State Papers. Washington, D.C.: Gales & Seaton, 1832–1861. The following volumes are especially concerned with the War of 1812: Class I—*Foreign Relations,* 6 vols., Vol. III; Class II—*Indian Affairs,* 2 vols., Vol. I; Class V—*Military Affairs,* 7 vols. Vol. I; Class X—*Miscellaneous,* 2 vols., Vols. I and II.

Annals of the Congress of the United States, 1789–1824. 42 vols. Washington, D.C.: Gales & Seaton, 1834–1856.

Armstrong, J. *Notices of the War of 1812.* 2 vols. New York: 1840.

Austin, S. *Apology of Patriots.* Worcester, Mass.: 1812.

Baring, Alexander. *Inquiry into the Causes and Consequences of the Orders in Council.*

Bartlett, J. Speech at the Republican Convention at Kingston Plains, September 10, 1812. Portsmouth, N.H.: 1812.

Bassett, J. S. (ed.). *Battles of the Late War . . . and Adventures of Corporal Samuel Stubbs.* Boston: 1817.

———. *Correspondence of Andrew Jackson.* 7 vols. Washington, D.C.: 1924–1933.

Beall, W. K. "Journal of W. K. Beall, July–August, 1812," *American Historical Review,* Vol. XVII.

Birbeck, M. *Notes on a Journey in America, from the Coast of Virginia to the Territory of Illinois.* Dublin: 1818.

Bonney, C. V. R. *A Legacy of Historical Gleanings.* 2 vols. Albany, N.Y.: 1875.

Boyd, John Parker. *Documents and Facts Relative to Military Events during the Late War.* Boston: 1816.

Brannan, J. *Official Letters of the Military and Naval Officers of the United States during the War with Great Britain.* Washington: 1823.

Bryce, J. (ed.). *A Great Peace Maker, the Diary of James Gallatin, Secretary Albert Gallatin, 1813–1817.* New York: 1914.

Brymner, D. *Report on Canadian Archives.* 1896.
Enumerates important letters of the War of 1812 in the archives. Some are given as a whole; others are briefly outlined.

Callan, J. F. *The Military Laws of the United States.* Philadelphia: 1863.

Captain's Letters. National Archives, Washington, D.C. Correspondence of naval commanders in the War of 1812.

Carter, C. E. (ed.). *The Territorial Papers of the United States.* 21 vols. Washington, D.C.: U.S. Government Printing Office, 1934–1954. See especially Vols. XIV–XVII.

Clift, G. G. (ed.). *War of 1812, Diary of William B. Northcutt.* Frankfort, Ky.: Kentucky Historical Society, 1958.

Cobbett, William. *Letters on the Late War between the United States and Great Britain.* New York: 1815.

Commager, Henry S., and Allan Nevins (eds.). *The Heritage of America.* Boston: Little, Brown, 1949.
Contains six interesting accounts of the war written by contemporaries.

Commercial Advertiser (New York), 1812–1815.

Conciliator. "Why Are We Still at War or the American Question Considered," *The Pamphleteer* (London), Vol. IV (Nov., 1814), 451–575.

Cruikshank, E. A. *Documentary History of the Campaign Upon the Niagara Frontier.* Welland, Ontario: 1907.
Composed of several volumes for each year of the war.

——. *Documents Relating to the Invasion of Canada and the Surrender of Detroit.* Ottawa: 1912.

——. "Letters of 1812 from Dominion Archives," *Niagara Historical Society Publications,* No. 23 (1925).

Cutts, L. B. (ed.). *Memoirs and Letters of Dolley Madison.* Boston: 1887.

Darnell, E. *A Journal . . . of . . . the Kentucky Volunteers and Regulars Commanded by General Winchester in . . . 1812–1813.* Philadelphia: 1854.

Duane, W. *A Handbook for Infantry.* Philadelphia: 1812.

Edgar, M. (ed.). *Ten Years of Upper Canada in Peace and War, 1805–1815; Being the Ridout Letters . . .* Toronto: 1890.

Esarey, L. (ed.). *Messages and Letters of William Henry Harrison.* 2 vols. Indianapolis: 1922.

Fairchild, G. M. (ed.). *Journal of an American Prisoner at Fort Malden and Quebec . . .* Quebec: 1909.

Fay, H. A. *A Collection of Official Accounts of all Battles Fought by Land and Sea during 1812–1815.* New York: 1817.

Forbes, J. G. *The Trial of Brig. General William Hull.* New York: 1814.

Green, E. "Some Graves in Lundy's Lane," *Niagara Historical Society Publications,* No. 22, 1912.

Hamersly, Thomas Holdup Steven. *Regular Army Register of the United States, 1770–1879.* Washington, D.C.: 1880.

Hamilton, S. M. (ed.). *The Writings of James Monroe.* 7 vols. New York: 1903.

Hansard, T. C. (ed.). *The Parliamentary Debates.* 94 vols. London: 1806–1825.

Hart, A. *Two for One . . . A Shilling's Worth of Good Sense and A Shilling's Worth of Common Sense.* New York: 1813.

Hastings, H. (ed.). *Public Papers of Daniel D. Tompkins.* 3 vols. Albany, N.Y.: 1902.

Hull, William. *Defense of Brigadier General William Hull.* Boston: 1814.

——. *Memoirs of the Campaign of the North-western Army of the United States,* 1812. Boston: True & Greene, 1824.

Hunt, G. (ed.). *The Writings of James Madison.* 9 vols. New York: 1900–1912.

Irving, L. H. *Officers of the British Forces in Canada during the War of 1812–1815.* Welland, Ontario: 1908.

Izard, G. *Official Correspondence with the Department of War, 1814–1815.* Philadelphia: 1816.

Johnson, R. M. "The Letters of Colonel R. M. Johnson of Kentucky," *Kentucky State Historical Society Register,* Vol. 38 (1940).

Kinzie, J. "Narrative of the Ft. Dearborn Massacre," *Illinois State Historical Society,* Vol. 46.

Knopf, R. C. (ed.). *Document Transcriptions of the War of 1812 in the Northwest.* 6, vols. Columbus, Ohio: Ohio Historical Society, 1957–1962. Prepared by the Anthony Wayne Parkway Board.

Lee, H. *Correct Account of the Conduct of the Baltimore Mob.* Winchester, Va.: 1814. (Pamphlet.)

Lindley, H. *Captain Cushing in the War of 1812.* Columbus, Ohio: Ohio Archaeological and Historical Society, 1944.

Log of the Frigate *Constitution.* National Archives, Washington, D.C.

Log of the Frigate *United States.* National Archives, Washington, D.C.

Lowe, J. W. *Catalogue of Books and Manuscripts of the War of 1812.* Chicago: 1917.

Lowell, J. *Analysis of the Late Correspondence between our Administration and Great Britain and France.* Boston: 1809.

———. *Mr. Madison's War.* Boston: 1812.

Melish, J. *Military and Topographical Map Atlas of the United States.* Philadelphia: 1815.

Michigan Pioneer and Historical Collection. 40 vols. Lansing: 1877–1929.

For British and United States relations in the War of 1812, see Vols. 15 and 16.

Moore, C. C. *A Sketch of Our Political Condition.* New York: 1813.

National Intelligencer (Washington, D.C.), 1812–1815.

Naval Documents Related to the United States Wars with the Barbary Powers. 6 vols. Washington, D.C.: Government Printing Office, 1934–1945.

Nevins, Allan (ed.). *The Diary of John Quincy Adams.* New York: 1928.

Niles Weekly (Baltimore), 1812–1815.

Ohio Historical Collections. 11 vols. Columbus, Ohio: 1951.

"Orderly Book of Harrisburg Volunteer Co.," *Pennsylvania Magazine of History and Biography,* Vol. 37.

Padover, S. K. *A Jefferson Profile.* New York: John Day, 1956.

"Papers and Orderly Book of Brigadier General J. Winchester," *Michigan Pioneer and Historical Society Collections,* Vol. 31.

Parish, J. C. (ed.). *The Robert Lucas Journal of the War of 1812 . . .* Iowa City, Iowa: 1906.

Paullin, C. C. *Guide to the Materials in London Archives for History of the ʻUnited States since 1783.* Washington, D.C.: Carnegie Institution, 1914.

Quaife, M. M. (ed.). *War on the Detroit*. Chicago: Lakeside Press, 1940. Consists of the "Chronicles of Thomas Vercheres de Boucherville" and "Capitulation by an Ohio Volunteer."

Richardson, J. D. (ed.). *Messages and Papers of the Presidents, 1789–1908*. 11 vols. Washington, D.C.: 1908.

Roach, Isaac. "Journal of Major Isaac Roach," *Pennsylvania Magazine of History and Biography* (July and October, 1893).

Schillinger, W. "Journal of Ensign W. Schillinger," *Ohio Archaeological and Historical Quarterly* (January 1932).

Sloan, J. *An Address to Citizens of the United States*. Philadelphia: 1812.

Thian, R. P. *Legislative History of the General Staff of the Army of the United States, 1775–1901*. Washington, D.C.: 1901.

Valpey, J., Jr. *Journal of 1813–1815, With Other Papers Relating to His Experience in Dartmoor Prison*. Detroit: 1922.

Van Rensselaer, Solomon. *A Narrative of the Affair of Queenston . . .* New York: 1836.

Walker, A. *A Journal of Two Campaigns of the Fourth Regiment of U.S. Infantry . . . During the Years of 1811–1812*. Keene, N.H.: 1816.

Wilkinson, J. *Memoirs of My Own Times*. 3 vols. Philadelphia: 1816.

Wood, E. D. "Journal of E. D. Wood, covering Northwestern Campaign of 1812–1813 under W. H. Harrison," in G. W. Cullum (ed.), *Campaigns of the War of 1812–15*. New York: Miller, 1879.

Wood, W. *Select British Documents of the Canadian War of 1812*. 3 vols. Toronto: 1923.

Secondary Sources

Abbott, Willis J. *Blue Jackets of 1812*. New York: 1887.

——. *The Naval History of the United States*. New York: Dodd, Mead, 1896.

Adams, Henry. "Count Edward de Crillon," *American Historical Review*, Vol. I (1895).

——. *History of the United States, 1801–1817*. 9 vols. New York: Scribner, 1889–1891. Based on this history, H. A. De Weerd has compiled *The War of 1812* (Washington, D.C.: Infantry Journal, 1944).

Adams, John Quincy. *The Lives of James Madison and James Monroe*. Boston: 1850.

Adams, J. S. *Atlas of American History*. New York: Scribner, 1943.

Allen, Gardner W. *Our Naval War with France.* Boston: Houghton Mifflin, 1909.

———. *Our Naval War with the Barbary Corsairs.* Boston: Houghton Mifflin, 1905.

Armstrong, K. *Review of T. L. McKenny's Narrative* . . . New York: 1846. (Pamphlet.)

Atwater, C. *The Indians of the Northwest, their Manners, Customs* . . . Columbus, Ohio: 1850.

Auchinleck, G. *The War of 1812* . . . Toronto: 1862.

Babcock, L. L. *The War of 1812 on the Niagara Frontier.* Buffalo, N.Y.: 1927.

Baldwin, S. F., and J. S. Barry. "The Hartford Convention," in C. F. Horne (ed.), *The Great Events by Famous Historians.* New York: 1904–1905. Vol. 15.

Bancroft, George. *History of the Battle of Lake Erie.* New York: Robert Bonners' Sons, 1891.

Bassett, J. S. *The Life of Andrew Jackson.* New York: 1928.

Beirne, F. F. *The War of 1812.* New York: Dutton, 1949.

Bernardo, C. Joseph, and E. H. Bacon. *American Military Policy.* Harrisburg, Pa.: Military Service Publishing Co., 1955.

Bingham, R. H. *The Cradle of the Queen City.* Buffalo, N.Y.: Buffalo Historical Society, 1931.

Birkhimer, W. E. *Historical Sketch of the Organization, Administration, etc. of the Artillery, U.S. Army.* Washington, D.C.: 1884.

Blakeslee, Fred Gilbert. *Uniforms of the World.* New York: 1929.

Bowers, D. G. *Jefferson in Power.* Boston: Houghton Mifflin, 1936.

Brackenridge, H. M. *History of the Late War.* Baltimore: 1816.

Bradford, S. S. "Fort McHenry, 1814," *Maryland Historical Magazine,* LIV (June 1959), 188–210.

Brant, Irving. *James Madison, Commander-in-Chief.* Indianapolis: Bobbs-Merrill, 1961.

———. *James Madison, The President.* Indianapolis: Bobbs-Merrill, 1956.

———. *James Madison, Secretary of State.* Indianapolis: Bobbs-Merrill, 1953.

Brown, S. R. *Views of the Campaigns of the Northwestern Army.* Troy, N.Y.: 1814.

Bruce, W. C. *John Randolph of Roanoke.* New York: 1922.

Buck, S. J., and E. H. Buck. *The Planting of Civilization in Western Pennsylvania.* Pittsburgh: University of Pittsburgh Press, 1939.

Burt, A. L. *The United States, Great Britain, and British North Amer-*

ica from the Revolution to the Establishment of Peace after the War of 1812. New Haven, Conn.: Yale University Press, 1940.

Calver, W. L. "United States Army Buttons of the War of 1812," *New York Historical Society Quarterly Bulletin,* Vol. 16.

Campbell, M. H. *Revolutionary Service and Civil Life of General William Hull . . .* New York: 1848.

Chapelle, Howard I. *The History of the American Sailing Navy.* New York: Norton, 1949.

Chapin, C. *Review of Armstrong's Notices of the War of 1812.* New York: Black Rock, 1836.

Chidsey, D. B. *The Battle of New Orleans.* New York: Crown, 1961.

Claiborne, J. F. H. *Life and Times of General Sam Dale.* New York: 1860.

Claiborne, N. H. *Notes on the War in the South.* Richmond, Va.: 1819.

Clark, J. F. *History of the Campaign of 1812 and Surrender of the Post of Detroit.* New York: 1858.

Cleaves, F. *Old Tippecanoe.* New York: Scribner, 1939.

Cooper, James Fenimore. *History of the Navy of the United States of America.* Philadelphia: Thomas, Cowperthwait & Co., 1841.

——. *Lives of Distinguished American Naval Officers.* Philadelphia: Carey & Hart, 1846.

Cotterill, R. S. *The Southern Indians.* Norman: University of Oklahoma Press, 1954.

Cox, I. J. *The Indians as a Diplomatic Factor in the History of the Old Northwest.* Chicago: 1907.

Cruikshank, E. *Drummond's Winter Campaign of 1813.* Welland, Ontario: 1900.

Cullum, G. W. (ed.). *Campaigns of the War of 1812–15.* New York: Miller, 1879.

Dallas, A. J. *An Exposition of the Causes and Character of the Late War.* Washington: 1815.

Dawson, H. B. *Battles of the United States by Sea and Land.* 2 vols. New York: 1958.

Dearborn, H. A. S. *Defense of General Henry Dearborn Against the Attack of General William Hull.* Boston: 1824.

Delafield, J. *Biographies of Francis Lewis and Morgan Lewis.* 2 vols. New York: 1877.

Dewey, D. R. *Financial History of the United States.* New York: Longmans, Green, 1922.

Dictionary of American Naval Fighting Ships. Washington, D.C.: U.S. Department of the Navy, 1963. Vol. II.

Dillon, J. B. *A History of Indiana . . . to the Close of the Territorial Government in 1816.* Indianapolis: 1859.

Dobbins, W. W. *History of the Battle of Lake Erie.* Erie, Pa.: Ashby Printing Company, 1929.

Dolph, E. A. *Sound Off—Soldier Songs from Yankee Doodle to Parley Voo.* New York: 1929.

Dupuy, R. Ernest. *Where They Have Trod.* New York: Stokes, 1940.

Dupuy, R. Ernest, and Trevor N. Dupuy. *Brave Men and Great Captains.* New York: Harper, 1959.

Dwight, T. *History of the Hartford Convention.* New York: 1833.

Eggleston, G. C. *Red Eagle and the Wars of the Creek Indians of Alabama.* New York: 1878.

Elliott, C. W. *Winfield Scott, the Soldier and the Man.* New York: Macmillan, 1937.

Engelman, F. L. *The Peace of Christmas Eve.* New York: Harcourt, Brace & World, 1962.

Fearon, H. B. *Sketches of America.* London: 1819.

Fisher, R. L. "The Western Prologue to the War of 1812," *Missouri Historical Review* (April 1936).

Forester, C. S. *The Age of Fighting Sail.* Garden City, N.Y.: Doubleday, 1956.

Fortescue, John W. *A History of the British Army.* 10 vols. London: 1899–1920.

Frost, Holloway Halstead. *We Build a Navy.* Annapolis, Md.: U.S. Naval Institute, 1929.

Frost, John. *The Book of the Army: Comprising a General Military History of the United States.* New York: 1845.

———. *The Pictorial Book of Commodores.* New York: Nafis & Cornish, 1845.

Gardiner, A. B. "The Uniforms of the American Army," *Magazine of American History* (August 1877).

Gilleland, J. *History of the Late War Between the United States and Great Britain.* Baltimore: 1817.

Gleig, G. R. *A Narrative of the Campaigns of the British Army at Washington and New Orleans.* London: 1836.

———. *A Subaltern in America.* Philadelphia: 1833.

Goodman, W. H. "The Origins of the War of 1812," *Mississippi Historical Review,* Vol. 28 (1941).

Hall, H. *Capture of Fort George.* Philadelphia: 1817.

Hamilton, P. J. "Early Roads of Alabama," *Transactions of the Alabama Historical Society,* Vol. 2 (1897–1898).

Hammond, J. H. *Quaint and Historic Forts of North America.* Philadelphia: 1915.

Hanney, James. *History of the War of 1812.* Toronto: 1905.

Hansen, M. L. *The Mingling of the Canadian and American People.* New Haven, Conn.: Yale University Press, 1940.

Hare, J. S. "Military Punishments in the War of 1812," *Journal of the American Military Institute* (Winter 1940).

Harris, Thomas, M.D. *Life and Services of Commodore William Bainbridge.* Philadelphia: Carey Lea & Blanchard, 1837.

Hatch, W. S. *A Chapter of the . . . War of 1812 in the Northwest.* Cincinnati: 1872.

Hatcher, H. *Lake Erie.* Indianapolis: Bobbs-Merrill, 1945.

Headley, J. T. *The Second War with England.* 2 vols. New York: 1853.

Heitman, Francis B. *Historical Register and Dictionary of the United States Army.* 2 vols. Washington, D.C.: Government Printing Office, 1903.

Hill, Frederic Stanhope. *Romance of the American Navy.* New York: Putnam, 1910.

——. *Twenty-six Historic Ships.* New York: Putnam, 1903.

Hollis, Ira N. *The Frigate Constitution, The Central Figure of the Navy Under Sail.* Boston: Houghton Mifflin, 1900.

Hollon, W. E. *The Lost Pathfinder.* Norman: University of Oklahoma Press, 1949.

Horsman, R. *The Causes of the War of 1812.* Philadelphia: University of Pennsylvania Press, 1962.

Hough, F. B. *A History of Jefferson County . . . New York.* Albany, N.Y.: 1854.

Howe, Henry. "Narrative of the Cruise of the *Essex*," *Adventures and Achievements of Americans.* Cincinnati: Henry Howe, 1860.

Hunt, G. *Life in America One Hundred Years Ago.* New York: 1914.

——. (ed.). *The First Forty Years of Washington Society as Portrayed in the Letters of Mrs. S. H. Smith.* New York: 1906.

Ingersoll, C. J. *Historical Sketch of the Second War between the United States . . . and Great Britain.* 3 vols. Philadelphia: 1845.

Ingraham, E. D. *Sketch of Events which Preceded the Capture of Washington.* Philadelphia: 1849.

Jacobs, James R. *Tarnished Warrior: Major General James Wilkinson.* New York: Macmillan, 1938.

James, Marquis. *The Life of Andrew Jackson.* Indianapolis: Bobbs-Merrill, 1938.

James, W. . . . *Military Occurrences of the Late War between Great Britain and the United States*. London: 1818.

Jenkins, J. S. *The Generals of the Last War with Great Britain*. Auburn, N.Y.: 1849.

Johnson, R. *A History of the War of 1812–1815*. New York: 1882.

Kerr, W. B. "The Occupation of York (Toronto) 1813," *Canadian Historical Review*, Vol. V (1924).

Kimball, Horace. *Naval Temple*. Boston: Barber Badger, 1816.

King, G. *Creole Families of New Orleans*. New York: 1921.

Kirkpatrick, John Ervin. *Timothy Flint, Pioneer, Missionary, Author, Editor, 1780–1840*. Cleveland: 1911.

Knox, Dudley W. *A History of the United States Navy*. New York: Putnam, 1936.

Landon, F. *Western Ontario and the American Frontier*. New Haven, Conn.: Yale University Press, 1941.

Latimer, M. K. "South Carolina—A Protagonist of the War of 1812," *American Historical Review* (July 1956).

Latour, A. L. *Historical Memoir of the War in West Florida and Louisiana in 1814–1815*. Philadelphia: 1829.

Lewis, Charles Lee. *The Romantic Decatur*. Philadelphia: University of Pennsylvania Press, 1937.

Lossing, Benson J. *Pictorial Field Book of the War of 1812*. New York: Harper, 1869.

Lucas, C. P. *The Canadian War of 1812*. Oxford: 1906.

Macdonough, R. *Life of Commodore Macdonough*. Boston: 1909.

Mackenzie, Alexander Slidell. *Life of Commodore Oliver Hazard Perry*. New York: Harper, 1840.

———. *Life of Stephen Decatur, A Commodore of the Navy of the United States*. Boston: Little, Brown, 1846.

Mahan, Alfred T. *Sea Power in its Relations to the War of 1812*. 2 vols. Boston: Little, Brown, 1905.

Mann, J. M. *Medical Sketches of the Campaigns of 1812, 13, 14*. Dedham, Mass.: 1816.

Marine, W. M. *The British Invasion of Maryland*. Baltimore: 1913.

Marriott, J. A. R. *George Canning and His Times*. London: 1907.

McAfee, R. B. *History of the Late War in Western Country*. Lexington, Ky.: 1816.

Meyer, L. W. *The Life and Times of Colonel Richard M. Johnson of Kentucky*. New York: Columbia University Press, 1932.

Montgomery, H. *The Life of Major General Zachary Taylor*. Auburn, N.Y.: 1847.

New York State Commission Plattsburgh Centenary. *The Battle of Plattsburgh, What Historians Say About It.* Albany, N.Y.: 1914.

Niles, J. M. *The Life of Oliver Hazard Perry.* Hartford, Conn.: 1821.

O'Connor, T. *History of the War between the United States and Great Britain.* New York: 1817.

Palmer, John M. *America in Arms.* New Haven, Conn.: Yale University Press, 1941.

Palmer, P. S. *History of Lake Champlain . . . 1609–1814.* New York: 1853.

Parton, James. *Life of Andrew Jackson.* 3 vols. New York: 1859–1860.

Patrick, R. W. *Florida Fiasco.* Athens: University of Georgia Press, 1954.

Perkins, B. *Prologue to War.* Berkeley: University of California Press, 1961.

Peterson, C. J. *The Military Heroes of the War of 1812.* Philadelphia: 1854.

Pickett, A. J. *History of Alabama.* 2 vols. Charleston, S.C.: 1851.

Pratt, Fletcher. *The Heroic Years.* New York: Smith and Hass, 1934.

———. *The Navy: A History. The Story of a Service in Action.* Garden City, N.Y.: Doubleday, 1938.

Pratt, Julius W. *Expansionists of 1812.* Gloucester, Mass.: Peter Smith, 1957.

Prentiss, H. P. "Timothy Pickering as the Leader of New England Federalism, 1800–1815," *Essex Institute Historical Collections,* 1933–1934.

Quaife, M. M. *Chicago and the Old Northwest, 1673–1835.* Chicago: 1913.

Quisenberry, A. C. *Kentucky in the War of 1812.* Frankfort, Ky.: 1915.

Richardson, J. *The War of 1812.* Brockville, Canada: 1842.

Roosevelt, Theodore. *The Naval War of 1812.* New York: Putnam, 1894.

Russell, J. *History of the War between the United States and Great Britain.* Hartford, Conn.: 1815.

Sellar, R. *The U.S. Campaign of 1814 to Capture Montreal.* Quebec: Huntingdon, 1914.

Short, A., and A. G. Doughty (eds.). *Canada and Its Provinces.* 22 vols. Toronto: 1914.

Sinclair, H. *The Port of New Orleans.* Garden City, N.Y.: Doubleday, 1942.

Smith, G. C. M. (ed.). *The Autobiography of Lieutenant General Sir Harry Smith.* London: 1903.

Smith, J. E. *One Hundred Years of Hartford's Courant.* New Haven, Conn.: Yale University Press, 1949.

Smith, M. *A Geographical View of the Province of Upper Canada.* Hartford, Conn.: 1913.

Sonneck, O. G. T. *The Star Spangled Banner.* Washington: 1914.

Sprout, H., and M. Sprout. *The Rise of American Naval Power, 1776–1918.* Princeton, N.J.: Princeton University Press, 1939.

Squires, J. D. *The Granite State of the United States.* New York: American Historical Co., 1956.

Stoddard, A. *Sketches, Historical and Descriptive, of Louisiana.* Philadelphia: 1812.

Styron, A. *The Last of the Cocked Hats.* Norman: University of Oklahoma Press, 1955.

Swanson, N. H. *The Perilous Fight.* New York: Farrar & Rinehart, 1945.

Symons, J. *The Battle of Queenston Heights.* Toronto: 1859.

Thompson, J. L. *Historical Sketches of the Late War between the United States and Great Britain.* Philadelphia: 1816.

Tucker, Glenn. *Dawn Like Thunder: The Barbary Wars and the Birth of the U.S. Navy.* Indianapolis: Bobbs-Merrill, 1963.

———. *Poltroons and Patriots.* 2 vols. Indianapolis: Bobbs-Merrill, 1963. An account of the War of 1812.

———. *Tecumseh.* Indianapolis: Bobbs-Merrill, 1956.

Tuckerman, H. T. *Life of John Pendleton Kennedy.* New York: 1871.

Updyke, F. A. *The Diplomacy of the War of 1812.* Baltimore: 1915.

Upton, E. *Military Policy of the United States.* Washington: 1912.

Walker, Alexander, *Jackson and New Orleans.* New York: 1856.

———. *The Life of Andrew Jackson.* New York: Derby & Jackson, 1859.

Walsh, R. "The Star Fort, 1814," *Maryland Historical Magazine* (September 1949).

White, L. D. *The Jeffersonians.* New York: Macmillan, 1951.

White, S. *History of the American Troops during the Late War under the Command of Colonels Fenton, Campbell, Gaines.* Baltimore: 1830.

Williams, J. S. *History of the Invasion and Capture of Washington.* New York: 1857.

Wiltse, C. M. *John C. Calhoun, Nationalist.* Indianapolis: Bobbs-Merrill, 1944.

Wood, E. O. *Historic Mackinac.* 2 vols. New York: 1918.

Index

215